MW00788599

FREE Study Skills Videos/DVD Offer

Dear Customer,

Thank you for your purchase from Mometrix! We consider it an honor and a privilege that you have purchased our product and we want to ensure your satisfaction.

As part of our ongoing effort to meet the needs of test takers, we have developed a set of Study Skills Videos that we would like to give you for FREE. These videos cover our *best practices* for getting ready for your exam, from how to use our study materials to how to best prepare for the day of the test.

All that we ask is that you email us with feedback that would describe your experience so far with our product. Good, bad, or indifferent, we want to know what you think!

To get your FREE Study Skills Videos, you can use the **QR code** below, or send us an **email** at studyvideos@mometrix.com with *FREE VIDEOS* in the subject line and the following information in the body of the email:

- The name of the product you purchased.
- Your product rating on a scale of 1-5, with 5 being the highest rating.
- Your feedback. It can be long, short, or anything in between. We just want to know your impressions and experience so far with our product. (Good feedback might include how our study material met your needs and ways we might be able to make it even better. You could highlight features that you found helpful or features that you think we should add.)

If you have any questions or concerns, please don't hesitate to contact me directly.

Thanks again!

Sincerely,

Jay Willis
Vice President
jay.willis@mometrix.com
1-800-673-8175

Alcohol and Drug Counselor

Exam Secrets Study Guide

ADC Test Review for the International Examination for Alcohol & Drug Counselors

Written and edited by Mometrix Test Prep

Printed in the United States of America

This paper meets the requirements of ANSI/NISO Z39.48-1992 (Permanence of Paper).

Paperback
ISBN 13: 978-1-62733-021-3
ISBN 10: 1-6273-3021-6

Ebook
ISBN 13: 978-1-5167-0453-8
ISBN 10: 1-5167-0453-3

Hardback
ISBN 13: 978-1-5167-1850-4
ISBN 10: 1-5167-1850-X

DEAR FUTURE EXAM SUCCESS STORY

First of all, **THANK YOU** for purchasing Mometrix study materials!

Second, congratulations! You are one of the few determined test-takers who are committed to doing whatever it takes to excel on your exam. **You have come to the right place.** We developed these study materials with one goal in mind: to deliver you the information you need in a format that's concise and easy to use.

In addition to optimizing your guide for the content of the test, we've outlined our recommended steps for breaking down the preparation process into small, attainable goals so you can make sure you stay on track.

We've also analyzed the entire test-taking process, identifying the most common pitfalls and showing how you can overcome them and be ready for any curveball the test throws you.

Standardized testing is one of the biggest obstacles on your road to success, which only increases the importance of doing well in the high-pressure, high-stakes environment of test day. Your results on this test could have a significant impact on your future, and this guide provides the information and practical advice to help you achieve your full potential on test day.

Your success is our success

We would love to hear from you! If you would like to share the story of your exam success or if you have any questions or comments in regard to our products, please contact us at **800-673-8175** or **support@mometrix.com**.

Thanks again for your business and we wish you continued success!

Sincerely,
The Mometrix Test Preparation Team

TABLE OF CONTENTS

Introduction

Thank you for purchasing this resource! You have made the choice to prepare yourself for a test that could have a huge impact on your future, and this guide is designed to help you be fully ready for test day. Obviously, it's important to have a solid understanding of the test material, but you also need to be prepared for the unique environment and stressors of the test, so that you can perform to the best of your abilities.

For this purpose, the first section that appears in this guide is the **Secret Keys**. We've devoted countless hours to meticulously researching what works and what doesn't, and we've boiled down our findings to the five most impactful steps you can take to improve your performance on the test. We start at the beginning with study planning and move through the preparation process, all the way to the testing strategies that will help you get the most out of what you know when you're finally sitting in front of the test.

We recommend that you start preparing for your test as far in advance as possible. However, if you've bought this guide as a last-minute study resource and only have a few days before your test, we recommend that you skip over the first two Secret Keys since they address a long-term study plan.

If you struggle with **test anxiety**, we strongly encourage you to check out our recommendations for how you can overcome it. Test anxiety is a formidable foe, but it can be beaten, and we want to make sure you have the tools you need to defeat it.

Secret Key #1 – Plan Big, Study Small

There's a lot riding on your performance. If you want to ace this test, you're going to need to keep your skills sharp and the material fresh in your mind. You need a plan that lets you review everything you need to know while still fitting in your schedule. We'll break this strategy down into three categories.

Information Organization

Start with the information you already have: the official test outline. From this, you can make a complete list of all the concepts you need to cover before the test. Organize these concepts into groups that can be studied together, and create a list of any related vocabulary you need to learn so you can brush up on any difficult terms. You'll want to keep this vocabulary list handy once you actually start studying since you may need to add to it along the way.

Time Management

Once you have your set of study concepts, decide how to spread them out over the time you have left before the test. Break your study plan into small, clear goals so you have a manageable task for each day and know exactly what you're doing. Then just focus on one small step at a time. When you manage your time this way, you don't need to spend hours at a time studying. Studying a small block of content for a short period each day helps you retain information better and avoid stressing over how much you have left to do. You can relax knowing that you have a plan to cover everything in time. In order for this strategy to be effective though, you have to start studying early and stick to your schedule. Avoid the exhaustion and futility that comes from last-minute cramming!

Study Environment

The environment you study in has a big impact on your learning. Studying in a coffee shop, while probably more enjoyable, is not likely to be as fruitful as studying in a quiet room. It's important to keep distractions to a minimum. You're only planning to study for a short block of time, so make the most of it. Don't pause to check your phone or get up to find a snack. It's also important to **avoid multitasking**. Research has consistently shown that multitasking will make your studying dramatically less effective. Your study area should also be comfortable and well-lit so you don't have the distraction of straining your eyes or sitting on an uncomfortable chair.

The time of day you study is also important. You want to be rested and alert. Don't wait until just before bedtime. Study when you'll be most likely to comprehend and remember. Even better, if you know what time of day your test will be, set that time aside for study. That way your brain will be used to working on that subject at that specific time and you'll have a better chance of recalling information.

Finally, it can be helpful to team up with others who are studying for the same test. Your actual studying should be done in as isolated an environment as possible, but the work of organizing the information and setting up the study plan can be divided up. In between study sessions, you can discuss with your teammates the concepts that you're all studying and quiz each other on the details. Just be sure that your teammates are as serious about the test as you are. If you find that your study time is being replaced with social time, you might need to find a new team.

Secret Key #2 – Make Your Studying Count

You're devoting a lot of time and effort to preparing for this test, so you want to be absolutely certain it will pay off. This means doing more than just reading the content and hoping you can remember it on test day. It's important to make every minute of study count. There are two main areas you can focus on to make your studying count.

Retention

It doesn't matter how much time you study if you can't remember the material. You need to make sure you are retaining the concepts. To check your retention of the information you're learning, try recalling it at later times with minimal prompting. Try carrying around flashcards and glance at one or two from time to time or ask a friend who's also studying for the test to quiz you.

To enhance your retention, look for ways to put the information into practice so that you can apply it rather than simply recalling it. If you're using the information in practical ways, it will be much easier to remember. Similarly, it helps to solidify a concept in your mind if you're not only reading it to yourself but also explaining it to someone else. Ask a friend to let you teach them about a concept you're a little shaky on (or speak aloud to an imaginary audience if necessary). As you try to summarize, define, give examples, and answer your friend's questions, you'll understand the concepts better and they will stay with you longer. Finally, step back for a big picture view and ask yourself how each piece of information fits with the whole subject. When you link the different concepts together and see them working together as a whole, it's easier to remember the individual components.

Finally, practice showing your work on any multi-step problems, even if you're just studying. Writing out each step you take to solve a problem will help solidify the process in your mind, and you'll be more likely to remember it during the test.

Modality

Modality simply refers to the means or method by which you study. Choosing a study modality that fits your own individual learning style is crucial. No two people learn best in exactly the same way, so it's important to know your strengths and use them to your advantage.

For example, if you learn best by visualization, focus on visualizing a concept in your mind and draw an image or a diagram. Try color-coding your notes, illustrating them, or creating symbols that will trigger your mind to recall a learned concept. If you learn best by hearing or discussing information, find a study partner who learns the same way or read aloud to yourself. Think about how to put the information in your own words. Imagine that you are giving a lecture on the topic and record yourself so you can listen to it later.

For any learning style, flashcards can be helpful. Organize the information so you can take advantage of spare moments to review. Underline key words or phrases. Use different colors for different categories. Mnemonic devices (such as creating a short list in which every item starts with the same letter) can also help with retention. Find what works best for you and use it to store the information in your mind most effectively and easily.

Secret Key #3 – Practice the Right Way

Your success on test day depends not only on how many hours you put into preparing, but also on whether you prepared the right way. It's good to check along the way to see if your studying is paying off. One of the most effective ways to do this is by taking practice tests to evaluate your progress. Practice tests are useful because they show exactly where you need to improve. Every time you take a practice test, pay special attention to these three groups of questions:

- The questions you got wrong
- The questions you had to guess on, even if you guessed right
- The questions you found difficult or slow to work through

This will show you exactly what your weak areas are, and where you need to devote more study time. Ask yourself why each of these questions gave you trouble. Was it because you didn't understand the material? Was it because you didn't remember the vocabulary? Do you need more repetitions on this type of question to build speed and confidence? Dig into those questions and figure out how you can strengthen your weak areas as you go back to review the material.

Additionally, many practice tests have a section explaining the answer choices. It can be tempting to read the explanation and think that you now have a good understanding of the concept. However, an explanation likely only covers part of the question's broader context. Even if the explanation makes perfect sense, **go back and investigate** every concept related to the question until you're positive you have a thorough understanding.

As you go along, keep in mind that the practice test is just that: practice. Memorizing these questions and answers will not be very helpful on the actual test because it is unlikely to have any of the same exact questions. If you only know the right answers to the sample questions, you won't be prepared for the real thing. **Study the concepts** until you understand them fully, and then you'll be able to answer any question that shows up on the test.

It's important to wait on the practice tests until you're ready. If you take a test on your first day of study, you may be overwhelmed by the amount of material covered and how much you need to learn. Work up to it gradually.

On test day, you'll need to be prepared for answering questions, managing your time, and using the test-taking strategies you've learned. It's a lot to balance, like a mental marathon that will have a big impact on your future. Like training for a marathon, you'll need to start slowly and work your way up. When test day arrives, you'll be ready.

Start with the strategies you've read in the first two Secret Keys—plan your course and study in the way that works best for you. If you have time, consider using multiple study resources to get different approaches to the same concepts. It can be helpful to see difficult concepts from more than one angle. Then find a good source for practice tests. Many times, the test website will suggest potential study resources or provide sample tests.

Practice Test Strategy

If you're able to find at least three practice tests, we recommend this strategy:

Untimed and Open-Book Practice

Take the first test with no time constraints and with your notes and study guide handy. Take your time and focus on applying the strategies you've learned.

Timed and Open-Book Practice

Take the second practice test open-book as well, but set a timer and practice pacing yourself to finish in time.

Timed and Closed-Book Practice

Take any other practice tests as if it were test day. Set a timer and put away your study materials. Sit at a table or desk in a quiet room, imagine yourself at the testing center, and answer questions as quickly and accurately as possible.

Keep repeating timed and closed-book tests on a regular basis until you run out of practice tests or it's time for the actual test. Your mind will be ready for the schedule and stress of test day, and you'll be able to focus on recalling the material you've learned.

Secret Key #4 – Pace Yourself

Once you're fully prepared for the material on the test, your biggest challenge on test day will be managing your time. Just knowing that the clock is ticking can make you panic even if you have plenty of time left. Work on pacing yourself so you can build confidence against the time constraints of the exam. Pacing is a difficult skill to master, especially in a high-pressure environment, so **practice is vital**.

Set time expectations for your pace based on how much time is available. For example, if a section has 60 questions and the time limit is 30 minutes, you know you have to average 30 seconds or less per question in order to answer them all. Although 30 seconds is the hard limit, set 25 seconds per question as your goal, so you reserve extra time to spend on harder questions. When you budget extra time for the harder questions, you no longer have any reason to stress when those questions take longer to answer.

Don't let this time expectation distract you from working through the test at a calm, steady pace, but keep it in mind so you don't spend too much time on any one question. Recognize that taking extra time on one question you don't understand may keep you from answering two that you do understand later in the test. If your time limit for a question is up and you're still not sure of the answer, mark it and move on, and come back to it later if the time and the test format allow. If the testing format doesn't allow you to return to earlier questions, just make an educated guess; then put it out of your mind and move on.

On the easier questions, be careful not to rush. It may seem wise to hurry through them so you have more time for the challenging ones, but it's not worth missing one if you know the concept and just didn't take the time to read the question fully. Work efficiently but make sure you understand the question and have looked at all of the answer choices, since more than one may seem right at first.

Even if you're paying attention to the time, you may find yourself a little behind at some point. You should speed up to get back on track, but do so wisely. Don't panic; just take a few seconds less on each question until you're caught up. Don't guess without thinking, but do look through the answer choices and eliminate any you know are wrong. If you can get down to two choices, it is often worthwhile to guess from those. Once you've chosen an answer, move on and don't dwell on any that you skipped or had to hurry through. If a question was taking too long, chances are it was one of the harder ones, so you weren't as likely to get it right anyway.

On the other hand, if you find yourself getting ahead of schedule, it may be beneficial to slow down a little. The more quickly you work, the more likely you are to make a careless mistake that will affect your score. You've budgeted time for each question, so don't be afraid to spend that time. Practice an efficient but careful pace to get the most out of the time you have.

Secret Key #5 – Have a Plan for Guessing

When you're taking the test, you may find yourself stuck on a question. Some of the answer choices seem better than others, but you don't see the one answer choice that is obviously correct. What do you do?

The scenario described above is very common, yet most test takers have not effectively prepared for it. Developing and practicing a plan for guessing may be one of the single most effective uses of your time as you get ready for the exam.

In developing your plan for guessing, there are three questions to address:

- When should you start the guessing process?
- How should you narrow down the choices?
- Which answer should you choose?

When to Start the Guessing Process

Unless your plan for guessing is to select C every time (which, despite its merits, is not what we recommend), you need to leave yourself enough time to apply your answer elimination strategies. Since you have a limited amount of time for each question, that means that if you're going to give yourself the best shot at guessing correctly, you have to decide quickly whether or not you will guess.

Of course, the best-case scenario is that you don't have to guess at all, so first, see if you can answer the question based on your knowledge of the subject and basic reasoning skills. Focus on the key words in the question and try to jog your memory of related topics. Give yourself a chance to bring the knowledge to mind, but once you realize that you don't have (or you can't access) the knowledge you need to answer the question, it's time to start the guessing process.

It's almost always better to start the guessing process too early than too late. It only takes a few seconds to remember something and answer the question from knowledge. Carefully eliminating wrong answer choices takes longer. Plus, going through the process of eliminating answer choices can actually help jog your memory.

Summary: Start the guessing process as soon as you decide that you can't answer the question based on your knowledge.

How to Narrow Down the Choices

The next chapter in this book (**Test-Taking Strategies**) includes a wide range of strategies for how to approach questions and how to look for answer choices to eliminate. You will definitely want to read those carefully, practice them, and figure out which ones work best for you. Here though, we're going to address a mindset rather than a particular strategy.

Your odds of guessing an answer correctly depend on how many options you are choosing from.

Number of options left	5	4	3	2	1
Odds of guessing correctly	20%	25%	33%	50%	100%

You can see from this chart just how valuable it is to be able to eliminate incorrect answers and make an educated guess, but there are two things that many test takers do that cause them to miss out on the benefits of guessing:

- Accidentally eliminating the correct answer
- Selecting an answer based on an impression

We'll look at the first one here, and the second one in the next section.

To avoid accidentally eliminating the correct answer, we recommend a thought exercise called **the $5 challenge**. In this challenge, you only eliminate an answer choice from contention if you are willing to bet $5 on it being wrong. Why $5? Five dollars is a small but not insignificant amount of money. It's an amount you could afford to lose but wouldn't want to throw away. And while losing $5 once might not hurt too much, doing it twenty times will set you back $100. In the same way, each small decision you make—eliminating a choice here, guessing on a question there—won't by itself impact your score very much, but when you put them all together, they can make a big difference. By holding each answer choice elimination decision to a higher standard, you can reduce the risk of accidentally eliminating the correct answer.

The $5 challenge can also be applied in a positive sense: If you are willing to bet $5 that an answer choice *is* correct, go ahead and mark it as correct.

Summary: Only eliminate an answer choice if you are willing to bet $5 that it is wrong.

Which Answer to Choose

You're taking the test. You've run into a hard question and decided you'll have to guess. You've eliminated all the answer choices you're willing to bet $5 on. Now you have to pick an answer. Why do we even need to talk about this? Why can't you just pick whichever one you feel like when the time comes?

The answer to these questions is that if you don't come into the test with a plan, you'll rely on your impression to select an answer choice, and if you do that, you risk falling into a trap. The test writers know that everyone who takes their test will be guessing on some of the questions, so they intentionally write wrong answer choices to seem plausible. You still have to pick an answer though, and if the wrong answer choices are designed to look right, how can you ever be sure that you're not falling for their trap? The best solution we've found to this dilemma is to take the decision out of your hands entirely. Here is the process we recommend:

Once you've eliminated any choices that you are confident (willing to bet $5) are wrong, select the first remaining choice as your answer.

Whether you choose to select the first remaining choice, the second, or the last, the important thing is that you use some preselected standard. Using this approach guarantees that you will not be enticed into selecting an answer choice that looks right, because you are not basing your decision on how the answer choices look.

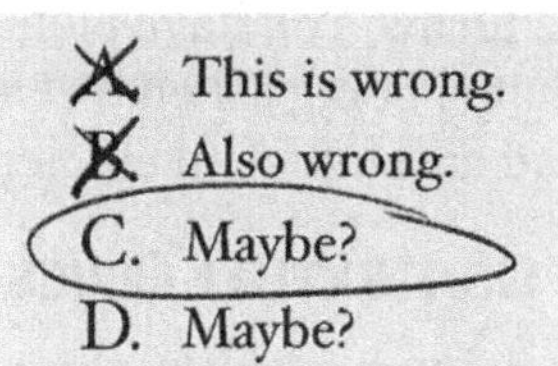

This is not meant to make you question your knowledge. Instead, it is to help you recognize the difference between your knowledge and your impressions. There's a huge difference between thinking an answer is right because of what you know, and thinking an answer is right because it looks or sounds like it should be right.

Summary: To ensure that your selection is appropriately random, make a predetermined selection from among all answer choices you have not eliminated.

Test-Taking Strategies

This section contains a list of test-taking strategies that you may find helpful as you work through the test. By taking what you know and applying logical thought, you can maximize your chances of answering any question correctly!

It is very important to realize that every question is different and every person is different: no single strategy will work on every question, and no single strategy will work for every person. That's why we've included all of them here, so you can try them out and determine which ones work best for different types of questions and which ones work best for you.

Question Strategies

☑ Read Carefully

Read the question and the answer choices carefully. Don't miss the question because you misread the terms. You have plenty of time to read each question thoroughly and make sure you understand what is being asked. Yet a happy medium must be attained, so don't waste too much time. You must read carefully and efficiently.

☑ Contextual Clues

Look for contextual clues. If the question includes a word you are not familiar with, look at the immediate context for some indication of what the word might mean. Contextual clues can often give you all the information you need to decipher the meaning of an unfamiliar word. Even if you can't determine the meaning, you may be able to narrow down the possibilities enough to make a solid guess at the answer to the question.

☑ Prefixes

If you're having trouble with a word in the question or answer choices, try dissecting it. Take advantage of every clue that the word might include. Prefixes can be a huge help. Usually, they allow you to determine a basic meaning. *Pre-* means before, *post-* means after, *pro-* is positive, *de-* is negative. From prefixes, you can get an idea of the general meaning of the word and try to put it into context.

☑ Hedge Words

Watch out for critical hedge words, such as *likely, may, can, sometimes, often, almost, mostly, usually, generally, rarely,* and *sometimes.* Question writers insert these hedge phrases to cover every possibility. Often an answer choice will be wrong simply because it leaves no room for exception. Be on guard for answer choices that have definitive words such as *exactly* and *always.*

☑ Switchback Words

Stay alert for *switchbacks.* These are the words and phrases frequently used to alert you to shifts in thought. The most common switchback words are *but, although,* and *however.* Others include *nevertheless, on the other hand, even though, while, in spite of, despite,* and *regardless of.* Switchback words are important to catch because they can change the direction of the question or an answer choice.

✓ Face Value

When in doubt, use common sense. Accept the situation in the problem at face value. Don't read too much into it. These problems will not require you to make wild assumptions. If you have to go beyond creativity and warp time or space in order to have an answer choice fit the question, then you should move on and consider the other answer choices. These are normal problems rooted in reality. The applicable relationship or explanation may not be readily apparent, but it is there for you to figure out. Use your common sense to interpret anything that isn't clear.

Answer Choice Strategies

✓ Answer Selection

The most thorough way to pick an answer choice is to identify and eliminate wrong answers until only one is left, then confirm it is the correct answer. Sometimes an answer choice may immediately seem right, but be careful. The test writers will usually put more than one reasonable answer choice on each question, so take a second to read all of them and make sure that the other choices are not equally obvious. As long as you have time left, it is better to read every answer choice than to pick the first one that looks right without checking the others.

✓ Answer Choice Families

An answer choice family consists of two (in rare cases, three) answer choices that are very similar in construction and cannot all be true at the same time. If you see two answer choices that are direct opposites or parallels, one of them is usually the correct answer. For instance, if one answer choice says that quantity *x* increases and another either says that quantity *x* decreases (opposite) or says that quantity *y* increases (parallel), then those answer choices would fall into the same family. An answer choice that doesn't match the construction of the answer choice family is more likely to be incorrect. Most questions will not have answer choice families, but when they do appear, you should be prepared to recognize them.

✓ Eliminate Answers

Eliminate answer choices as soon as you realize they are wrong, but make sure you consider all possibilities. If you are eliminating answer choices and realize that the last one you are left with is also wrong, don't panic. Start over and consider each choice again. There may be something you missed the first time that you will realize on the second pass.

✓ Avoid Fact Traps

Don't be distracted by an answer choice that is factually true but doesn't answer the question. You are looking for the choice that answers the question. Stay focused on what the question is asking for so you don't accidentally pick an answer that is true but incorrect. Always go back to the question and make sure the answer choice you've selected actually answers the question and is not merely a true statement.

✓ Extreme Statements

In general, you should avoid answers that put forth extreme actions as standard practice or proclaim controversial ideas as established fact. An answer choice that states the "process should be used in certain situations, if..." is much more likely to be correct than one that states the "process should be discontinued completely." The first is a calm rational statement and doesn't even make a definitive, uncompromising stance, using a hedge word *if* to provide wiggle room, whereas the second choice is far more extreme.

✓ Benchmark

As you read through the answer choices and you come across one that seems to answer the question well, mentally select that answer choice. This is not your final answer, but it's the one that will help you evaluate the other answer choices. The one that you selected is your benchmark or standard for judging each of the other answer choices. Every other answer choice must be compared to your benchmark. That choice is correct until proven otherwise by another answer choice beating it. If you find a better answer, then that one becomes your new benchmark. Once you've decided that no other choice answers the question as well as your benchmark, you have your final answer.

✓ Predict the Answer

Before you even start looking at the answer choices, it is often best to try to predict the answer. When you come up with the answer on your own, it is easier to avoid distractions and traps because you will know exactly what to look for. The right answer choice is unlikely to be word-for-word what you came up with, but it should be a close match. Even if you are confident that you have the right answer, you should still take the time to read each option before moving on.

General Strategies

✓ Tough Questions

If you are stumped on a problem or it appears too hard or too difficult, don't waste time. Move on! Remember though, if you can quickly check for obviously incorrect answer choices, your chances of guessing correctly are greatly improved. Before you completely give up, at least try to knock out a couple of possible answers. Eliminate what you can and then guess at the remaining answer choices before moving on.

✓ Check Your Work

Since you will probably not know every term listed and the answer to every question, it is important that you get credit for the ones that you do know. Don't miss any questions through careless mistakes. If at all possible, try to take a second to look back over your answer selection and make sure you've selected the correct answer choice and haven't made a costly careless mistake (such as marking an answer choice that you didn't mean to mark). This quick double check should more than pay for itself in caught mistakes for the time it costs.

✓ Pace Yourself

It's easy to be overwhelmed when you're looking at a page full of questions; your mind is confused and full of random thoughts, and the clock is ticking down faster than you would like. Calm down and maintain the pace that you have set for yourself. Especially as you get down to the last few minutes of the test, don't let the small numbers on the clock make you panic. As long as you are on track by monitoring your pace, you are guaranteed to have time for each question.

✓ Don't Rush

It is very easy to make errors when you are in a hurry. Maintaining a fast pace in answering questions is pointless if it makes you miss questions that you would have gotten right otherwise. Test writers like to include distracting information and wrong answers that seem right. Taking a little extra time to avoid careless mistakes can make all the difference in your test score. Find a pace that allows you to be confident in the answers that you select.

⊘ Keep Moving

Panicking will not help you pass the test, so do your best to stay calm and keep moving. Taking deep breaths and going through the answer elimination steps you practiced can help to break through a stress barrier and keep your pace.

Final Notes

The combination of a solid foundation of content knowledge and the confidence that comes from practicing your plan for applying that knowledge is the key to maximizing your performance on test day. As your foundation of content knowledge is built up and strengthened, you'll find that the strategies included in this chapter become more and more effective in helping you quickly sift through the distractions and traps of the test to isolate the correct answer.

Now that you're preparing to move forward into the test content chapters of this book, be sure to keep your goal in mind. As you read, think about how you will be able to apply this information on the test. If you've already seen sample questions for the test and you have an idea of the question format and style, try to come up with questions of your own that you can answer based on what you're reading. This will give you valuable practice applying your knowledge in the same ways you can expect to on test day.

Good luck and good studying!

Scientific Principles of Substance Use and Co-Occurring Disorders

Substance Use Disorder

Categories of Psychoactive Substances

Psychoactive substances are categorized by their mechanism of action. **Central nervous system (CNS) depressants** work by increasing gamma-aminobutyric acid (GABA), which inhibits or slows brain activity. CNS depressants include sedative-hypnotics (e.g., benzodiazepines, barbiturates, and sleep aids), alcohol, and opioids.

On the opposite end of the spectrum are **stimulants.** Stimulants increase CNS activity by releasing catecholamines (epinephrine, norepinephrine, and dopamine), which are hormones secreted from the adrenal glands. Examples of CNS stimulants include amphetamines, cocaine, nicotine, and caffeine.

The next category is **hallucinogens.** Hallucinogens work by affecting the parasympathetic nervous system (PNS). The primary neurotransmitter in the PNS is acetylcholine, which is part of the autonomic nervous system. Hallucinogens also affect the neuronal actions of dopamine, serotonin, and epinephrine. Examples of hallucinogens include D-lysergic acid diethylamide (LSD), mushrooms, MDMA (Ecstasy), ketamine, and synthetic cannabinoids.

There are also separate categories for **cannabis, inhalants,** and **performance-enhancing drugs.** Cannabis works by stimulating cannabinoid receptors that produce tetrahydrocannabinol (THC) and cannabidiol (CBD) chemical compounds. Inhalants include gases, aerosols, and volatile solvents that work by suppressing the action of the CNS. Nitrites are inhalants that work as vasodilators. Performance-enhancing drugs, such as anabolic steroids, activate androgen receptors and increase calcium levels.

Substance Use Disorders (SUD) as Described in the DSM-5-TR

The two groups of DSM-5-TR substance-related disorders are **substance use disorders (SUD)** and **substance-induced disorders**. There are 10 categories of substances with DSM-5-TR diagnostic criteria for SUD. These categories are:

- Alcohol
- Caffeine
- Cannabis
- Hallucinogens (including phencyclidine [PCP] or similar hallucinogens, such as LSD)
- Inhalants
- Opioids
- Sedatives
- Hypnotics or anxiolytics
- Stimulants (including amphetamine-type substances, cocaine, and other stimulants)
- Tobacco

Other (Unknown) Substance-Related Disorders as Described in the DSM-5-TR

The DSM-5-TR also includes criteria for other substance-related disorders that are due to unknown substances. **Other (unknown) substance-related disorders include:**

- **Other (unknown) substance use disorder**: The problematic use of a substance not listed in the 10 substances of substance use disorder criteria.
- **Other (unknown) substance intoxication**: This category includes substance intoxication delirium, along with additional disorders that result from the use of substances capable of producing euphoria or a "high." Substance intoxication can develop with:
    - Marijuana
    - Cocaine
    - Heroin
    - Stimulants
    - Hallucinogens
- **Other (unknown) substance withdrawal**: The state experienced with the reduction or cessation of a substance that has been misused for a period of time. Withdrawal symptoms can be mild, moderate, or severe and may vary based on the psychoactive substance and the length of time that the substance was misused.
- **Other (unknown) substance-induced mental disorders**: Those in which the use of a substance creates behavior similar to that of a mental health disorder such as depression, anxiety, or psychosis (hallucinations and delirium).

DSM-5-TR Criteria for SUD

The DSM-5-TR criteria for SUD include the following:

- **Amount:** Substance intake increases in volume or amount. Substance use may also last for a longer amount of time than was originally intended.
- **Control:** An inability to stop or cut down substance use.
- **Time:** Spending an excessive duration of time obtaining, using, or recovering from substances.
- **Cravings:** Craving involves the unwavering urge to use the substance.
- **Obligations:** Failing to fulfill promises or duties, including activities at work, home, and/or school.
- **Social:** Continuing to use the substance, despite relationship difficulties.
- **Importance:** Prioritizing substance use over relationships, work, or recreational activities.
- **Risk:** Continuing to use a substance despite dangerous consequences or the threat of dangerous consequences.
- **Harm:** Experiencing detrimental outcomes with substance use (e.g., physical harm, psychological harm).
- **Tolerance:** Requiring more and more of a substance to achieve the desired effect.
- **Withdrawal**: Symptoms that occur after discontinued substance use. Withdrawal is also associated with the need to use a substance to avoid the onset of symptoms.

Stages of Substance Use and the Progression of Psychoactive Substance Use

Not everyone who has used drugs or alcohol has a problem with substance abuse. The counselor must determine if the client has a pathological addiction or just engages in experimental use. The first step is to grade the client on the continuum of drug use, based on a five-stage progression.

Stage 1: Abstinence	This stage refers to the client who is abstinent or involved in self-denial of use. Abstinence may allow for an occasional glass of wine. However, the person who chooses this route probably was heavily addicted to alcohol in the past and completely abstains now to keep from falling back into old, addictive ways. Twelve-step programs such as AA and Narcotics Anonymous advocate complete abstinence; these self-help groups are complementary reinforcement for formal therapy because meetings are held daily in most metropolitan areas and peer pressure can help prevent a relapse. In cases involving a past addiction, the therapist's role is to help the client stay "on the wagon" of abstinence. Having even one drink can be detrimental to an alcoholic because it can trigger a drinking binge.
Stage 2: Experimental Use (No SUD)	Teens and young adults partake of a chemical to find out what it feels like. It is an expected rite of passage for many segments of our culture. Problems involved with experimentation include drunk driving and date rape. Gamma-hydroxybutyric acid (GHB) is often dissolved in alcohol at social events like raves because it enhances the libido and lowers inhibitions. Victims enter a dreamlike state and act drunk. They relax sometimes to the point of unconsciousness, have problems seeing clearly, are confused, and have no recollection of events or the passage of time while drugged.
Stage 3: Social Use (Mild SUD)	The test to determine if a person is a social user or is addicted is whether or not the person can stop drug use. For example, a social drinker can drink a controlled amount and does not need it to function normally. But if a person needs alcohol or a drug to satisfy cravings, to prevent unpleasant withdrawal symptoms, or as a means of coping with daily life, then it is considered an addiction. Counseling involves an educational group to develop coping skills and relationship skills with peers.
Stage 4: Abuse (Moderate SUD)	The client's problem can be physiological or psychological in nature, or both. The addiction is detrimental to personal safety, family relationships, academic life, and work functions. Spousal and child abuse often coincide with drug abuse. Drunk driving and theft to support a habit are societal problems resulting from addictive behavior. Friends and associates are probably uncomfortable around the abuser by the time the addiction is visibly evident. At this point, the employer can insist that the abuser get help on a professional level through an employee assistance program or public programs as a condition of continued employment. Abusers benefit from psychological counseling on a weekly basis and an intervention program to stop the alcohol or drug abuse. Antabuse (disulfiram), methadone, levo-alpha-acetylmethadol, buprenorphine, and naltrexone are useful adjuncts to counseling to wean the abuser off the drugs of abuse. Intensive outpatient programs may be sufficient for recovery.

Stage 5: Chemical Dependency/ Addiction (Severe SUD)	The addict experiences withdrawal symptoms when the drug or alcohol is not available for consumption. The addict builds up a tolerance to the drug to the point that more and more is needed just to keep from experiencing physical withdrawal. The high is harder and harder to reach. The addict is now at increased risk for unintentional overdose, because street drugs have inconsistent strengths. The addict is also on the verge of failing in marriage, academics, and work. The addict experiences serious medical issues such as ventricular tachycardia and atrial fibrillation, and more powerful drugs such as clonidine (Catapres patches or tablets) are used to prevent death. Permanent damage from Korsakoff syndrome or Wernicke encephalopathy may result from a poor diet lacking in vitamins. Long-term inpatient rehabilitation programs are crucial in most cases. Intensive outpatient programs may be sufficient for a minority of addicts.

Tolerance, Dependence, and Withdrawal

Substance Dependence

Substance dependence occurs when an individual experiences significant clinical and functional impairment from the repeated use of a substance. The consequences of dependency can be emotional, physical, mental, or psychological. Susceptibility to substance dependence begins with an initial rewarding experience that occurs with psychoactive substance use, followed by reinforced behavior or frequent use, which can create a pathway leading to substance abuse. When substances are misused or abused regularly, the body and brain begin to adapt to this use, resulting in tolerance and dependence. When an individual becomes psychologically dependent on a substance, craving can occur with abstinence (i.e., discontinued use).

The amount of a substance required to cross the threshold for dependence varies from person to person. An individual's risk for dependency is influenced by many biological and environmental factors, including genetics, brain chemistry, gender, interpersonal stressors, and emotional well-being.

Psychological and Physical Forms of Drug Dependence

Drug dependence can present in the form of psychological and/or physical symptoms. Psychological dependence comes in the form of cravings, urges, and the desire for substance use, whereas physical dependence is the result of brain changes due to drug use, in which the brain starts to require the heightened state of activity produced by the drug and therefore creates physical reactions when the drug is absent.

Withdrawal consists of the physical reactions that occur when a person suddenly stops using a substance that he or she is dependent on. Common withdrawal symptoms include nausea, muscle aches, anxiety, and depression. Tolerance is another physical reaction; tolerance is the change in which a person's body requires higher doses of a substance to produce the same effects attained when the substance was first used.

Physical and psychological dependence describe states in which a person only feels functionally "normal" in the presence of the substance that he or she has become dependent on. When a person is dependent, the brain's natural state of homeostasis is disrupted, creating a state of disequilibrium. The brain is then challenged with restoring balance in the presence of neuropathways altered by chronic substance use.

Connection Among Psychoactive Substance Use, Brain Functioning, and Dependency

An individual who engages in **psychoactive substance use** experiences physiological and psychological symptoms. These symptoms can include physical illness or disease and impairments in mood, cognition, behavior, and judgment. When individuals use psychoactive substances, their **brain functioning** is altered, and the person is at risk for substance dependency.

Dependency is viewed as a brain disease characterized by an uncontrollable desire to consume increased quantities of a psychoactive substance. When the repeated consumption of a substance follows this compulsion, the brain becomes altered, and the person becomes dependent on that substance. When altered, the brain can only function normally with continued substance use. When this level of dependency is reached, habituation or **addiction** is likely to occur. The mechanisms involved in dependency are individualized, and each person has varying thresholds. These thresholds are influenced by the complex interaction of various biopsychosocial factors (e.g., genetics, emotional distress, interpersonal relationships).

Individuals with substance dependence continue to use psychoactive substances despite encountering harmful consequences, including the risk of long-term complications. When substances continue to be misused, **tolerance** occurs, which causes the individual to require an increased amount of the substance to attain the desired effect.

Molecular Mechanisms of Tolerance to Psychoactive Substances

Tolerance to psychoactive substances occurs when individuals must consume larger quantities of substances to receive the same effect or intensity as experienced with previous smaller doses. Over time, repeated consumption of a psychoactive substance can lead to tolerance. Substances that rapidly develop tolerance in users include methamphetamine and heroin.

Various **forms of tolerance** include the following:

- **Behavioral tolerance** occurs when individuals display behaviors that mask the effects of substance use from others, including changes in disposition, attitude, or speech associated with psychoactive substance intoxication.
- **Dispositional or metabolic tolerance** happens when a person's body tries to accelerate metabolism to rid itself of chemically toxic substances. Substance misuse disrupts this natural process, creating the need for more and more of the substance to be consumed.
- **Cross-tolerance** develops when people become tolerant of psychoactive substances in the same pharmaceutical family as those previously tolerated. For example, a person who is tolerant to heroin may become tolerant to all other opioids.
- **Pharmacodynamic tolerance or cellular-adaptive tolerance** occurs when neurotransmitters are altered so that the brain has become desensitized to the substance. This cellular adaptation lessens the effects of a substance as it loses its ability to change brain activity.
- **Reverse tolerance** happens when a person becomes more sensitive to the substance because the substance has harmed neuronal activity. For example, a person who is tolerant to alcohol has begun to experience liver damage. Liver damage then causes a decrease in tolerance because the liver can no longer break down alcohol.
- **Select tolerance** occurs when some effects of a drug are experienced and others are not. For example, some people may not feel the euphoric effects of a substance, but the substance continues to affect other parts of their body.

Stages of Withdrawal

Withdrawal describes the physiological symptoms associated with discontinuing a substance upon which a person is physically dependent. Withdrawal is highly personalized, with signs and symptoms varying among those who are physiologically dependent. Withdrawal is also substance-specific, and it can vary based on the amount of time the substance was used. The **stages of withdrawal** include the following:

- **Stage 1** describes the initial symptoms of withdrawal, and it can occur within a few hours or within 24 hours after the last dose. The timelines vary based on the substance used. For example, withdrawal symptoms from alcohol may present hours after the last drink, whereas benzodiazepine withdrawal generally begins within 1–4 days after the last dose.
- **Stage 2** is characterized by the intensification of symptoms and can include body aches, sleep disturbances, depression, tremors, and anxiety. Acute symptoms of withdrawal can last days or weeks as the detoxification process begins.
- **Stage 3** is the post-acute phase, which is marked by a sharp peak and then a decline in symptoms. In this stage, medical professionals may intervene to help alleviate acute symptoms. This phase can last several weeks or months, and it may include persistent insomnia, emotional lability, memory impairment, and anxiety.
- After a person has experienced the stages of withdrawal, he or she may transition into **post-acute withdrawal syndrome**, which can last anywhere from several months to years. The symptoms of post-acute withdrawal syndrome vary from person to person and affect multiple elements of biopsychosocial functioning. Its biopsychosocial symptoms often include memory impairment, difficulty thinking clearly, mood swings, cravings, anhedonia, suicidal ideation, fatigue, muscle aches, social withdrawal, and pain sensitivity.

Detoxification in the Recovery Process

Detoxification (casually referred to as detox) is the first step of recovery for individuals diagnosed with SUD. **Medical detox** is warranted for individuals at risk for life-threatening withdrawal symptoms who may require sedation, whereas **social or supervised detox** is reserved for individuals with nonlethal withdrawal symptoms (e.g., seizures). Alcohol and benzodiazepine misuse are associated with hazardous or lethal withdrawal symptoms.

Detoxification management generally occurs in the following **three phases or steps**:

1. **Screening, assessment, and evaluation:** During this initial stage of treatment for SUD, the existence of a psychoactive substance and its concentration are measured through blood work and other means. Clients are also assessed for co-occurring mental and physical disorders.
2. **Stabilization:** This step involves guiding individuals through all phases of withdrawal as they begin SUD treatment and recovery. Medication management may be used to help clients through the detoxification process. A treatment plan is built, and when appropriate, family members and social supports are identified and included in the client's treatment.
3. **Treatment engagement:** Detox is not viewed as a treatment modality for SUD but instead as the first phase in the continuum of recovery that allows a person to experience physiological and psychological withdrawal symptoms in a safe environment.

SUD and the Brain

Blood-Brain Barrier

Microvascular endothelial cells protect the brain by forming a **blood-brain barrier**. Because endothelial cells are compact and tightly wound, many substances are prevented from leaving the blood and reaching the brain. However, small or fat-soluble substances (e.g., alcohol, cocaine) pass through the barrier without difficulty. The body produces transporter proteins to help larger and water-soluble substances (e.g., insulin) reach the brain from the bloodstream.

Once a substance enters the bloodstream, it remains in the circulatory proteins and plasma for a period of time. A substance's **half-life** is the duration of time that it takes for half of the substance to be eliminated from the body. **Metabolism** is the process through which a substance is eliminated from the body. This happens primarily in the liver, but it can also occur in the gastrointestinal tract, kidneys, lungs, and plasma.

Classification of SUD as a Disease That Affects the Brain and Behavior

SUD is classified as a brain disease due to its direct and often long-lasting effects on the nervous system, primarily with the brain, which is part of the central nervous system (CNS), and then on the peripheral nervous system (i.e., the somatic and autonomic nervous systems).

The **autonomic nervous system** is part of the peripheral nervous system. It controls various bodily functions, including breathing, gastrointestinal functions, heart rate, emotions, temperature, and digestion. The autonomic nerve pathways transmit **acetylcholine**, which is part of the parasympathetic system, and **norepinephrine**, which is part of the sympathetic nervous system. Acetylcholine elicits an inhibiting effect, whereas norepinephrine produces a stimulating or excitatory effect.

When a psychoactive substance is introduced into the body, the brain compensates by attempting to maintain stability. Psychoactive substances can alter the brain's chemistry in the areas required to sustain life and may lead to various behaviors contributing to addiction, such as compulsive drug seeking and use. The brain's structural alterations are responsible for causing a person to use substances despite detrimental consequences.

Effects of Psychoactive Substance Use on the Brain

When an individual consumes one or more psychoactive substances, the CNS and its subsystems become altered. This alteration can occur with licit (i.e., legal) or illicit (i.e., illegal) substances. The main areas of the brain that are altered with psychoactive substance use include the following:

- **Amygdala:** It is responsible for emotion, motivation, and memory formation, particularly in relation to stress and fear responses. These are most relevant in the withdrawal experience.
- **Reticular activating system:** It is responsible for an individual's state of arousal.
- **Basal ganglia:** The basal ganglia control the portion of the brain responsible for motivation, movement-related functions, and the formation of habits. The basal ganglia also control the psychoactive substance use's pleasurable and rewarding effects.
- **Cerebellum:** The cerebellum controls coordination, posture, motor skills, and movement.
- **Prefrontal cortex:** The prefrontal cortex is responsible for thinking, planning, and problem solving. Impulse control is also a prefrontal cortex function, making adolescents especially vulnerable to the influence of SUD on the prefrontal cortex, as development and maturity of the prefrontal cortex is at its height during adolescence.

- **Hypothalamus:** The hypothalamus controls hormone production and sends hormones to other bodily organs through the pituitary gland. It plays an essential role in regulating the body's stress response.

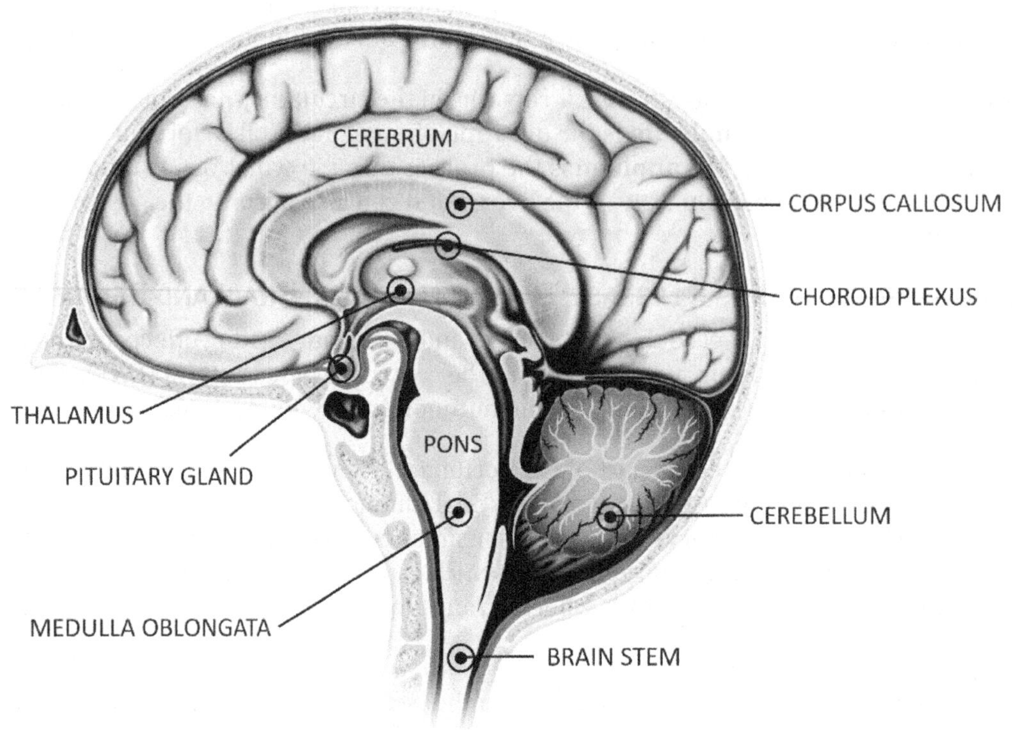

Components of the Brain's Communication Pathways

Key components of the brain's communication pathways include the following:

- **Neurons** are the specialized cells that send and receive biochemical information. Neurons use synapses to send and receive messages. Neurons are made of three main parts: **dendrites, the axon, and the soma.**
- The **synapses** deliver neurotransmitters, such as dopamine and serotonin, from neuron to neuron.
- **Dendrites** are tree-like extensions of the neuron that receive synaptic inputs from axons.
- The **axon** is the portion of the brain cell that determines whether or not the neuron will be fired to signal the release of neurotransmitters.
- **The soma** is the cell body, which contains the nucleus. The soma's function is to send proteins through the axon and dendrites.

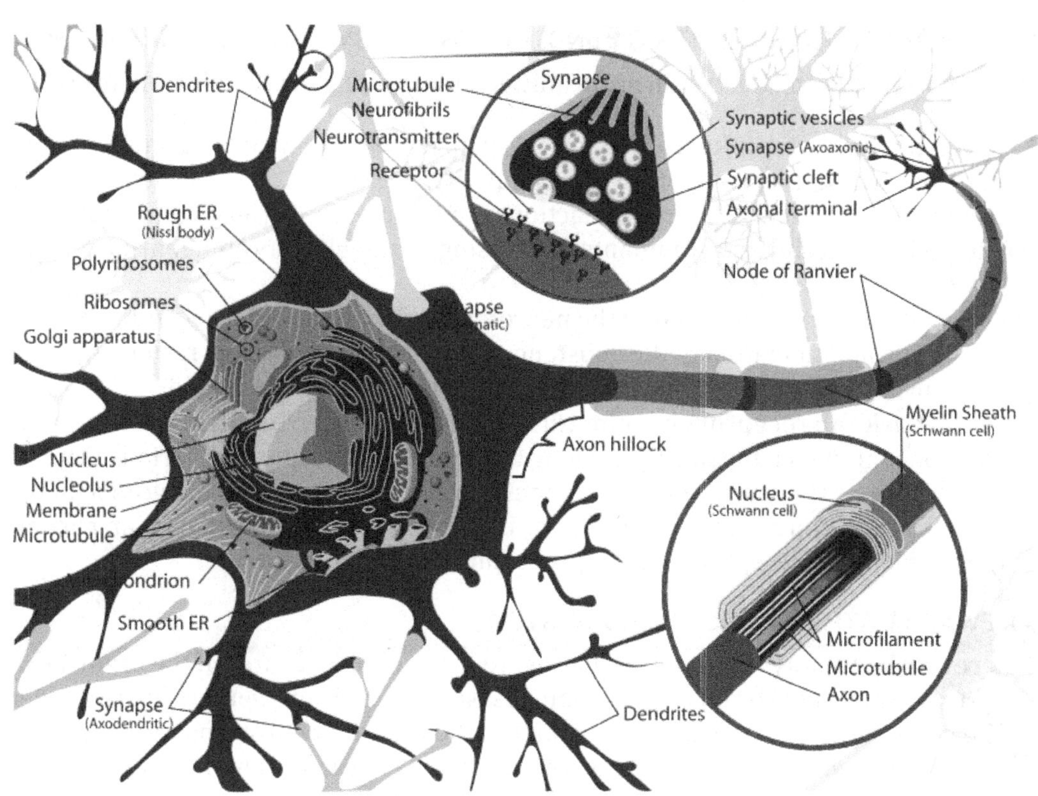

Cross Section of a Neuron

Neurotransmitters Activated by Psychoactive Substances

The most common neurotransmitters activated by psychoactive substances include the following:

- **Acetylcholine** is responsible for memory, attention, and mood and is affected by nicotine, caffeine, and hallucinogens.
- **Dopamine** is responsible for the functions of movement, memory, concentration, and pleasure. Substances that affect dopamine levels include cocaine, methamphetamine, alcohol, and opioids.
- **Serotonin** is responsible for sleep, sexual desire, emotions, and digestion. Substances that affect serotonin levels include MDMA, hallucinogens, and cocaine.
- **Endogenous opioids** (endorphins and enkephalins) affect areas of the brain responsible for regulating pain, mood, responses to stress, and sedation. Endogenous opioids are affected by heroin, morphine, and prescription medications (e.g., oxycodone, codeine, hydrocodone).
- **Epinephrine** (i.e., adrenaline) is responsible for the fight-or-flight brain function and is affected by nicotine, stimulants, MDMA, and hallucinogens. Epinephrine is a neurotransmitter and a hormone produced in the adrenal gland.
- **Norepinephrine** controls movement, sleep, memory, and anxiety and is affected by cocaine, methamphetamine, and MDMA.
- **Glutamate** affects functions associated with memory, learning, and cognition and is affected by ketamine, alcohol, and PCP.
- **Gamma-aminobutyric acid (GABA)** is responsible for slowed neuronal activity, anxiety, and anesthesia. GABA is affected by alcohol, tranquilizers, and sedative-hypnotics.

Altering of a Neurotransmitter's Functioning by Psychoactive Substances

Psychoactive substances can alter a neurotransmitter's functioning in the following ways:

- They can **prevent reuptake** from occurring, which is when a neurotransmitter is blocked from being absorbed by its appropriate synapse, thereby increasing the neurotransmitter's concentration in the brain. This is the action of antidepressants (increasing the level of serotonin in the brain) and stimulants (increasing the level of norepinephrine and/or dopamine).
- They can affect the **metabolism** of the neurotransmitter by interfering with the breakdown and subsequent elimination of the substance's non-usable parts. This results in neurotransmitters activating specific receptors for longer than intended.
- They can **trick the receptors** by mimicking their action (e.g., the effects of methamphetamine on dopamine), causing the receptor to respond in various ways. If the substance causes the receptors to react or activate, the substance is an **agonist**. Substances that block this action are **antagonists** (e.g., naltrexone). Some substances can partially trigger or block the reception (e.g., buprenorphine).

Brain's Reward Pathway and Limbic System

The **brain's reward pathway and limbic system** are located in the center of the brain. Because the limbic system controls the brain's motivation, pleasure, and reward centers, it is designed to seek and repeat pleasurable experiences. Dopamine is the primary neurotransmitter associated with emotionally heightened feelings of pleasure. Dopamine is produced in the ventral tegmental area and is then carried to the nucleus accumbens and the prefrontal cortex.

The reward pathway is responsible for pleasurable survival-related functions and behaviors, such as eating, drinking, and sex. This pathway can be altered, influenced, and/or harmed by psychoactive substance use. The brain's reward pathway also affects memory and behavior. When a substance is introduced to the body, the brain learns a new or "artificial" way to seek pleasure and avoid pain. The hypothalamus is also located in the limbic system and works with the CNS and the autonomic nervous system to help the body reach and maintain homeostasis.

How Neurotransmitters Are Implicated in the Development of SUD

Dopamine is the primary neurotransmitter implicated in the development of SUD. Dopamine occurs naturally in the brain when a person engages in pleasurable activities. The reward centers of the brain work to reinforce and repeat pleasurable behaviors. Psychoactive substances increase dopamine levels, which produces euphoric feelings or highs.

Some substances can release up to 10 times the amount of dopamine as pleasurable activities such as sex or eating, and they are often longer lasting. In addition, when administration methods include smoking or injection into the vein, the dopamine surge and subsequent euphoria are almost immediate.

SUD occurs when the brain remembers euphoric episodes and seeks to repeat them again and again. A drug-induced high is the result of dopamine overload triggered by the brain in reaction to drug use, and the brain responds by producing less dopamine as a means of maintaining homeostasis. The individual then begins to feel sad or hopeless without the substance and seeks the drug just to experience moods equivalent to their previous baseline levels. Chronic exposure to a substance creates tolerance and contributes to the development of SUD. These brain changes persist long after the substance is stopped.

Changes in Adolescent Brains Increasing Risk for SUD

Compared to other adolescents, those who misuse drugs and alcohol are at greater risk for **cognitive, emotional, and social deficits**. Although teens are more likely to experiment with drugs and alcohol, not all develop SUD in adulthood. There is well-supported evidence that prolonged and chronic psychoactive substance use adversely affects the normal growth and development of the brain. However, longitudinal studies are currently needed to determine the influence of preexisting neurobiological networks on the development of SUD and whether the brain can recover from the harmful effects of substance use.

During adolescence, synaptic refinement affects biopsychosocial development, which, along with **myelination,** reduces gray matter and makes the brain more efficient. This process, known as **synaptic pruning**, occurs in the **temporal cortex and subcortical structures**. In addition, the adolescent brain's **prefrontal regions and limbic system** are responsible for increased risk taking, making teens more vulnerable to SUD. The prefrontal cortex is one of the most affected areas of the brain, and it does not reach full maturity until young adulthood (i.e., ages 21–25). The prefrontal cortex is the part of the brain responsible for executive functioning (e.g., planning, organization, problem solving) and emotional regulation (e.g., self-control, decision making)

Routes of Administration

The most common routes of psychoactive drug administration include the following:

Route	Description	Common Drugs	Complications
Oral	Taken by mouth in pill or liquid form	Opioids, steroids, LSD, cannabinoids, alcohol, CNS stimulants and depressants	Gastrointestinal damage, bleeding, oral lesions and caries, tooth loss, and the development of various carcinomas.
Inhaled	Smoked into the lungs	Nicotine, ketamine, PCP	Damage to the lungs and lung cancer are risks of smoke (and other substance) inhalation.
Intravenous (IV)	Injected into the vein	Heroin, cocaine, methamphetamine, amphetamine, ketamine, PCP	Offers an immediate high, placing a person at the most significant risk for dependency and/or overdose. Individuals who use IV drugs are also at an increased risk for infectious diseases (e.g., HIV/AIDS and hepatitis B and C).
Intramuscular (IM)	Injected into the muscle	Ketamine	Abscesses and infectious diseases at the location of insertion that may become systemic if untreated.
Subcutaneous	Injected beneath the skin—often used when venous access has deteriorated due to chronic drug use	Heroin, cocaine, amphetamine, methamphetamine	Abscesses and infectious diseases at the location of insertion that may become systemic if untreated.

Route	Description	Common Drugs	Complications
Nasal	Snorted through the nasal passage	Cocaine, ketamine, heroin	Places individuals at risk for developing perforations in the nasal cavity. The effects of substances administered nasally are rapid, increasing a person's risk for dependency.
Sublingual	Absorbed under the tongue	LSD, nicotine	Chronic sublingual drug use can lead to poor oral health, including oral lesions, tooth loss, and carcinomas.
Transdermal	Absorbed into the skin, usually in the form of a patch	Opioids (most commonly fentanyl), nicotine	Skin irritation, with the possibility of burns and wounds in severe cases.

Smoking is the fastest administration method for drugs, followed by—in order—injection, snorting, and substances placed in the mucous membranes. The slowest rate of absorption is with orally administered substances.

CNS Stimulants

Stimulants, which include caffeine, nicotine, cocaine, amphetamines, and methamphetamines, are the most commonly used substances in the world. This class of drugs increases CNS activity and is used medically and recreationally. Stimulants are primarily administered orally. When used recreationally, administration can occur by intramuscular and/or intravascular injection, smoking, and snorting. Stimulants can also be administered transdermally.

Stimulant medication is prescribed to medically treat the following conditions:

- Narcolepsy
- Attention-deficit/hyperactivity disorder (ADHD)
- Nasal and sinus congestion
- Asthma
- Weight loss
- Respiratory issues
- Depression
- Edema

Mechanism of Action and Effects of Stimulants

Stimulants increase the release of **catecholamines (epinephrine, norepinephrine, and dopamine)** from the adrenal glands. These are the main hormones involved in the fight-or-flight stress response of the sympathetic nervous system. Epinephrine is a neurotransmitter responsible for providing the physical response of increased heart and respiratory rates, increased blood glucose levels, and a temporary increase in energy. Norepinephrine causes vasoconstriction, leading to increased blood pressure along with increased heart rate. Dopamine is a feel-good hormone that elicits feelings of confidence and pleasure. The main effects of stimulants include increased mental awareness, excitation, euphoria, and aphrodisiacal effects. These side effects last for varying lengths of time depending on the drug and the route through which it was administered. Stimulants are primarily metabolized in the liver.

Adverse Effects of Stimulants

The adverse effects of stimulants depend upon the dosage, the method of delivery, tolerance to the substance, the user's body weight, and the type of stimulant. Stimulants can affect a person's metabolism, heart rate, respiratory functions, blood pressure, and body temperature.

The chief adverse effects of stimulants include the following:

- Decreased appetite
- Auditory hallucinations
- Agitation
- Respiratory failure
- Anxiety
- Malnutrition
- Psychosis
- Increased urination
- Dehydration
- Insomnia
- Delusions of grandeur
- Ringing in ears
- Elevated body temperature
- Seizures
- Cardiac arrest
- Chills
- Headaches
- Emotional lability
- Hyperglycemia
- Paranoia

Dependence, Withdrawal, and Toxicity Associated with the Misuse of Stimulants

Stimulant misuse is dangerous because it places users at a high risk for developing dependence and the rapid onset of tolerance. Psychological and physical dependence generally occurs within a month and varies based on the type of substance and the frequency of use. Stimulant misuse can lead to long-term heart problems.

Stimulants release between 2 and 10 times more dopamine than natural rewards, such as food or sex, and their absence is quickly recognized by the brain. Withdrawal symptoms of stimulants often begin with a "crash," which is followed by depression, lethargy, irritability, and poor concentration. Toxicity, or the dose at which the drug can induce possibly lethal effects, is dependent on the drug type, with cocaine being the strongest. For some stimulants, overdose may be fatal due to cardiac failure, seizures, dehydration, and/or stroke.

Amphetamines and Methamphetamine

Types, Medical Use, and Peak Responses of Amphetamines

Amphetamines are synthetic psychoactive substances with street names including uppers, crank, white crosses, bennies, black beauties, glass, white cross, ice, no doze, speed, whiz, meth, and crystal.

The most common types of amphetamines include amphetamine (amps) and methamphetamine (meth). These are prescribed medically in the treatment of ADHD and also to help individuals stay awake (in the case of narcolepsy) and to diminish appetite (in the case of obesity).

When amphetamines are orally ingested, the peak response is between 1 and 3 hours; when injected, the peak response occurs after 15 minutes. Effects may be experienced between 7 and 12 hours after use. The peak concentration of methamphetamine is just under 3 hours.

Legal Status

In 1970, Congress passed the **Controlled Substances Act**, which classified amphetamines as Schedule III drugs. In 1971, amphetamines were reclassified as Schedule II. This regulation was enacted in response to the amphetamine epidemic of the 1960s. At that time, there was an increase in misuse and dependency due to the psychoactive properties of the substance.

Methamphetamine is a Schedule II drug that can be chemically created in meth labs using ingredients found in over-the-counter (OTC) allergy medications. In 2005, the dangers of illegal methamphetamine production were addressed by the Combat Methamphetamine Epidemic Act (CMEA).

CMEA regulates the sale of OTC medications containing ephedrine, phenylpropanolamine, and pseudoephedrine—ingredients used to illegally produce methamphetamine. CMEA also provides regulations addressing the risk of child endangerment associated with the toxic effects of methamphetamine production. As a result, several states now carry stricter penalties for individuals manufacturing methamphetamine in homes shared with children.

Metabolism, General Mechanism of Action, Half-Life, and Health Risks of Methamphetamine

Methamphetamine triggers dopamine release and functions as a dopamine look-alike by dysregulating dopamine reuptake and transmission. Common street names for methamphetamine include black beauties, chalk, chicken feed, crank, peanut butter crank, crystal, glass, ice, meth, shards, speed, tina, tweak, and uppers. Desoxyn is the only FDA-approved methamphetamine and is used to treat obesity and ADHD.

Methamphetamine is primarily trafficked from Mexico, with some illegal production found in the United States. CMEA was passed in 2005 to regulate ingredients used in meth labs by requiring identification to purchase medications containing key ingredients used to make meth. When methamphetamine is smoked or transmitted intranasally, the half-life is just over 10.5 hours. When transmitted intravenously or orally, the half-life is an average of 11.5 hours.

Newborns exposed in utero are at risk for low birth weight, excessive crying, lethargy, and neurological problems. Methamphetamine-dependent newborns may also experience decreased arousal, and they may develop into toddlers and children with developmental delays and poor self-regulating behaviors. Other neonatal health risks include infectious diseases caused by shared needles (e.g., HIV, hepatitis). In addition, intrauterine brain hemorrhaging can occur, with potentially fatal complications.

Short- and Long-Term Effects

Short-term effects of amphetamines and methamphetamines include an increase in all of the following areas:

- Energy
- Cognition
- Libido
- Heart rate
- Self-esteem
- Respirations
- Euphoria
- Blood pressure

The **long-term effects** include all of the following:

- Cardiovascular events (e.g., cardiac arrest)
- Insomnia
- Poor dental hygiene
- Hyperthermia
- Anxiety
- Hallucinations of "meth bugs"
- Memory impairment
- Aneurysms, strokes, and seizures
- Depression
- Severe malnutrition
- Psychosis
- Poor decision making
- Muscle tension
- Akathisia (i.e., the inability to remain still)
- Irritability
- Paranoia
- Dermatillomania (i.e., skin picking)

Tolerance, Dependence, Withdrawal, and the Potential for Toxicity

Tolerance to amphetamines and methamphetamines develops quickly, which places the user at greater risk for toxicity because higher doses are required to attain the desired effect. Both forms of stimulant medication cause an increase in norepinephrine and dopamine, resulting in a surge of energy, as well as feelings of euphoria. In some individuals, a phenomenon known as sensitization occurs when selective events trigger memories associated with initial use of the stimulants. During these episodes, the individual exhibits a lower tolerance to the substances' perceived effects.

The potential for dependence is exceptionally high for amphetamines and methamphetamines. Psychological dependence is associated with chronic misuse, with withdrawal symptoms leading to extreme lethargy, increased appetite, irritability, and body aches. Withdrawal symptoms generally begin 1–2 days after the last dose and can last between 5 days and 3 weeks. For chronic users, protracted symptoms, such as psychosis, may last for years. Toxic effects include hypothermia, increased heart rate, hyperglycemia, and seizures. The effects of overdose are heightened with polydrug use—particularly when mixed with CNS depressants—and these effects may be fatal.

Cocaine Hydrochloride, Cocaine, and Crack Cocaine

Cocaine is a highly addictive CNS stimulant derived from coca plant leaves cultivated in the Andean highlands of South America. **Cocaine hydrochloride** is a Schedule II drug used medically as a local anesthetic and vasoconstrictor. Smoking is the only means of consuming crack cocaine, which increases the risk for addiction because the onset of euphoria occurs quickly. Cocaine hydrochloride, crack cocaine, and cocaine differ in a variety of ways (see the table below).

Drug	Method of Use	Medical Use	Onset of Action	Appearance	Street Names
Cocaine hydrochloride	Snorted, injected, smoked when combined with marijuana, absorbed through mucosal membranes	Medically used as a vasoconstrictor, topical solution, and anesthetic; lidocaine and procaine mimic the effects of cocaine hydrochloride.	When used topically, it is absorbed through mucous membranes, with effects experienced rapidly and persisting for 30 minutes.	Powder	Coke, snow white, toot, happy trails, and sugar
Crack cocaine	Smoked alone (i.e., freebasing) or with marijuana, or tobacco; also smoked with opioids (i.e., speedballing)	None	Instant high occurring between 7 and 10 seconds and persisting up to 10 minutes.	Irregular glass-like appearance, chunks hardened into crystalized rocks, achieved by dissolving powdered cocaine in a mixture of water and ammonia or baking soda	Rock, vases, and crack
Cocaine	Snorted; rubbed on gums or injected after dissolving in water	Rare uses (e.g., nosebleeds, oral surgery)	When snorted and rubbed on the gums, 1–3 minutes; when injected, 10–15 seconds	Powder, which is often diluted or cut with other substances	Coke, nose candy, flake, snow, blow, and toot

Solubility, Half-Life, Mechanism of Action, Metabolism

Cocaine is water-soluble, and crack cocaine is fat-soluble. The half-life of cocaine is brief (0.5–1.5 hours). Cocaine is rapidly metabolized in the liver.

Cocaine prevents the reuptake of dopamine, serotonin, and norepinephrine, causing a buildup of these hormones in the body. Increased concentrations of dopamine in the synaptic cleft or gap that separates neurons results in dopamine overload, leading to euphoria.

Short-Term Psychological Effects

The **short-term psychological effects** of cocaine include the following:

- Anxiety
- Paranoia
- Irritability
- Mental acuity
- Auditory hallucinations
- Enhanced confidence

Short-Term Physiological Effects and Long-Term Protracted Effects

The short-term physiological effects of cocaine use include vasoconstriction, sympathetic stress response (fight or flight), increased body temperature, tremors, pressured speech, and cardiovascular incidents. The long-term use of cocaine can lead to severe emotional, cardiovascular, neurological, and gastrointestinal complications, including coronary calcification, vasoconstriction, heart arrhythmia, headaches, seizures, strokes, and malnutrition.

Protracted use of cocaine may cause personality changes. Prolonged cocaine use can exacerbate sociocognitive deficits and aggression in individuals prone to violence. The physiological effects of prolonged use vary based on the specific route of administration.

Individuals who snort cocaine can lose their sense of smell or have difficulty swallowing. Prolonged vasoconstriction caused by administering cocaine intranasally can lead to chronic irritation, infection, or perforation of the nasal septum. Individuals who smoke cocaine are at an increased risk for gastrointestinal and respiratory difficulties. Gastrointestinal difficulties include tears, ulcers, and intestinal ischemia (blocking of blood vessels). In extreme cases, prolonged use can lead to malnutrition and bowel tissue complications. Respiratory problems include lung disease, pneumonia, asthma, and acute respiratory irritation. In addition, when individuals use cocaine intravenously, there is a heightened risk of developing an infectious disease, abscesses, and cellulitis.

Tolerance, Dependence, and the Risk for Toxicity and Overdose

Tolerance to cocaine develops quickly because higher doses are required to produce the same level of euphoria or assist with initial withdrawal symptoms. Psychological tolerance occurs due to the activation of the brain's mesolimbic dopamine pathway. For these reasons, cocaine dependence tends to happen more rapidly than with other psychoactive substances.

As with opioids, there is a risk of overdose due to cocaine's narrow therapeutic index or threshold, which is the ratio between the drug's toxicity and therapeutic dose. Cocaethylene is produced when cocaine is mixed with alcohol, which adds to its toxicity and increases incidents of overdose caused by cardiovascular events. Polydrug use increases cocaine's toxicity and risk of overdose.

Withdrawal Symptoms

Suddenly stopping cocaine use after periods of dependence can lead to impairment. As with other psychoactive drugs, neuropathways associated with the brain's reward circuits begin to adapt to chronic cocaine use by becoming less sensitive to the drug's effects. Tolerance occurs when more of the substance is required to reach the desired effect. This happens quickly with cocaine because of its rapid onset and short duration.

Once someone is dependent, the abrupt discontinuation of cocaine leads to symptoms of withdrawal. Withdrawal from cocaine does not have as many physiological symptoms as withdrawal from CNS depressants. For this reason, counselors need to assess common behavioral manifestations. Of particular concern are cravings, depression, and suicidal ideation. A pattern of binge use is often followed by a crash, with symptoms including lethargy, poor motivation, nightmares, and cognitive blunting. Individuals experiencing withdrawals often self-medicate with CNS depressants. For this reason, polysubstance detoxification is advised.

Effects of Cocaine Use During Pregnancy

Women who use cocaine while pregnant are at increased risk of neurological impairments, such as migraines, seizures, and strokes. Because pregnancy is already associated with expected changes in heart rate, using cocaine while pregnant can exacerbate these cardiovascular changes, leading to several adverse pathophysiological issues endangering the lives and health of mothers, the unborn fetus, and newborns. Women who use cocaine while pregnant are at increased risk for miscarriage, premature delivery, high blood pressure, and heart attack.

Children born to cocaine-dependent mothers are at higher risk for cognitive and behavioral deficits in infancy that may persist through early childhood. Children who are prenatally exposed to cocaine are at higher risk for poor concentration, difficulties with emotional regulation, working memory deficits, and developmental delays. Moreover, these difficulties can also continue through adolescence without individualized medical, educational, and socioemotional support. Maternal and child outcomes are also influenced by social determinants of health, including poor maternal nutrition, exposure to violence, and limited access to prenatal health care. For this reason, a multipronged approach is recommended to address changes within societal structures (e.g., child welfare, social justice, health care) on the micro and macro levels.

Nicotine

Prevalence of Use, Method of Delivery, and Chemicals Found in Nicotine

Nicotine is a stimulant drug found in tobacco leaves, and it can also be produced synthetically. In its various forms, nicotine can be smoked, sniffed, chewed, or vaporized. According to the 2020 National Survey on Drug Use and Health, just over 20% of individuals over the age of 12 were found to have used nicotine in the month prior to the survey. Age disparities exist for methods of delivery, with more than 60% of teens selecting vaping methods, compared to almost 90% of adults aged 26 and older using tobacco products.

Products containing nicotine include cigarettes, noncombusted (i.e., heated tobacco) products, most e-cigarettes, chewing tobacco (e.g., snuff, chew), and hookah tobacco. Combusted tobacco, which is not inhaled, is found in pipes, cigars, and cigarillos. When tobacco is burned, toxic gas and tar are released, containing thousands of harmful chemicals, with at least 250 known to cause adverse effects among smokers and passive smokers (i.e., those inhaling secondhand smoke). Harmful and cancer-causing chemicals released through smoking include ammonia, hydrogen cyanide, arsenic, acetaldehyde, and formaldehyde.

MECHANISM OF ACTION

Research indicates that nicotine is as addictive as heroin, cocaine, and alcohol. Nicotine consumption causes an increase in epinephrine (i.e., adrenaline) by acting on the adrenal glands, resulting in high adrenal cortical hormone levels. In addition, dopamine, a monoamine neurotransmitter, is released, activating the brain's reward circuits.

Nicotine also binds to nicotinic acetylcholine receptors, which are expressed in the brain stem and spinal cord. Acetylcholine receptors function to regulate breathing by depressing respiratory muscles. Although nicotine is classified as a stimulant, the effects of the acetylcholine receptors create paradoxical feelings of relaxation. When smoked, nicotine is rapidly absorbed, with effects occurring within 10 seconds. Smokeless nicotine is absorbed in the mucous membranes at a slower rate. Nicotine is mainly metabolized in the liver and is absorbed in the lungs, mucous membranes, mouth, and gastrointestinal tract.

ADVERSE EFFECTS

The chief adverse effects of nicotine include the following:

- Lung cancer
- Pneumonia
- Leukemia
- Erectile dysfunction and infertility
- Heart attack
- Cataracts
- Emphysema
- Decreased immunity
- Chronic bronchitis
- Increased blood pressure
- Macular degeneration
- Peptic ulcer disease
- Stroke
- Pancreatic cancer
- Kidney disease
- Gastroesophageal reflux disease, obesity, and chronic gastritis; diarrhea
- Type 2 diabetes
- Mouth cancer (primarily with smokeless tobacco)
- Osteoporosis
- Asthma

SHORT-TERM EFFECTS

Nicotine affects nearly every organ in the human body; its primary effects are seen in conditions of the heart, lungs, kidneys, and reproductive organs. Once inhaled, nicotine produces an immediate rush, leading to increased blood pressure, respiratory rate, and heart rate. The immediate effects of nicotine are influenced by an increase in dopamine and adrenaline, including memory effects, vasodilation, decreased appetite, and enhanced feelings of pleasure.

Vaping and smoking are tied to higher rates of lung cancer, and chewing tobacco is tied to higher rates of oral cancer. Conditions also include periodontal disease, reduced life expectancy, and peripheral arterial disease resulting from poor circulation. Adolescents who use nicotine are more likely to have difficulties with executive functioning, attention, and learning. Nicotine use while pregnant can cause early termination of pregnancy, low birth weight, and sudden infant death syndrome.

Nicotine Tolerance, Dependence, and Withdrawal

An increase in dopamine induces pleasurable sensations and cravings, leading to repeated nicotine use and the development of tolerance. Cigarette smokers may be at greater risk for nicotine dependence because when nicotine is smoked, its addictive properties are also enhanced by a decrease in the enzyme monoamine oxidase. This decrease—which is not detected in other forms of nicotine administration—results in an additional increase in dopamine and norepinephrine.

Once an individual who is dependent on nicotine stops use, withdrawal symptoms can occur. Because of its **short half-life** (1–2 hours), symptoms of nicotine withdrawal can happen quickly. Acute symptoms of withdrawal occur in the first 5 days, with the acuity and duration of symptoms contingent upon how long and at what frequency nicotine was used.

Withdrawal symptoms may include headache, irritability, hopelessness, increased appetite, fatigue, cough, inattention, and/or sleep disturbances. Overdose with nicotine is rare. Nicotine replacement therapy is possible with FDA-approved medications to assist with smoking cessation. This includes bupropion (Zyban), varenicline (Chantix), and nicotine replacement (gum, patches, lozenges).

Caffeine

Sources of Caffeine and Caffeine Content

Caffeine can be found naturally in the fruit, beans, and leaves of more than 60 plants, including coffee beans, cacao, guarana plants, tea leaves, and kola nuts. Energy supplements and drinks derived from the guarana seed contain nearly four times the amount of caffeine found in drinks made from coffee beans. Caffeine is also found in chocolate and can be made synthetically. In addition, it can be found in some supplements and OTC medications. The FDA recommends that adults consume no more than 400 mg of caffeine per day to avoid adverse effects.

The content of caffeine in coffee and tea varies depending on how the drinks are brewed, and sodas vary by manufacturer. The following list is a general guideline for the content found in drinks and supplements:

- An 8 oz cup of coffee = 95 mg
- An 8 oz cup of black tea = 47 mg
- An 8 oz cup of green tea = 28 mg
- A 12 oz can of soda = 40–55 mg
- 1 oz of dark chocolate = 24 mg
- A 16 oz energy drink = 170 mg
- Caffeine supplements (1 tablet) = 200 mg
- Energy shots (2 oz) = 200 mg
- OTC stimulants = 75–350 mg

Caffeine Metabolism and Its Mechanism of Action

Globally, caffeine is the most commonly used psychoactive substance, and consumption remains on the rise in the United States. Caffeine absorption occurs within 30–45 minutes, with a peak concentration in blood levels at 15–120 minutes, depending on certain conditions. For example, blood levels peak more quickly when caffeine is consumed on an empty stomach. Cigarette smoking also increases the rate of absorption. Caffeine is mainly metabolized in the liver and is fat- and water-soluble.

Caffeine works by speeding up the production of adenosine. Adenosine is a CNS neuromodulator that slows down activities responsible for regulating sleep and cardiovascular blood flow. Caffeine acts as an adenosine receptor antagonist—meaning it binds to the same receptors without reducing activity, causing increased arousal and wakefulness.

Like other psychostimulants, caffeine intake increases dopamine levels and causes the adrenal glands to increase adrenaline production. The hormone adrenaline causes a spike in energy levels. Because the adrenal glands also produce cortisol—the body's stress hormone—the effects of caffeine can include exhaustion, difficulty sleeping, nervousness, difficulty attending to tasks, and rapid heart rate. Higher rates of caffeine consumption increase the likelihood and severity of health effects.

Health Concerns and Medical Uses

Adverse health conditions are mainly associated with excessive caffeine use, which, in most studies, is greater than 800 mg/day—twice the amount of the FDA's recommended use.

Excessive caffeine use is associated with the following **health concerns**:

- Calcium deficiency
- Gastrointestinal disorders (ulcers, diarrhea)
- Convulsions
- Anxiety
- Adverse pregnancy outcomes
- Tinnitus
- Incoherent speech
- Diabetes
- Cardiovascular disease

The **FDA has approved** caffeine to treat the following medical conditions:

- Low heart rate and oxygen levels in newborns
- Postsurgical headaches
- Migraine headaches (when coupled with pain relievers)
- Tension headaches

Caffeine is also used to treat the following medical conditions:

- Asthma
- Obesity
- Gallbladder disease
- Sinus congestion
- Low blood pressure

Intrauterine, Neonatal, and Age-Related Health Risks

Pregnant women metabolize caffeine slowly, with blood levels detectable up to 15 hours after consumption. **Prenatal exposure** to caffeine can cause adverse effects such as intrauterine growth restriction because the fetus and placenta lack the enzymes required to metabolize caffeine properly. Infants that were exposed to caffeine in utero are at greater risk for heart disease, obesity, and diabetes. Caffeine intake while pregnant also increases the risk of miscarriage, increases blood pressure, and causes dehydration.

The American Academy of Pediatrics recommends that **children under the age of 12** refrain from caffeine use, with limited intake permissible for children over 12 and adolescents. The increase in blood pressure and poor sleep quality caused by caffeine can lead to behavioral and emotional difficulties. There is a greater risk for adolescents and adults who mix alcohol with caffeine. The stimulant effects of caffeine can mask the effects of alcohol, causing an increase in alcohol consumption, thus enhancing the risk of alcohol-related injuries and health consequences (e.g., unwanted pregnancy, sexually transmitted infections, violence, toxicity).

Tolerance, Dependence, Withdrawal, and Risk of Overdose

Although the effects are milder, caffeine carries the same addictive properties as other psychostimulants. Caffeine tolerance occurs through its pharmacological activity and mechanism of action. Dependence is more likely to happen with doses greater than 400 mg. Caffeine withdrawal symptoms include headaches, irritability, sluggishness, gastrointestinal issues, depressed mood, and sleep problems. Although rare, overdose can occur when extreme amounts of caffeine are ingested, which is generally caused by energy drinks or caffeine pills. Once caffeine reaches toxic levels, it can cause ventricular fibrillation or ventricular tachycardia, and its effects can be fatal.

Synthetic Cathinones

Synthetic cathinones, known by the slang term *bath salts*, are chemically similar to cathinone. Cathinone is derived from the khat shrub that is indigenous to East Africa and the Arabian Peninsula. Chewing the leaves of the plant produces a stimulant effect. Bath salts are similar to cathinone, but bath salts are more potent. Cathinones are marketed under a variety of names, including flakka, snow leopard, cloud nine, vanilla sky, white dove, and purple wave.

The psychological and physiological effects of synthetic cathinones include paranoia, hallucinations, increased energy, increased libido, suicidality, emotional connectedness, and agitation or violence. Synthetic cathinones are categorized as new psychoactive substances and are sold as cheaper alternatives to cocaine and amphetamines. Synthetic cathinones are often substituted for the chemical MDMA found in Ecstasy (i.e., Molly, "E") and can be swallowed, snorted, or injected. The stimulant effects are often 10 times those experienced with cocaine. Individuals who attempt to avoid drugs with stimulant properties when using Ecstasy are then exposed to the hidden dangers of cathinones.

Yohimbe

Yohimbe is a species of evergreen tree indigenous to certain parts of Africa. The bark of yohimbe contains the chemical yohimbine, which is used to treat erectile dysfunction and enhance libido. It is also used to dilate pupils and treat the sexual side effects of selective serotonin reuptake inhibitors. Yohimbine can be legally obtained with a prescription, whereas yohimbe cannot. Yohimbe is considered a supplement and is not concentrated or standardized. Adverse effects of yohimbine include skin rash, insomnia, anxiety, increased heart rate, headache, and gastrointestinal issues. High doses have been known to cause cardiac events, kidney failure, and liver disease.

Kratom

Kratom is a substance derived from a plant (*Mitragyna speciosa*) grown in Southeast Asia, and it is the most commonly used illegal substance in Thailand. Kratom functions as a stimulant and a CNS depressant, creating feelings of pleasure, rapid heart rate, and relaxation. Kratom leaves can be brewed as tea or taken as a powder. Anecdotally, kratom has been used to treat opioid withdrawal, fatigue, chronic pain, and depression. To date, its medicinal uses are still under investigation. Kratom is also used recreationally.

Although currently legal in 44 states, kratom is not regulated by the FDA. Kratom's stimulant and opioid properties increase its tolerance, dependence, and withdrawal potential. Withdrawal symptoms include nausea, diarrhea, labored breathing, tremors, anxiety, and anhedonia. Kratom can be toxic; however, instances leading to death are more common when kratom is combined with other substances or impurities.

Ephedra and Betel Nut

Ephedra is an evergreen tree indigenous to central Asia, Mongolia, and the United States, known for its stimulant properties. Many of these evergreen species of trees also contain the substance ephedrine. Ephedra is known for its stimulant effects and has been traditionally used in China to treat symptoms of colds and flu, including headaches, fever, and congestion. Side effects of ephedra include anxiety, headache, dizziness, and insomnia.

Ephedra was once used legally to treat obesity and chronic fatigue. It was also used to enhance athletic performance. However, in 2004, the FDA banned its use because of associated cardiovascular events, including stroke and heart attack. Additional effects are attributed to the stimulant property's effect on the respiratory and nervous systems. Ephedra is also banned by the National Collegiate Athletic Association, International Olympic Committee, and National Football League.

Betel nut is the seed of the areca palm (*Areca catechu*), a fruit-bearing tree. When chewed, betel nut produces stimulant effects and often leaves a deep red or purple stain around the lips and mouth. Betel nut is used worldwide but is most prevalent in several parts of the Pacific and Asia. It is used to increase energy and to experience euphoria. Adverse effects include cancers of the mouth and tooth decay. Due to its prevalence among some refugee communities, experts recommend inquiring about its use during routine domestic medical screenings. In addition, betel nuts contain muscarine, which can be fatal when high doses are consumed.

CNS Depressants

Categories of CNS Depressants

Major CNS depressants include the following:

- Alcohol
- Opioids
- Sedative-hypnotics (barbiturates, benzodiazepines, non-benzodiazepine sleep aids)

CNS depressants (i.e., downers) work by suppressing CNS activity. Minor depressants, which likewise suppress CNS activity, include muscle relaxants, antihistamines, and depressants purchased over the counter. The physiological effects of CNS depressants include slurred speech, impaired coordination, wobbly gait, shallow breathing, slowed heart rate, and sedation.

Some CNS depressants are used to treat pain medically. **Endorphins** are suppressed or inhibited with CNS depressant use, whereas the neurotransmitter GABA is increased, resulting in calming of the brain and, therefore, sedation. Individuals who combine multiple CNS depressants are at risk for long-term and potentially deadly side effects. Each substance presents with unique properties when combined with another. Combining two CNS depressants does not double their effect; instead, it results in a synergistic process that exponentially increases the effects of both substances, known as **potentiation.**

ALCOHOL

HOW ETHYL ALCOHOL IS PRODUCED, MEASURED, AND METABOLIZED

Ethyl alcohol is the most common and least toxic form of alcohol. Concentrations of ethyl alcohol in a drink must be **greater than 2%** for it to qualify as an alcoholic beverage. The **proof** of an alcoholic beverage is calculated by doubling the percentage of alcohol content (e.g., a drink that is 30% alcohol is 60 proof).

The following list gives **alcohol content** estimates for several drinks, from lowest to highest; all these drinks have approximately the same total amount of alcohol.

- 12 oz of beer: 5%
- 8–9 oz of malt liquor: 7%
- 5 oz glass of wine: 12%
- 1.5 oz of 80-proof distilled spirits: 40%

Alcohol is **metabolized** at a rate of 1 oz (i.e., 1.5 drinks) every 3 hours, with rates varying by gender. Due to higher levels of the liver enzyme alcohol dehydrogenase, males metabolize alcohol quicker than females. For this reason, when females and males drink the same number of drinks in the same amount of time, the blood alcohol concentration for males is lower than that for females.

Alcohol use has the potential to affect every organ in the human body. It decreases inhibitions; impacts the brain and liver; and affects cognitive, emotional, and psychological functioning.

LONG-TERM SYSTEMIC RISKS AND EFFECTS

The long-term systemic risks and effects of alcohol use disorder (AUD) include, but are not limited to, the following:

- **Mouth**: Oral mucosal lesions
- **Muscles**: Atrophy and "flabby" appearance
- **Circulatory system**: High blood pressure, irregular heart rhythm, and hardening of the arteries
- **Nervous system**: Alteration of neurotransmitters and decreased thiamine levels
- **Gastrointestinal and genitourinary systems (general)**: Gastroesophageal reflux disease, obesity, and chronic gastritis (i.e., stomach inflammation)
  - Duodenum (i.e., small intestine): Poor absorption of carbohydrates, fats, and proteins
  - Liver: Excessive fat, cirrhosis, jaundice, and pancreatitis (i.e., poor insulin production)
  - Kidneys: Chronic kidney disease due to progressive loss of renal function
- **Reproductive system**: Hormone imbalances, shrinking testicles, and decreased egg production
  - Pregnancy: Miscarriage, irreversible damage to an unborn fetus, and intellectual disabilities
- **Skeletal system**: Bone disease and anemia

Individuals with AUD are also at risk of developing cancer of the head and neck, esophagus, liver, breast, and colorectal regions.

Impact on Neurotransmitters and the Signs of Alcohol Intoxication

Alcohol's mechanism of action is through alterations of the following neurotransmitters:

- GABA (increased)
- Dopamine (increased)
- Glutamate (decreased)
- Serotonin (increased)

The effects of alcohol can be experienced within 5–10 minutes, with estimates varying based on gender, tolerance, body weight, food present in the digestive system, and the type of alcoholic beverage consumed. These factors also contribute to a person's blood alcohol level or blood alcohol concentration, with women having slower absorption rates than men.

Symptoms of **alcohol intoxication** include:

- Maladaptive behavior and psychological changes
- Slurred speech
- Poor coordination
- Unsteady gait
- Nystagmus (uncontrolled eye movements)
- Impaired attention and memory
- Stupor or coma

Maladaptive Behaviors and Psychological Changes

Maladaptive behaviors and **psychological changes** associated with alcohol intoxication include inappropriate sexual or aggressive behaviors, impaired judgment, and emotional lability.

Long-term health effects of alcohol use include, but are not limited to, all of the following:

- Brain dehydration and stroke
- Weakened immune system
- Cardiomyopathy
- Hepatitis
- Cirrhosis
- Pancreatitis
- Coma
- Death
- Depression

Alcohol Dependence, Metabolism, and the Stages of Alcohol Dependence

Research shows that alcohol dependence is a complex hereditary disorder. Alcohol dependence and AUD can also present with co-occurring mental disorders, particularly post-traumatic stress disorder (PTSD). Alcohol is metabolized in the liver. This metabolic process involves converting the enzyme **alcohol dehydrogenase** into acetaldehyde. **Acetaldehyde** is then metabolized by **acetaldehyde dehydrogenase**. Alcoholism is a progressive disease.

The stages of alcohol dependence include the following:

1. **Prodromal-stage alcohol dependence:** Individuals in the early stages of alcohol dependence exhibit a higher tolerance to alcohol, may use alcohol to ease anxiety in social situations, and may feel guilty about alcohol consumption. Binge drinking is common and is intermittently paired with increased blackouts (i.e., memory loss). Without intervention, individuals who have a genetic predisposition to AUD and those with co-occurring disorders are at an increased risk for advancing to the middle stage of alcohol dependence.
2. **Middle-stage alcohol dependence:** An individual's drinking reaches more serious proportions in this next phase. Individuals begin to experience alcohol-related consequences, including job loss, strained relationships with friends and families, and engaging in risky behaviors.
3. **Advanced-stage alcohol dependence:** Many individuals in this phase are drinking to stay alive. The body has developed a high tolerance to alcohol, and withdrawal symptoms are noted when alcohol use is abruptly stopped. Alcohol-related health issues are apparent in this stage.
4. **End-stage alcohol dependence:** In this final stage, individuals cannot stop drinking, and alcohol has affected vital organs. The heart, lungs, liver, and digestive system are often affected, leading to heart failure, pneumonia, cirrhosis, and cancer. Paranoia may develop and, in severe cases, Wernicke-Korsakoff syndrome (i.e., alcohol dementia).

Alcohol Withdrawal and Detoxification (Detox)

The effects of alcohol withdrawal vary. For individuals with severe AUD, withdrawal effects are experienced in the following ways:

Withdrawal Stage	Characteristics
8 hours	Tremors occur and increase in intensity between 24 and 36 hours. Nearly 90% of individuals with AUD experience withdrawal symptoms, including tremors, slurred speech, unsteady gait, disorientation, vomiting, increased heart rate, and sweating.
12–24 hours	Auditory and visual hallucinations are experienced by one out of four individuals with alcohol dependency experiencing withdrawal.
24–48 hours	Life-threatening seizures may occur as soon as 7 hours, but they primarily occur between 24 and 48 hours after drinking cessation. Just over 30% of individuals will eventually experience delirium tremens.
48–72 hours	Delirium tremens may last as long as 5 days. Symptoms include vivid hallucinations, tremors, fever, sleeplessness, agitation, and an increased heart rate. The fatality rate for individuals in this advanced state is 15%.

Detoxification from alcohol is generally supervised by a medical professional and can last up to 5 days. During this time, individuals are provided with nutritional therapy to address electrolyte imbalances. Thiamine is administered to prevent Wernicke-Korsakoff syndrome because many alcoholics are deficient in thiamine, which results in this dangerous condition. In addition, they are given medications such as clonidine and beta-blockers to assist with tremors and high blood pressure. Anticonvulsants (e.g., carbamazepine, sodium valproate) are used to prevent seizures.

Fetal Alcohol Syndrome (FAS)

Fetal alcohol syndrome (FAS) occurs when alcohol crosses the placental barrier and reaches the fetus. When the mother drinks alcohol during pregnancy, the fetus receives seven times the amount of alcohol that the mother does. Individuals with FAS encounter difficulties with cognitive tasks, memory, vision, and hearing. FAS is also associated with abnormal facial features, including a thin upper lip, an upturned nose, and a flat nasal bridge. Joint abnormalities may also occur.

Wernicke-Korsakoff Syndrome

Wernicke-Korsakoff syndrome is characterized by retrograde and anterograde amnesia and confabulation due to **thiamine deficiency.** It is a late sign of **Wernicke syndrome**, which is characterized by ataxia, abnormal eye movements, and confusion. In Korsakoff syndrome, the anterograde amnesia is more severe, especially for declarative memories. The retrograde amnesia seems to affect recent long-term memories more than those formed long ago. **Confabulation** occurs when an individual unconsciously attempts to compensate for memory loss by making up memories. It is associated with damage to the frontal lobe and basal forebrain.

Hepatic Coma (Hepatic Encephalopathy)

Hepatic coma or hepatic encephalopathy occurs when the liver's inability to remove ammonia and other toxins from the bloodstream causes a decrease in neurologic function. This can be a complication of late- to end-stage alcohol dependence. Hepatic encephalopathy often occurs in patients with severe liver disease, most commonly in patients diagnosed with cirrhosis of the liver. The fibrous tissue that forms in cirrhosis affects the liver structure and impedes the blood flow to the liver, ultimately causing the liver to fail. There are five stages of hepatic encephalopathy, ranging from grade 0 to grade 4. Grade 4 encephalopathy is defined as hepatic coma. Neurologic alterations may progress slowly, and if left untreated, may result in irreversible neurologic damage.

Signs and symptoms of hepatic encephalopathy include altered mental status, personality or mood changes, poor judgment, and poor concentration. As symptoms progress, patients may experience agitation, disorientation, drowsiness, increasing confusion, lethargy, slurred speech, tremors, and seizures. In grade 4 encephalopathy, patients become unresponsive and ultimately comatose.

First- and Second-Line Medication Treatments for AUD

Medication treatment for AUD is effective for moderate to severe symptoms of AUD. **Naltrexone** is FDA approved, and it is the preferred first-line treatment for AUD, mainly because it can be administered daily and individuals do not have to be abstinent from alcohol to begin treatment. Naltrexone is an opioid antagonist that can be taken orally or by a monthly long-acting injection.

Another first-line treatment, **acamprosate**, is FDA approved and is recommended as an alternative for those with contraindications to naltrexone (e.g., liver failure, concurrent opioid use). Acamprosate decreases cravings or urges to use alcohol by restoring balance to inputs from the inhibition-excitation neurotransmitters (i.e., glutamate, GABA). Acamprosate is used to help individuals with AUD maintain abstinence.

Second-line treatments can be considered for individuals who have not had a therapeutic response to the first-line treatments. **Disulfiram** (Antabuse) is a second-line FDA-approved treatment for AUD. Disulfiram works by arresting the acetaldehyde metabolism. Individuals who consume alcohol while taking disulfiram may become violently ill and experience severe headaches, vomiting, and shortness of breath.

Second-line treatment medications also include two antiseizure drugs, **topiramate** and **gabapentin.** Topiramate is recommended as a second-line treatment for those with a comorbid seizure disorder. Gabapentin is effective in treating symptoms of AUD, specifically cravings, dysphoria, and sleep difficulties.

Opiates and Opioids

Opiates vs. Opioids

The main difference between opiates and opioids is the way in which they are manufactured. Opiates occur naturally and are derived from opium poppy plants (e.g., morphine, codeine). Opioids are manufactured synthetically (e.g., meperidine, methadone, fentanyl) or partially synthetically (e.g., heroin, hydrocodone, oxycodone, hydromorphone).

Opiates and opioids are classified as CNS depressants and are primarily used medically for pain management. There are many formulations of opiates and opioids, with each differing according to their method of administration, potency, duration of action, and how quickly a person experiences their intended effects. Heroin is arguably the most dangerous and most addictive. Heroin and fentanyl are fat-soluble, and morphine is primarily water-soluble. Methadone is a medically approved synthetic opioid used to treat opioid use disorder.

Opioids' Mechanism of Action and Effects

Opiates and opioids are powerful **pain relievers,** and many are used medically for pain control. There are three types of opiate-related drugs: **agonists,** which increase the CNS effects; **antagonists,** which block these effects; and **mixed agonist-antagonists**. Opiates act by elevating the production of **dopamine** by increasing the neuronal firing rate of dopamine-producing cells. The opiate abuser's mood is elevated, resulting in a sense of euphoria brought on by the increased dopamine activity. Opioids also block the release of substance P, one of the major neurotransmitters responsible for communicating pain from the peripheral nervous system to the brain. Opiate receptors are located throughout the brain and body and are activated by endorphins.

Opioids cause a sense of euphoria, relaxation, pain relief, sedation, decreased sexual desire, impaired judgment, constricted pupils, nausea, slurred speech, and memory and concentration impairments.

Opioid Overdose, Tolerance, Dependence, and Withdrawal Symptoms

Opioid overdose is common, with an increased probability for individuals who mix opioids with other CNS depressants (e.g., benzodiazepines and alcohol). **Opioid tolerance** and **dependence** tend to develop quickly with heavy opioid use. Combining opiates and stimulants (i.e., speedballing) is known to cause heart damage, stroke, or respiratory failure. Naloxone (Narcan) is an antagonist used to treat opioid overdose. The primary cause of fatalities by **overdose** is respiratory failure. Three main symptoms of opioid overdose are a combination of the following:

- Unconsciousness
- Pinpoint pupils
- Respiratory depression

For individuals who are opioid dependent, withdrawal symptoms occur with sudden cessation or reduction of use. **Withdrawal symptoms** include watery eyes, runny nose, yawning, dilated pupils, goose bumps, diaphoresis, gastrointestinal upset, insomnia, anorexia, flushing, hypertension, paresthesia, headaches, and fatigue.

The same symptoms occur when an opioid antagonist is administered.

Risk Factors for Developing Opioid Use Disorder

While anyone who takes opioids is at risk of opioid dependency, there are additional factors that place a person at an increased risk for developing opioid use disorder, including the following:

- Personal history
- Family history
- Poverty
- Joblessness
- Heavy tobacco use
- Mental disorders
- Chronic pain

Older adults are at an increased risk for opioid use disorder because they metabolize drugs slowly and generally receive more prescription pain medications, making them more vulnerable to drug-drug interactions. When compared to men, women are more likely to develop opioid use disorder because they are more likely to have chronic pain, receive opioid prescriptions, and use opioids for an extended period.

Opioid Toxicity and Overdose Risk Factors

Individuals with opioid use disorder are at greater risk for overdose if they return to use after a period of abstinence, mix opioids with other sedatives, and have comorbid mental or physical health issues. Common health issues for individuals at risk for opioid overdose include HIV, depression, lung disease, and liver disease. White non-Hispanic males and young adults aged 20–40 have the highest rates of opioid overdose.

Heroin is associated with increased toxicity and overdose, primarily because dealers "cut" (i.e., dilute) heroin with other, less expensive, psychoactive substances to increase profits. With the opioid fentanyl, overdose is fatal in smaller doses because it is 50 times more potent than heroin and 100 times more potent than morphine. As a result, many fentanyl overdoses result in unintentional deaths. Additionally, for some opioids, therapeutic drug errors have been linked to overdose.

Sedative-Hypnotics

Examples of sedative-hypnotics, classified by group, include the following:

Barbiturates	Benzodiazepines	Sleep Aids
Mephobarbital (Mebaral) Phenobarbital (Luminal) Pentobarbital sodium (Nembutal)	Diazepam (Valium) Clonazepam (Klonopin) Alprazolam (Xanax) Triazolam (Halcion) Estazolam (Prosom)	Zolpidem (Ambien) Eszopiclone (Lunesta) Zaleplon (Sonata)

Barbiturates

Mechanism of Action, Solubility, and Administration Methods for Barbiturates

Derived from barbituric acid, barbiturates are prescribed for anxiety, panic, migraine headache, and epileptic seizures. Barbiturates are fat-soluble, and they come in capsule, tablet, liquid, and injectable forms. Some of the street names for barbiturates include downers, yellow jackets, reds, purple hearts, and pinks. As a CNS depressant, barbiturates work by increasing the activity of

GABA, an inhibitory neurotransmitter that slows neuronal activity, resulting in sedation. Barbiturates are metabolized in the liver.

Barbiturates can be long acting (e.g., phenobarbital, mephobarbital), intermediate acting (e.g., amobarbital, aprobarbital, pentobarbital, secobarbital), or short acting (e.g., methohexital, thiamylal, thiopental). In general, long-acting barbiturates are prescribed for seizures, and short-acting barbiturates are reserved for anesthetic purposes. Flumazenil (Romazicon) is a reversal agent used to treat benzodiazepine overdose and postoperative sedation.

Short-Term Physiological Effects and Psychological Effects of Barbiturates

Physiological and psychological effects of barbiturates include the following:

Physiological Effects	Psychological Effects
Unsteady gait, impaired coordination	Nightmares
Drowsiness	Insomnia
Blackouts	Euphoria
Dizziness	Paranoia
Sedation	Hallucinations
Lowered blood pressure	Impaired judgment
Slurred speech	Mood lability
Memory impairment	
Respiratory depression	
Liver damage and failure	

Barbiturate Tolerance, Dependence, Toxicity, and Risk of Overdose

Barbiturate tolerance can manifest in the following ways:

- Metabolic tolerance occurs when repeated use reduces drug concentrations as liver cells respond by shortening its half-life.
- Reduced responsiveness happens when repeated use causes nerves and tissues to become less sensitive to the drug's effects.

Barbiturates are addictive and can cause physical, psychological, and physiological dependence, even when used as prescribed. Physiological dependence occurs when higher doses are taken daily for 1 month or longer. In addition, individuals who use barbiturates for sleep are at an increased risk of psychological dependence.

Barbiturates are extremely toxic, with higher risks for coma or death, because the correct dosage is difficult to predict. When not taken as prescribed, there is a high risk for overdose because of the drug's narrow therapeutic index (i.e., therapeutic threshold), which is the range between the drug's toxicity and therapeutic dose.

Barbiturate Withdrawal Symptoms and Detoxification

Symptoms of barbiturate withdrawal generally peak at around 48–72 hours and can begin 6–8 hours after the substance was last used. Withdrawal symptoms include nausea, vomiting, insomnia, sweating, and agitation. If a person is physiologically dependent, he or she is at a higher risk for severe withdrawal symptoms. Severe withdrawal symptoms include seizures, delirium, high blood pressure, psychosis, and loss of consciousness. Newborns exposed to barbiturates in utero may also experience withdrawal.

There are currently no FDA-approved medications used to treat barbiturate withdrawal, although medications can be prescribed to manage the physical and physiological symptoms. Medically supervised detoxification is recommended, which includes gradually tapering down barbiturate dosages. Polydrug use can intensify the effects of withdrawal, particularly steroidal hormones, anticoagulants, and certain psychotropic medications.

Benzodiazepines

Classifications

Benzodiazepines are among the most widely prescribed medications that treat anxiety and insomnia. They are Schedule IV substances and are classified according to their half-life.

Examples of **long-acting** benzodiazepines include the following:

- Flurazepam
- Diazepam
- Chlordiazepoxide
- Clorazepate

Examples of **intermediate-acting** benzodiazepines include the following:

- Lorazepam
- Alprazolam
- Clonazepam
- Oxazepam

Examples of **short-acting** benzodiazepines include the following:

- Midazolam
- Triazolam

Medical Uses of Benzodiazepines

Benzodiazepines have fewer side effects than barbiturates and are classified as **anxiolytics** due to their ability to treat anxiety effectively. Examples of street names for benzodiazepines include benzos, candy, downers, mind erasers, tranx, qual, z-bars, sleeping pills, and goofballs. Benzodiazepines are designed for the short-term treatment (≤30 days) of generalized anxiety and panic disorder, and they have also been FDA approved for treatment of insomnia, seizures, and certain phobias.

Commonly used benzodiazepines and their main medical uses include the following:

- **Alprazolam** (Xanax) is used to manage depression and anxiety or depression alone.
- **Triazolam** (Halcion) is recommended for the short-term (7–10 days) treatment of insomnia.
- **Diazepam** can be used for muscle spasms and seizures. Diazepam is also used to manage acute alcohol withdrawal symptoms, including convulsions, psychomotor agitation, and the progression of delirium tremens. It is also used intravenously to eradicate traumatic memories and lessen apprehension associated with surgical procedures.

Effects, Mechanism of Action, and Solubility of Benzodiazepines

The main effects of benzodiazepines include the following:

- Fatigue
- Drowsiness
- Blurred vision
- Euphoria
- Confusion
- Mood swings
- Paranoia
- Short-term memory impairment

Benzodiazepines enhance the effects of GABA, an inhibitory neurotransmitter that slows neuronal activity associated with anxiety and stress, while also causing a surge in dopamine and serotonin, which contribute to feelings of euphoria. They go through the process of chemical conversion in the liver, which strengthens their potency. Benzodiazepines are fat-soluble, and long-acting versions can have a half-life as long as 80 hours.

Benzodiazepine Tolerance, Dependence, and Withdrawal

Long-term use of benzodiazepines is associated with tolerance, dependence, and withdrawal. Benzodiazepine tolerance develops less quickly as one ages (i.e., age-dependent reverse tolerance). Sedative tolerance to benzodiazepines develops before tolerance to its anxiolytic properties. As a result, benzodiazepines are more effective when managing short-term symptoms of conditions such as insomnia. Research shows that benzodiazepines are rarely effective after 4–6 months of continuous use.

Benzodiazepine dependence is substance-specific and varies according to dosage and the length of time that the substance is used. **Physical dependence** occurs when benzodiazepines are used in high doses (i.e., 10–20 times) over 1–2 months. The risk of dependence is higher with short-acting (i.e., more potent) forms of benzodiazepines. When taken as prescribed, benzodiazepine dependence can develop after 1 or more years.

Psychological dependence is associated with successfully managing anxiety and other related mental disorders. When a person with benzodiazepine dependence goes off the medication, withdrawal symptoms can occur. Because withdrawal symptoms mimic anxiety, there is the risk of developing a cycle of tolerance and dependence as more of the substance is consumed.

Benzodiazepine Toxicity, the Potential for Overdose, Withdrawal, and Detoxification

Benzodiazepines have a higher therapeutic or safety index, the ratio between the substance's therapeutic dose and toxicity. The risk of overdose is higher with polydrug use, mainly when the substance is alcohol. Benzodiazepine overdose may occur if 50–100 pills are ingested. Flurazepam and lorazepam block the activation of benzodiazepines and can be used to treat/reverse the effects.

A timeline for benzodiazepine withdrawal depends on the half-life of the benzodiazepine. Symptoms generally emerge within 6–12 hours after the last dose, with acute symptoms peaking around the second week. Gradually reducing (tapering) a person's benzodiazepine dose over time is the best way to minimize withdrawal symptoms. Medically supervised detoxification is recommended due to the severity of benzodiazepine withdrawal, which can be protracted and can last as long as several months after the last dose.

When a person who is benzodiazepine-dependent suddenly stops the medication, withdrawal symptoms are likely. Withdrawal symptoms can include sleep disturbance, anxiety, yawning, paranoia, headaches, seizures, and convulsions. Protracted abstinence syndrome, a term used to describe prolonged withdrawal symptoms, can occur with benzodiazepines, with effects lasting several months. Chronic neuroadaptation is thought to cause protracted withdrawal, making detox difficult, even when the substance is gradually decreased or tapered down.

Sleep Aids

Mechanism of Action, the Effects, and Withdrawal of Non-benzodiazepine Sleep Aids

Non-benzodiazepine sleep aids (also known as Z-hypnotics) and other sedative-hypnotics are used to induce sleep, manage generalized anxiety, and treat seizures and nerve pain. They are CNS depressants that mimic benzodiazepines but have slightly different chemical structures.

The effects of non-benzodiazepine sleep aids include the following:

- Aggression
- Diarrhea
- Vertigo
- Headaches
- Loss of balance
- Drowsiness
- Decreased respiration rate
- Memory and learning impairment

Tissue dependence may occur with chronic misuse of Z-hypnotics. Z-hypnotic withdrawal symptoms can be severe and may include seizures; these symptoms must be carefully monitored when Z-hypnotics are abruptly discontinued. There are no FDA-approved medications available for sedative dependence and withdrawal. The toxicity of Z-hypnotics increases with alcohol use.

Treating Insomnia

There are several non-benzodiazepine sedative-hypnotics indicated for the treatment of insomnia. Non-benzodiazepine hypnotic agents are used to help individuals fall asleep (sleep latency) and stay asleep (sleep maintenance). Examples of non-benzodiazepine sedative-hypnotics include the following:

- **Ethchlorvynol** was the first hypnotic substance used to treat insomnia, but it has been replaced by more effective benzodiazepines.
- **Zolpidem** (Ambien, Ambien CR, Intermezzo, Edluar, Zolpimist, Stilnox): Zolpidem is rapidly absorbed, making it effective for falling asleep because the onset of action occurs within 30 minutes. Zolpidem is also effective for increasing sleep duration and is used as a short-term treatment for insomnia.
- **Zaleplon** (Sonata, Starnoc, Andante): Zaleplon is effective for sleep latency but is less effective for sleep maintenance.
- **Eszopiclone** (Lunesta): Eszopiclone is used for sleep, and unlike zolpidem and zaleplon, it is not limited to short-term use.
- **Zopiclone** (Imovane, Zimovane, Imrest): Zopiclone is used as a short-term treatment for sleep maintenance.

Z-Hypnotics and Other Sedative-Hypnotics Used to Treat Mental Disorders

Z-hypnotics and sedative-hypnotics are known for their anxiolytic effects and include the following:

- **Buspar** treats generalized anxiety disorder and can be combined with a selective serotonin reuptake inhibitor to treat depression. Buspar is not associated with significant substance misuse.
- **Ocinaplon** is a $GABA_A$ receptor modulator used for the treatment of generalized anxiety disorder.
- **Pagoclone** was developed to treat symptoms of panic and anxiety but has not been commercialized. It is known for decreasing anxiety without the sedative side effects and is a currently promising treatment for stuttering.
- **Quetiapine** (Seroquel) is primarily indicated to relieve symptoms of schizophrenia and bipolar disorders.

Z-Hypnotics and Other Sedative-Hypnotics Commonly Used Illicitly

In the United States, several sedative-hypnotics are known primarily for their illicit use. These include the following:

- **Chloral hydrate** is no longer available in the United States due to the increased risk of dependence and toxic overdose. Chloral hydrate has been used as a date rape drug. Street names include knockout drops and Mickey Finn.
- **Gamma-hydroxybutyric acid** (GHB) is also known as a date rape drug. GHB rapidly decreases inhibitions, induces euphoria, and causes sedation. The effects of GHB are similar to **flunitrazepam** (i.e., roofies). Flunitrazepam can be combined with alcohol to cause significant memory impairment, sedation, and muscle relaxation. Street names for GHB include easy lay, G, Georgia home boy, soap, goop, liquid Ecstasy, and scoop.
- **Gamma-butyrolactone** is an illicit prodrug that is converted into GHB. Gamma-butyrolactone is generally more potent and produces effects more quickly than GHB. Street names include blue nitro vitality, revivarant, firewater, and gamma-g.
- **Methaqualone** (quaalude, Mandrax) produces effects similar to alcohol, including disinhibition, sedation, and euphoria. In the United States, quaaludes were produced legally until 1983. Street names include quad, ludes, lemons, flowers, and quack.

Hallucinogens

The American Psychological Association defines a hallucinogen as "a substance capable of producing a sensory effect (visual, auditory, olfactory, gustatory, or tactile) in the absence of an actual stimulus." Hallucinogens occur naturally and are also produced synthetically. The psychedelic effects of hallucinogens are caused by activating the serotonin 5-hydroxytryptamine 2A receptor (5-HT 2A) neurotransmitter sites. Substances that mainly act on the serotonin system are known as indolealkylamines. **Common classic hallucinogens** include the following:

- **DMT (N,N-dimethyltryptamine):** DMT occurs naturally in plants and can also be made synthetically. DMT can be administered orally or smoked.
- **LSD (D-lysergic acid diethylamide):** LSD is derived from a fungus on rye and other grain breads and can be taken orally or absorbed in the mucous membrane.
- **Peyote (mescaline):** Peyote is a cactus plant containing the hallucinogen mescaline. Mescaline can also be produced synthetically. In liquid form, it can be swallowed or consumed raw. It can also be brewed into a tea.
- **Psilocybin (4-phosphoryloxy-N,N-dimethyltryptamine):** Psilocybin is found in mushrooms located in subtropical areas. It can be brewed into a tea or eaten raw.

Short-Term Effects of Classic Hallucinogens

The effects of classic hallucinogens can be experienced within 20 to 90 minutes and can last between 15 minutes and 12 hours, with synthetic DMT producing shorter experiences and LSD having more prolonged effects. The primary **effects of hallucinogens** include the following:

- Mixed sensory experiences (i.e., seeing sounds and hearing colors)
- Tremors
- Dizziness
- Cognitive processing difficulties
- Dry mouth
- Impulsivity
- Psychosis
- Dilated pupils
- Loss of appetite
- Increased blood pressure
- Panic
- Bizarre behaviors
- Feelings of relaxation and euphoria
- Sleeplessness
- Paranoia
- Depersonalization
- Increased heart rate
- Nausea
- Sweating
- Slowed conception of time

Long-Term Effects of Classic Hallucinogens

Although rare, two long-term conditions that are associated with classic hallucinogen use are **persistent psychosis** and **hallucinogen persisting perception disorder (HPPD).** These conditions can occur together. They can also happen to first-time or chronic hallucinogen users.

Each condition involves reexperiencing the same perceptual sensations that were experienced when under the influence of a hallucinogen. Symptoms of persistent psychosis include disorganized thinking, emotional lability, distrustfulness of others, and visual disturbances.

HPPD is recognized in the DSM-5-TR with criteria that include a cluster of hallucinogen effects, which are primarily visual. The **perceptual hallucinations** occurring with HPPD include the following:

- Pelopsia (i.e., objects appearing nearer than they are) and teleopsia (i.e., objects appearing farther away than they are)
- Micropsia (i.e., objects appearing smaller than they are) and macropsia (i.e., objects appearing larger than they are)
- Visual trailing (i.e., seeing stationary objects follow behind moving objects)
- Ego-dystonic psychosis (i.e., thinking that is misaligned with one's self-concept)
- Visual snow with additional geometric hallucinations
- Halos around objects
- Flashes of light

D-Lysergic Acid Diethylamide (LSD)

D-lysergic acid diethylamide (LSD) is a classic hallucinogen derived from ergot alkaloids found in a fungus that grows on rye and other grains. It is a synthetic substance that is colorless, odorless, and crystalline in appearance. LSD is one of the most potent psychoactive substances. LSD is nearly undetectable on blotter paper or other forms of administration.

Street names for LSD include acid, blotter, microdot, yellow sunshine, electric Kool-Aid, mellow yellow, window pane, and goofballs. It is available in liquid form, added to blotter paper, or saturated in sugar cubes (i.e., microdots). LSD is categorized as a Schedule I drug with a high potential for abuse and no accepted medical use. LSD does not induce the addictive properties of dependence and withdrawal; however, tolerance can develop. Cross-tolerance can develop with peyote and psilocybin.

Mechanism of Action and the Effects of LSD

LSD is a classic hallucinogen that produces psychedelic effects via the serotonin 5-hydroxytryptamine 2A receptor (5-HT 2A) sites. Its effects can be experienced within 30–60 minutes and, in some instances, may last for days. LSD causes cognitive, emotional, and perceptual distortions fueled by increased sympathetic nervous system activity. These fight-or-flight responses include an increase in heart rate, sleep disturbances, nausea, excessive sweating, and poor appetite.

LSD hallucinations are likened to drug-induced psychosis, causing a person to experience disorganized thoughts, a distorted sense of time, emotional lability, and mixed sensory experiences. LSD is known to produce a long-lasting high, consisting of "trips" that include visual distortions, delusions, euphoria, hallucinations, and an overall sense of transcendence.

Short-term effects can include "bad trips," accompanied by traumatic feelings of insanity, terror, and a looming fear of death. Symptoms of a bad trip can also include panic attacks, paranoia, and suicidality. Individuals with certain mental health conditions (e.g., psychosis) are more likely to have a bad trip. The long-term effects of LSD include flashbacks, which often manifest as disturbing perceptual distortions akin to those experienced while under the influence of LSD. In addition, individuals who use LSD are at a higher risk for persistent psychosis and HPPD.

N,N-Dimethyltryptamine, or Dimethyltryptamine (DMT)

N,N-dimethyltryptamine, or dimethyltryptamine (DMT), is a natural substance in certain plants indigenous to the Amazon rainforest. The plants can be brewed into a tea known as ayahuasca. Ayahuasca is brownish-red in appearance. Street names for ayahuasca include aya, hoasca, and yage. DMT is a classic hallucinogen that has been used in religious ceremonies and rituals to help users achieve spiritual insight.

DMT has the appearance of a white crystalline powder. More commonly, it appears in its impure form, which is a yellow, orange, or pink powder or solid. Synthetic DMT is generally smoked through a pipe, but it can also be vaporized, snorted, or injected. DMT has a strong odor that some compare to burnt plastic.

Like other classic hallucinogens, DMT is a Schedule I substance with a high potential for abuse and no accepted medical use. Street names of DMT include changa, Dimitri, businessman's trip, the Rogan, fantasia, the spirit molecule, and 45-minute psychosis. Tolerance can occur with regular use. Physical dependence and withdrawal are not associated with DMT use; however, psychological cravings, mood swings, and irritability may happen when detoxing from the substance. DMT overdose is rare; however, the DEA states that poison control reports of respiratory distress, consequent respiratory failure, and coma are associated with DMT exposure.

Mechanism of Action and the Effects of DMT

DMT is a **tryptamine hallucinogen** that works best when combined with a substance that inhibits monoamine oxidase, an enzyme used to metabolize DMT. Because the neurotransmitter serotonin creates the hallucinogenic effects of DMT, there is the risk of serotonin syndrome, a potentially fatal condition associated with high serotonin levels. Therefore, individuals who mix DMT with antidepressants are at higher risk of serotonin syndrome. DMT differs from other classic hallucinogens in that the effects are very rapid but generally last between 20 and 45 minutes.

The **effects of DMT** include changes in mood, perception, and thinking, and consist of the following:

- Visual hallucinations
- A distorted sense of body image
- Depersonalization
- Euphoria
- Synesthesia or "mixed" senses
- Altered perceptions of space and time
- Sensory distortions
- Feelings similar to those involving a near-death experience

Physiological effects of DMT include the following:

- High blood pressure
- Tightness in the chest
- Agitation
- Seizures
- Dilated pupils
- Poor muscle coordination
- Rapid eye movements (nystagmus)
- Dizziness

Mescaline and Peyote

Mescaline is derived from the **peyote cactus plant** indigenous to the Southwest United States and areas of Mexico and Peru. Peyote is button-like or disc-shaped in appearance and has a bitter taste. Its active ingredient is mescaline, which carries the hallucinogenic effect. Mescaline is also synthetically produced. In powdered form, mescaline is off-white and can be contained in a capsule or sprinkled on a marijuana joint or cigarette. Mescaline can be chewed, smoked, ingested after it is saturated in water, or made into a tea.

Street names include buttons, britton, tops, mesc, black button, half moon, nubs, cactus, shaman, hikori, and Texas medicine. Mescaline is a Schedule I substance that is illegal in all states, unless it is harvested, sold, and used for Native American religious purposes (under the American Indian Religious Freedom Act Amendments of 1994). Tolerance can occur quickly with regular use and in as few as 3 days. Individuals can also develop cross-tolerance to psilocybin and LSD. Physiological dependence and withdrawal are not associated with mescaline use; however, psychological withdrawal symptoms may occur, including depression or dysphoria.

Mechanism of Action and the Effects of Mescaline

As with other classic hallucinogens, the effects of mescaline vary among individuals, with factors such as drug history, expectations, mental health issues, and environmental surroundings influencing perceptual disturbances. Mescaline produces psychedelic effects via the serotonin 5-hydroxytryptamine 2A receptor (5-HT 2A) and stimulates dopamine receptors. Mescaline differs from other hallucinogens in that it is categorized as a phenethylamine, as opposed to the group of psychedelics known as indoles (e.g., LSD). Phenethylamine is a natural intoxicant that contributes to the synthesis of potent hallucinogens and is responsible for causing effects associated with vasoconstriction (i.e., the constriction of blood vessels). Effects occur within 1–2 hours and can last up to 12 hours.

The **effects of mescaline** include the following:

- Upset stomach
- Tremors
- Nausea and vomiting
- Appetite suppression
- Excessive sweating
- Visual disturbances
- Chills
- Distorted sense of reality
- Paranoia
- Mental confusion
- Sleeplessness

Individuals who consume mescaline are at risk of experiencing a bad trip, persistent psychosis, and HPPD.

Psilocybin and Psilocin

Psilocybin and **psilocin** are psychoactive substances, but psilocybin is responsible for the major hallucinogenic effects of **magic mushrooms**. Indigenous to Central and South America, these classic hallucinogens have been used in religious ceremonies for thousands of years. Fresh mushrooms have long white or light gray stems, a dark brown underside, dark brown edges, and white and light brown caps. Dried mushrooms have an orange-brown tint interspersed with cream-colored areas. Synthetic psilocybin resembles a white crystalline powder. The liberty cap (*Psilocybe semilanceata*) is the most prominent and potent species of psilocybin.

Street names for psilocybin and psilocin include boomers, purple passion, little smoke, shrooms, tweezers, musk, silly putty, mushies, champiñones, simple Simon, and God's flesh. When psilocybin is combined with MDMA, it is known as flower flipping or hippie flip. Psilocybin can be taken orally, used as an additive to foods, or brewed into a tea. It can also be smoked, injected, or sniffed. Tolerance can develop with repeated use, and cross-tolerance occurs with LSD and mescaline. Psilocybin is a Schedule I substance with a slight risk for psychological withdrawal symptoms, including fatigue and difficulty discerning what is real and what is not. Overdose is rare but can occur.

Mechanism of Action and the Effects of Psilocybin

The major hallucinogenic effects of mushrooms are attributed to psilocybin. Psilocybin is converted into psilocin upon ingestion. The mood-altering and psychedelic effects of psilocybin are caused by its interaction with the serotonin 5-hydroxytryptamine 2A receptor (5-HT 2A) located in the CNS and PNS. The effects of psilocybin are experienced within 15–45 minutes and can last up to 6 hours. The **effects of psilocybin** include the following:

- Euphoria
- Depersonalization
- Auditory and visual hallucinations
- Muscle spasms
- Mood swings
- Feelings of enlightenment or transcendence
- Altered sense of reality
- Heightened senses
- Anxiety
- Nausea
- Dizziness
- Increased heart rate and blood pressure
- Psychosis
- Insomnia
- Numbness

Dissociative Drugs

Dissociative drugs are a category of hallucinogens known for causing users to feel detached from their bodies. Dissociative drugs also produce a numbing or anesthetic effect. Examples of **common dissociative drugs** include the following:

- **Phencyclidine (PCP):** PCP was originally used as an anesthetic for surgery. It can be administered orally in a capsule, liquid, or tablet. It can also be smoked, snorted, or injected. It has the appearance of a white crystalline powder.
- **Ketamine:** Ketamine is used medically as an anesthetic, sedative, and pain reliever, or to treat depressive symptoms. It is misused recreationally and comes in liquid form or a white powder.
- **Dextromethorphan (DXM):** DXM is a potent hallucinogen when taken in large doses. It is commonly found in OTC liquid cough medications.
- ***Salvia divinorum*:** *S. divinorum* is a plant indigenous to Central and South America. The leaves can be chewed, dried, and smoked, or they can be brewed into a tea.

The mechanism of action for PCP, ketamine, and DXM is through the disruption of glutamate on specific nerve cells responsible for memory, emotions, and experiences of pain. For PCP, dopamine receptors are also implicated. The mechanism of action is different for *S. divinorum* in that the effects are caused by activating an opioid receptor that differs from those activated by commonly known opioids (e.g., morphine, heroin).

Short-Term Effects of Dissociative Drugs

The common effects of dissociative drugs can be experienced quickly and can last up to 1.5 hours. There is a shortage of empirical evidence on the long-term effects of dissociative drugs. The primary short-term effects vary by substance and dosage.

Common effects associated with **low doses** of most dissociative drugs include the following:

- Confusion
- Feeling as if one is floating
- Nausea and vomiting
- Changes in sensory perceptions, including shapes, visions, and misperceptions of time
- Hallucinations

Common effects associated with **higher doses** of dissociative drugs include the following:

- Paranoia
- Rapid mood swings (unique to salvia)
- Sleepiness (unique to ketamine)
- Terror (unique to ketamine)
- Intense fear or panic
- Extremely high blood pressure
- Memory loss (mainly associated with ketamine)
- Violence (unique to PCP)
- Poor coordination
- Seizures (unique to PCP)

PCP

PCP is a dissociative drug that can be consumed orally in the form of a capsule or tablet. It can also be smoked, snorted, or injected. PCP is generally combined with marijuana, mint, parsley, oregano, or tobacco when smoked. Historically, PCP has been used as a surgical anesthetic and an animal tranquilizer. Because of its adverse effects, PCP is no longer used medically with humans and is rarely used in veterinary medicine. As a powder, PCP has a white, crystalline appearance. In liquid form, it is light brown or yellow.

Street names for PCP include animal tranq, angel dust, magic dust, lethal weapon, ozone, happy sticks, rocket fuel, dust joint, love boat, dipper, embalming fluid, horse tranquilizer, Peter Pan, and superweed. When PCP is mixed with marijuana or tobacco, the street names include wet, fry, or illy. PCP is a Schedule II substance due to the high probability of misuse and dependence. Tolerance can develop over time, and withdrawal symptoms have been reported.

Mechanism of Action for PCP

PCP inhibits the actions of glutamate and acetylcholine. PCP also targets serotonin receptors and is an indirect agonist of dopamine, specifically the D2 receptor. D2 is responsible for the schizophrenic-like effects of PCP. PCP also inhibits the actions of acetylcholine. When moderate doses are consumed, PCP inhibits the reuptake of dopamine, serotonin, and norepinephrine. The effects of PCP can be experienced within 2–5 minutes when smoked and can last between 4 and 6 hours. When PCP is administered orally, effects occur between 20 and 90 minutes and last between 6 and 24 hours.

Depending on the dose, PCP can act as a stimulant, anesthetic, or painkiller. There are several CNS sites involved that act together to provide stimulant, anesthetic, and analgesic effects. Over half of individuals who use PCP present with involuntary eye movements (i.e., nystagmus), aggression, increased heart rate, hypertension, and an inability to feel pain.

Symptoms of Toxicity and Binge "Runs" Associated with PCP Use

PCP's clinical effects are dose dependent, with adverse effects occurring primarily with high doses or polydrug exposure (see the table below). High doses of PCP can cause stupor, convulsions, hyperthermia, and death. Some individuals who use PCP, including one-time users, may experience effects for up to 14 days.

In individuals with a history or predisposition for psychosis, PCP use risks triggering symptoms of the disorder. High doses of PCP can be toxic and can lead to a condition known as rhabdomyolysis, causing kidney damage and the breakdown of muscle tissue. Infants and children can become intoxicated by PCP's secondhand smoke or the ingestion of PCP-laced cigarettes. Symptoms for infants and newborns include faltering weight and growth, irritability, agitation, and lethargy.

Significant risk occurs in individuals who go on **PCP binge runs**. PCP runs consist of a person using PCP multiple times for two or three consecutive days, during which time the person does not sleep or eat. Once the run is completed, there is a prolonged period of sleep. With repeated cycles, runs can cause dehydration and malnutrition, which increases the risk of internal organ failure. **Dose-dependent effects** include the following:

Dosage	Effects
2–5 mg	CNS stimulation and depression cause symptoms to wax and wane. Symptoms include agitation, anxiety, and lethargy.
5–25 mg	Symptoms are similar to acute schizophrenia (e.g., hallucinations, delusions, paranoia, agitation), coma, and stupor.
≥25 mg	Hyperthermia, convulsions, and possible death.

Short-Term Physiological and Psychological Effects

The **short-term physiological effects** of PCP include the following:

- Chills
- Fever
- Dizziness
- Sedation
- Increased heart rate
- Nystagmus
- Convulsions
- Seizures
- Vomiting
- Garbled or slurred speech
- Poor coordination
- Coma

- Respiratory depression
- Reduced response to pain
- Rigid muscles

The **short-term psychological effects** of PCP include the following:

- Rage or combativeness
- Paranoia
- Irrational thoughts
- Suicidality
- Delusions
- Confusion
- Psychosis
- Hallucinations
- Memory loss
- Severe anxiety
- Euphoria
- Catatonia
- Agitation
- Perceived invincibility

Withdrawal Symptoms and Long-Term Effects

Regular use of PCP can lead to dependence and withdrawal. Withdrawal symptoms include diarrhea, headaches, sweating, fever, chills, tremors, apathy, and mental confusion. In addition, its long-term use can produce flashbacks, hallucinations, persistent anxiety, and depression. If PCP is taken for an extended period, **long-term effects** may include the following:

- Depression
- Flashbacks
- Changes in speech fluency
- Poor judgment
- Social isolation
- Memory loss
- Weight loss
- Psychosis
- Cognitive dysfunction

Long-term symptoms are dose dependent. Symptoms of depression and memory loss may last up to 1 year after detoxification, with other symptoms potentially lasting months. Individuals who undergo detoxification treatment for PCP are provided inpatient supportive medical care. This may include the short-term use of benzodiazepines to control seizures or extreme emotional disturbances.

Ketamine

Ketamine has been a potent surgical anesthetic for people and animals for more than 60 years. It is a dissociative drug and comes in a white or off-white powder or liquid form. Powdered ketamine is packaged in small glass vials, capsules, or baggies, or folded into aluminum foil. Ketamine can be snorted, injected, smoked, or swallowed. Misuse primarily occurs when the substance is taken from veterinary clinics, sold illegally, and used recreationally. Ketamine has been misused since the

1970s. Street names for ketamine include special K, kit kat, blind squid, super acid, purple, jet, honey oil, K-ways, and vitamin K.

Ketamine is used to facilitate date rape or sexual assault. Its odorless and tasteless properties enable it to be secretly added to a drink, with victims experiencing sedation, blackout, and memory loss. Ketamine is also known as one of the club drugs and is commonly mixed with other club drugs such as MDMA (i.e., Ecstasy) or stimulants.

Tolerance and dependence can develop with ketamine. There is a higher risk for psychological dependence than physiological dependence. Symptoms of withdrawal include agitation, insomnia, anxiety, depression, decreased respiratory functions, and cardiovascular events. Because of its anesthetic properties, there is a risk of overdose and toxicity.

Medical Uses for Ketamine Hydrochloride (Ketalar) and Esketamine (Spravato)

Ketamine hydrochloride (Ketalar) and esketamine (Spravato) are Schedule III substances, each with different medical uses and both carrying the potential for abuse. The FDA has approved Ketalar for general anesthesia when used intravenously or intramuscularly but not for compound intranasal use. Compound substances place individuals at risk due to their lack of safety standardization, the potential for abuse, and the risk of adverse effects.

In 2019, the FDA approved a ketamine derivative to treat refractory unipolar depression with suicidality. Ketamine is composed of mirror-image enantiomers: S-ketamine and R-ketamine. S-ketamine is known as esketamine and is commonly sold under the brand name Spravato. Spravato generally takes effect within hours and is less apt to cause adverse reactions, such as dissociation and sedation. However, because those risks still exist, the FDA strictly monitors dispensing and administering Spravato. As a result, Spravato must only be distributed, administered, and monitored in medically supervised health-care pharmacies and settings certified by the FDA.

Mechanism of Action for Ketamine

Ketamine is a dissociative anesthetic with structural and chemical properties similar to PCP. Like PCP, ketamine inhibits the actions of glutamate through activity at the N-methyl-D-aspartate (NMDA) receptors. Ketamine works as an NMDA antagonist to produce anesthetic properties, including decreased breathing, sedation, immobility, and amnesia. In part, ketamine's use as an anesthetic is superior to PCP because ketamine is less potent, has a quicker onset of action, and has a shorter half-life.

Ketamine is characterized as a dissociative anesthetic because of its tendency to break apart and attach to multiple receptors, including mu, kappa, and delta opioid receptors. Its antidepressive effects are attributed to its interaction with serotoninergic pathways. Ketamine inhibits serotonin, dopamine, and norepinephrine.

Effects of Ketamine

The common **short-term effects** of ketamine are dose dependent and include the following:

- Pain relief
- Confusion
- Lethargy
- Muscle tremors
- Sedation
- Increase in blood pressure
- Respiratory depression

- Memory loss
- Poor attention span
- Decreased learning abilities
- Poor coordination
- Vocal tics
- Perceptual distortions
- Delirium
- Immobility
- Increased muscle tone

The long-term effects of ketamine include the following:

- Bladder pain and ulcers
- Learning problems
- Abdominal pain
- Memory loss
- Speech problems
- Kidney dysfunction
- Anxiety
- Depression

Slang expressions used to describe experiences with ketamine include the following:

- **K-hole**: K-hole refers to a dissociative paralysis that some liken to a near-death experience, whereas others describe a lost sense of space and time.
- **The God phase**: The God phase is a term to describe the belief that the person has total control of the universe. This delusion may be coupled with hallucinations of meeting God.
- **Baby food**: Ketamine is referred to as baby food because it is said to send the person using it into a state of pleasurable immobility. This state is associated with the simplicity of an infant's existence.
- **K-land:** K-land describes a mellow psychedelic transcendence and escape from reality.

Salvia (Salvia Divinorum)

Salvia (*Salvia divinorum*) is a mint plant found in the Sierra Mazateca region of southern Mexico. Historically, it has been used in religious ceremonies among indigenous tribes in that area. Salvia can be consumed raw or dried, or it can be brewed into a tea. It can also be inhaled, vaped, or smoked. The effects can be experienced in less than 1 minute and can last between 15 and 30 minutes.

Street names for salvia include diviner's sage, Maria Pastora, Sally-D, leaf of prophecy, magic mint, sage of the seers, shepherdess's herb, lady salvia, lady Sally, and purple sticky._The primary mechanism of salvia is through the kappa opioid receptor, which is different from receptors involved with opioids such as morphine and heroin.

Effects include the following:

- Hallucinations
- Depersonalization
- Feelings of levitation
- Mixed senses (i.e., seeing sounds or hearing colors)

- Emotional lability
- Irrepressible laughter
- Hypersensitivity to sight and sound
- Profuse sweating

MDMA (Ecstasy)

3,4-methylenedioxy-methamphetamine (MDMA) is a hallucinogen and stimulant that alters perception and mood. MDMA, commonly known as Ecstasy or Molly, initially gained popularity as a club drug in the 1990s. There was also an increase in prevalence among high school students during that time, with a decline in overall use seen between 2002 and 2003.

MDMA is a synthetic drug that comes in capsule, liquid, or tablet form. It is also sometimes crystallized to be smoked or snorted. Street names for MDMA include Molly, Scooby snacks, Ecstasy, Adam, beans, disco biscuits, clarity, and e bombs. The euphoria produced by MDMA is said to increase emotional closeness and enhance sexual intimacy, earning it the street names love drug, hug, or lover's speed.

MDMA is a Schedule I drug; however, tolerance and dependency are difficult to predict. Research shows that MDMA affects the same neurotransmitter pathways as other addictive substances, and data provide evidence of pharmacodynamic tolerance. However, the mechanisms by which this occurs are largely unknown. There are some reports of psychological withdrawal and cravings.

Mechanism of Action and Short-Term Effects

When administered orally, MDMA generally takes effect within 45 minutes and lasts approximately 3 hours, with some effects potentially lasting days. The effects of MDMA are said to be comparable to a mix between mescaline and amphetamine. MDMA's mechanism of action is to increase the activity of serotonin, dopamine, and norepinephrine. These neurotransmitters are responsible for the following effects:

- **Dopamine:** Enhanced dopamine production affects the brain's reward centers and contributes to its stimulant effect.
- **Norepinephrine:** Norepinephrine is responsible for cardiac effects, including increasing heart rate and blood pressure.
- **Serotonin:** Serotonin regulates sleep, mood, and appetite and is mainly responsible for MDMA's euphoric effect.

Because MDMA blocks the reuptake of serotonin, the aftereffects **cause serotonin depletion**, resulting in depression and difficulties with memory and concentration. In addition, MDMA is known to decrease libido, which has prompted the misuse of Viagra and MDMA—a practice known as "sextasy." This practice can result in permanent damage to sexual performance and functioning. The **short-term effects of MDMA** also include the following:

- Enhanced sensory (e.g., visual, tactile) perception
- Muscle tension and cramping
- Nausea
- Clenching teeth
- Dangerously high fever
- Sweating
- Dizziness
- Dehydration/heat exhaustion

Additional Substances Contained in Tablets

Tablets marketed as Ecstasy or Molly either contain different concentrations of MDMA or no MDMA at all. For this reason, individuals who use MDMA are at greater risk for unpredictable outcomes. Frequently, MDMA has either been replaced by or mixed with substances such as amphetamine, ketamine, or cathinones. In the mid-2000s, the DEA reported that seized Ecstasy tablets actually contained methylone—a synthetic substance found in bath salts. In 2015, a chemical analysis of seized Ecstasy tablets found that methylone had since been replaced with ethylone, a synthetic cathinone.

In 2022, the dangers of synthetic cathinones and their increase in supply prompted the European Monitoring Centre for Drugs and Drug Addiction to adopt new measures to control the dispersion of this widely reported new psychoactive substance. Cathinone is derived from the khat shrub and produces effects such as hallucinations, paranoia, suicidality, and rage. In addition, synthetic cathinones are 10 times as strong as cocaine, with the potential to cause adverse effects such as hyperthermia and a spike in fever, potentially resulting in heart failure or death.

Dextromethorphan (DXM)

Dextromethorphan (DXM) is a cough suppressant found in more than 120 OTC cold medications. DXM is a legal substance that is not controlled or regulated by the federal government. Most OTC products combine DXM with antihistamines, expectorants, analgesics, or decongestants. DXM is found in products such as Robitussin and NyQuil, with labels commonly marked "maximum strength." Misuse of DXM produces hallucinations and euphoria, with dissociative effects compared to ketamine or PCP. DXM is commonly used with marijuana or alcohol, increasing the risk of severe health effects.

DXM is generally administered orally and comes in liquid, tablets, or gel capsules. It can also be injected, but this method of administration is rare. DXM is often mixed with soda to enhance the flavor. When taken in large doses, DXM produces effects similar to dissociative hallucinogens (e.g., ketamine, PCP). Street names for DXM include skittles, red devil, robo, cousin, orange crush, triple C, dex, poor man's PCP, dexies, rojo, black beauties, and velvet. Illegal misuse of DXM is referred to as robotripping, tussin toss, skittling, pharming, leaning, or dexing.

Effects of DXM

The **effects of DXM** include the following:

- Confusion
- Out-of-body experiences
- Poor coordination
- Difficulty breathing
- Lethargy
- Numbness
- Nausea
- Hypertension
- Paranoia
- Excessive sweating
- Agitation
- Audio and visual hallucinations

The standard dosage for immediate-release DXM is 10–20 mg every hour or 30 mg every 6–8 hours. There are different stages or plateaus of toxicity. DXM produces the following **dose-dependent toxic effects**:

Plateau	Dosage	Effects
Plateau 1	100–200 mg	Mild euphoria, restlessness
Plateau 2	200–500 mg	Closed-eye hallucinations, decreased motor functioning, cognitive disturbances
Plateau 3	500–1,000 mg	Strong intoxication, mania, partial dissociation
Plateau 4	>1,000 mg	Altered consciousness; complete dissociation; and difficulty with walking, swallowing, and sleeping

Mechanism of Action and Toxic Effects of DXM

When high doses (i.e., 300 to >1,500 mg) of DXM are used, DXM works as an N-methyl-D-aspartate receptor (NDMA) antagonist. In normal doses, this stops an individual from coughing. In high doses, DXM blocks NDMA, which creates symptoms of dissociation. DXM misuse leads to a steep rise in serotonin levels. Individuals who misuse DXM or combine use with psychotropic antidepressants are at higher risk of serotonin syndrome, a potentially fatal condition. Serotonin syndrome is also thought to contribute to depression.

DXM also inhibits the reuptake of catecholamine, resulting in adverse adrenergic effects, including severe sweating and cardiac conditions. Because DXM is often combined with analgesics (e.g., acetaminophen), there are more severe risks with high doses, including liver failure, stroke, or heart attack. Additionally, up to 10% of Caucasians are found to have difficulty metabolizing DXM, placing them at increased risk for overdose and death.

Amanita Muscaria and Embalming Fluid

Amanita muscaria is a highly toxic mushroom with CNS effects leading to coma or, in rare instances, death. Effects include hallucinations, poor muscle coordination, and seizures. Street names for *A. muscaria* are death cap, fly, or fly agaric. Death cap refers to its highly toxic properties. It is often taken by mistake, which underscores the importance of correctly identifying the species. *A. muscaria* has an orange, red, or tan cap with white spots.

Embalming fluid contains formaldehyde, methanol, ethanol, and other solvents. It is used to prevent a body from decomposing after death. It is typically added to tobacco or marijuana to be smoked. Dipping cigarettes or joints in embalming fluid or PCP is known as smoking a "wet" drug. Street names for wet drugs include fry, happy sticks, dippers, illy, clickem, and crazy Eddie. When smoked, embalming fluid produces hallucinations.

Scopolamine and Nutmeg Myristicin

Scopolamine is used for nausea and vomiting caused by surgical anesthesia or motion sickness. It is an anticholinergic drug and is found naturally in the jimsonweed plant. Anticholinergic syndrome may lead to toxicity and enhance the risk of overdose. Symptoms of anticholinergic syndrome include increased heart rate, hallucinations, and hyperthermia. Scopolamine is known to worsen psychosis. Other effects include agitation, paranoia, and delusions.

Nutmeg myristicin can be highly toxic when taken in higher-than-normal quantities, and in rare cases, it can lead to death and organ failure, particularly when combined with other substances. Doses of 2 teaspoons (10 g) of nutmeg can cause adverse effects. Severe effects are noted when 50 g or more are ingested. The chemical responsible for the euphoric effects of nutmeg is myristicin, a compound found in nutmeg's essential oils. The effects of nutmeg myristicin include hallucinations, confusion, seizures, lethargy, and dry mouth.

Marijuana and Its Derivatives

Marijuana comes from a grayish-green mixture of dried leaves, seeds, stems, and flowers of the *Cannabis sativa* or *Cannabis indica* plant. **THC,** or **tetrahydrocannabinol,** provides marijuana's psychoactive effects. Street names for marijuana include weed, ganga, chronic, herb, pot, grass, gangster, 420, Mary Jane, blunts, hash, indo, reefer, and kif. Despite its legalization in many states, marijuana is still in Schedule I under federal law and is therefore illegal. Marijuana remains the most commonly used illicit substance in the United States.

The strength of the cannabis plant depends on factors such as its purity, species, and environment, as well as how it is harvested. Marijuana can be inhaled or ingested orally. The most common method is inhalation. Marijuana can be smoked in a pipe, bong, hand-rolled joint, or hollowed-out cigar. Hollowed-out cigars are referred to as "blunts." Marijuana can also be brewed into a tea or ingested in the form of edibles (e.g., brownies, candy). Vaping is another method of administration. Street names for vaping devices include e-cigs, mods, vape pens, tank systems, and Juuls.

FDA-Approved Medicinal Use

Marijuana is legal for recreational or medicinal purposes in nearly three-fourths of the United States. However, marijuana remains a Schedule I medication due to its high potential for abuse, and it has no formally approved medical use. Marijuana cannabinoids used to treat medical conditions are THC and CBD. The FDA has not approved the marketing of cannabis and cannabis-derived substances that are claiming therapeutic benefits. The FDA has approved the following brands of drugs to be safe and effective for their intended use:

- **CBD or cannabidiol (Epidiolex):** A cannabis-derived medication that is FDA approved to treat seizures associated with Lennox-Gastaut syndrome or Dravet syndrome in adults and children age 1 and older. Under the Controlled Substances Act of 1970, Epidiolex is a Schedule V drug.
- **Dronabinol capsules (Marinol), dronabinol oral solution (Syndros), and nabilone (Cesamet):** Synthetic cannabinoid medications that are FDA approved to treat chemotherapy-induced nausea, as well as anorexia resulting from weight loss in patients with AIDS. Under the Controlled Substances Act of 1970, Marinol is a Schedule III drug, and Syndros and Cesamet are Schedule II drugs.

Currently, there is emerging empirical evidence supporting the medical use of cannabis and cannabis-derived substances for adults with chronic pain, muscle spasms related to multiple sclerosis, fibromyalgia, and sleep apnea. However, there is also ample empirical evidence suggesting that medical marijuana has the potential to accelerate cannabis use disorder and exacerbate or induce mental disorders, such as schizophrenia, in individuals who are predisposed.

Positions on Recreational and Medicinal Use

The FDA has only approved one cannabis-derived medication, Epidiolex, and three cannabis-related medications, Marinol, Syndros, and Cesamet. The FDA has sent warning letters to industries using unlawful marketing strategies to promote CBD products containing cannabis and cannabis-derived compounds. This marketing directly violates the Federal Food, Drug, and Cosmetic Act. These violations include cannabis products that are unlawfully marketed as effective treatments for health conditions. Other violations include product labeling that inaccurately reflects the product's potency and purity.

The **DEA;** the **Association for Addiction Professionals (NAADAC);** the **National Academies of Sciences, Engineering, and Medicine (NASEM);** and the **American Psychiatric Association** do not support recreational or medicinal marijuana use. Additionally, the CDC issued a public health advisory in 2021 regarding adverse events associated with insufficient labeling of products containing delta-8 THC and CBD. The adverse effects reported were associated with marijuana intoxication (e.g., lethargy, low blood pressure, coma).

NAADAC currently opposes any legislative measures promoting the use of cannabis for medicinal or recreational purposes. Further, NAADAC "finds no benefit to legalizing cannabis use since decriminalization alone will address many social injustices—specifically within the criminal justice system—and stimulate greater social change." NAADAC stands with **NASEM** in reporting barriers to evidence-based research resulting from federal cannabis laws. One such barrier is the complex and lengthy process of approval involving systems within the National Institute on Drug Abuse (NIDA), FDA, and DEA. All marijuana eligible for research purposes must be obtained through NIDA. Since 2015, NIDA has contracted with the University of Mississippi to provide a secure plot of land dedicated to cannabis growth, harvesting, and storage. This sole resource is said to limit the availability of variations and strains of cannabis accessible to investigators for clinical studies.

History of Marijuana Legislation in the United States

Until 1914, marijuana was largely unrestricted. The history of marijuana policy and legislation in the United States includes the following:

- In 1914, the Harrison Act was enacted, making drug use a crime.
- In 1915, possession of cannabis became illegal in the state of California.
- In 1956, cannabis was included in substances covered by the Federal Narcotics Control Act.
- In 1970, the Controlled Substances Act categorized cannabis as a Schedule I drug.
- In 1978, New Mexico became the first state to recognize the medical use of cannabis.
- In 1996, California became the first state to legalize the medical use of cannabis.
- In 2013, the Cole Memorandum directed the Justice Department to allow states in which marijuana was legalized to impose appropriate regulatory standards. In 2018, this directive was rescinded.
- In 2018, the Agriculture Improvement Act, also known as the Farm Bill, provided state regulatory systems and the USDA authority to regulate hemp as a cannabis derivative with THC concentrations equal to 0.3%.
- In both 2020 and 2022, the Marijuana Opportunity Reinvestment and Expungement Act was passed in the House but stalled in the Senate. This bill decriminalizes marijuana.

Marijuana remains illegal at the federal level. To date, small amounts of recreational marijuana are legal in 23 states, Washington, D.C., and Guam for adults over the age of 21. In 2023, Michigan became the most recent state to legalize recreational marijuana. As of May 2023, 38 states have legalized the medical use of marijuana. The District of Columbia and four territories have also legalized medical marijuana.

Mechanism of Action for Marijuana

The THC in marijuana is mainly responsible for its psychoactive effects. THC attaches to cannabinoid receptors in the brain and body and alters neurological functioning. Cannabinoid receptors include CB1, which regulates the CNS, and CB2, which regulates the peripheral nervous system.

Endocannabinoids, or endogenous cannabinoids, attach to cannabinoid receptors. Endocannabinoids are naturally occurring neurotransmitters that send signals to the parts of the brain responsible for multiple functions, including lessening pain, reducing anxiety, creating pleasure, and enhancing learning. There is now empirical evidence suggesting that endocannabinoids, rather than endorphins, are likely responsible for the runner's high produced through exercise.

Marijuana's euphoric high is also produced by a surge in dopamine, which is caused by activating cannabinoid receptors in brain areas such as the nucleus accumbens. THC alters the hippocampus, an area of the brain that controls memory and complex thought processes. THC also disrupts activity in the cerebellum and basal ganglia. The cerebellum and basal ganglia work to integrate reward-based motivation and action, sensorimotor skills, coordination, balance, and reaction times.

Locations of Cannabinoid Receptors in the Brain

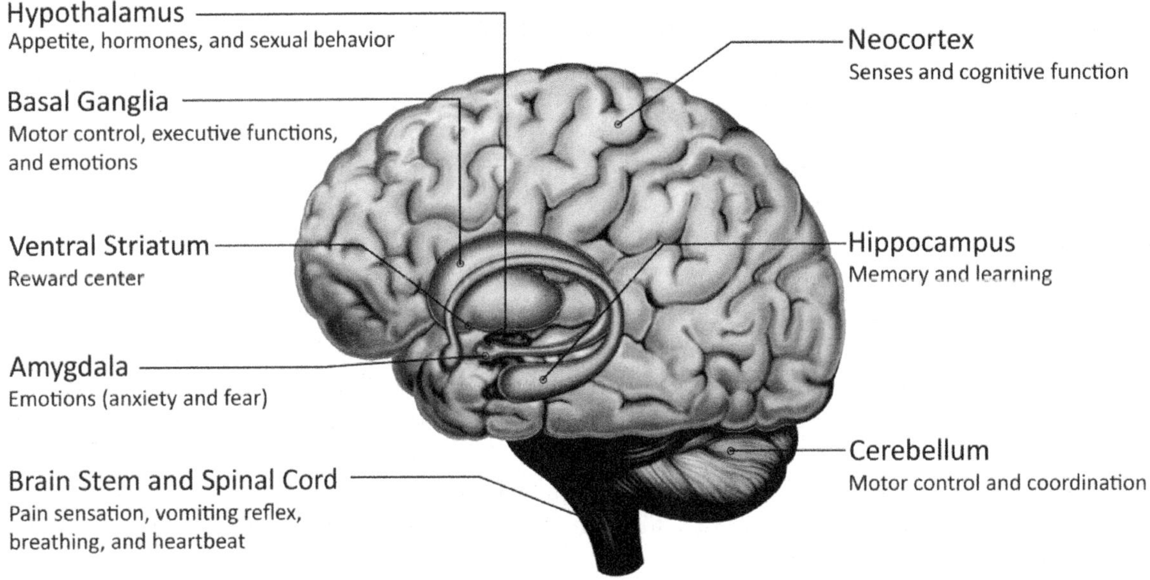

Short-Term Effects of Chronic Marijuana Use

THC works on the **endocannabinoid system,** resulting in the following **short-term effects:**

- Increased appetite
- Enhanced sensory experiences
- Delusions and hallucinations with high potency or higher doses
- Anxiety, panic, and paranoia
- Drowsiness
- Difficulty attending to tasks, and learning difficulties
- Lowered reaction time
- Relaxation

- Bloodshot eyes
- Memory impairment
- Increased risk of stroke
- Altered sense of time
- Low blood pressure
- Kidney damage
- Euphoria
- Impaired balance and coordination

When marijuana is inhaled, the high is felt within the first 10–15 seconds and lasts close to 4 hours. The effects of oral ingestion occur within 30 minutes and can last up to 6 hours.

Adverse Health Conditions Associated with Marijuana Use

Chronic marijuana use can lead to several adverse health conditions, including the following:

- **Cannabinoid hyperemesis syndrome:** A condition caused by long-term marijuana use that involves repetitive cycles of vomiting and dehydration.
- **Amotivational syndrome:** A condition characterized by the loss of drive, or apathy. This is common with schizophrenia. There is anecdotal evidence correlating loss of initiative with ongoing marijuana use. There is empirical evidence suggesting that chronic marijuana users are less satisfied with life and tend to drop out of high school at higher rates than those who do not use marijuana.
- **Relationship difficulties:** Chronic marijuana users report difficulty with interpersonal and intimate relationships. Research findings indicate a causal relationship between victims of intimate partner violence and chronic marijuana use.
- **Respiratory problems:** Frequent and ongoing marijuana use is associated with an increased risk of chronic lung disease and infection.
- **Heart attack:** Chronic marijuana use also increases a person's risk of a heart attack.

Effect of In Utero Cannabinoid Exposure on the Brain Development of the Fetus

The extent to which in utero cannabinoid exposure affects the brain development of the fetus depends on a variety of factors, including the amount and potency of the THC consumed, the frequency of use, and whether the pregnant mother is concurrently using additional substances. The long-term effects of marijuana are also confounded by genetics and sociodemographic factors. Longitudinal studies on neonatal outcomes have produced mixed results, with some researchers challenged by the fact that the potency of THC has rapidly increased over the past 2 decades.

Mounting empirical evidence has begun to show a relationship between in utero cannabinoid exposure and cognitive functioning, particularly in the areas of learning, problem solving, attention, and memory. There is also emerging evidence suggesting an association between in utero cannabinoid exposure and depression. Prenatal exposure is also linked to psychosis, fetal growth restriction, low birth weight, and preterm delivery.

Effects of Child, Adolescent, and Young Adult Marijuana Use on Brain Development

Because the brain is not fully developed until age 25, individuals younger than age 25 who use marijuana are particularly vulnerable to its adverse neurological effects. The severity of these effects is contingent upon the user's age, the frequency of use, and the THC potency consumed. Those who started frequently using high-potency marijuana at a younger age are at greater risk for long-term effects.

Researchers conducting longitudinal studies have found an association between frequent marijuana use beginning in adolescence and decreased IQ scores later in life. Participants lost an average of 8 IQ points, with the decline remaining even after participants stopped using marijuana. There is also empirical evidence showing that early marijuana use contributes to poor coordination, memory problems, and learning difficulties. Regular use of high-potency marijuana is related to the onset of mental disorders, particularly for those who are already predisposed. These disorders include anxiety, depression, schizophrenia, and psychosis. Some studies suggest that, compared to individuals who have never used marijuana, younger individuals who smoke high-potency marijuana daily are five times more likely to develop psychosis. Finally, early marijuana use is a predictor of SUD in adulthood.

Tolerance, Dependence, and Withdrawal from Marijuana

Cannabis is a **Schedule I** drug with no accepted/evidence-supported medical purpose and a high potential for abuse. Prolonged and heavy marijuana use can lead to tolerance, dependence, and withdrawal. Tolerance to marijuana often develops quickly, with higher doses required to reach the desired effect. Chronic marijuana use can lead to physical dependence, psychological dependence, or both.

High levels of THC increase the risk for dependence and withdrawal. Marijuana potency has risen sharply over time. For example, in 1990, marijuana samples seized by the DEA contained almost 4% THC, compared to those seized in 2019, which contained just over 14%. Marijuana concentrates and extracts are products that tend to have higher THC content. Concentrates include all products extracted from marijuana, whereas extracts generally refer to products made using solvents.

Symptoms of withdrawal can include the following:

- Cravings
- Difficulty sleeping
- Anorexia
- Fever
- Irritability
- Anxiety
- Stomach pain
- Depression

Methods for Producing THC Extracts and Concentrates

Cannabis extracts and concentrates are made using solvents (e.g., butane, alcohol, propane) or nonflammable methods (e.g., dry ice processing, water-based processing). Although the terms are often used interchangeably, *extracts* refers to solvent-based products, whereas *concentrates* refers to solventless products. *Concentrates* is also used to describe all extracted products.

Marijuana concentrates are commercially produced by using parts of the marijuana plant known as trichomes. Trichomes are the tiny hairs found on the surface of cannabis flowers; they have a high concentration of THC. Trichomes also contain CBD, terpenes, and other compounds. Concentrates, extracts, and dabs can be vaped or inhaled. Vaping is the act of inhaling THC from vapor from an electronic device, such as an electronic cigarette (e-cig, e-cigarette). This method, also known as "dabbing," has risen in popularity among teens and young adults. In 2020, marijuana consumption was highest among adults aged 18–25, with 34.5% reporting use within the prior 12 months.

Solvent-Based Methods

The most common way to manufacture marijuana concentrate is by using butane, a flammable solvent found in lighter fluid. This method produces **butane hash oil (BHO).** This method leaves behind extracts in the form of vape oil (i.e., hash oil or honey oil), wax (i.e., budder), or shatter, which is solidified hash oil. BHO concentrate yields products with a THC content as high as 90%. This is significantly higher than top-shelf marijuana, which has a THC content of around 20%. Individuals using BHO concentrates report longer-lasting euphoric effects.

BHO products carry an additional risk due to the potential for pesticide contaminants and other impurities that remain on the product. When solvents and pesticides are inhaled, adverse effects, including death, can occur. Individuals who produce BHO concentrates using butane, or other flammable products (e.g., alcohol, propane), are at an increased risk of burns and injuries caused by fires or explosions. Manufacturing BHO is illegal in several states. Street names for BHO include 710, honey oil, budder, shatter, and butane hash oil.

Supercritical Fluid Extraction Method

Supercritical fluid extraction is a solventless technique used to produce THC concentrates. This method allows carbon dioxide (CO_2) to reach a supercritical state (i.e., 1,071 psi and 88 °F [31 °C]), enabling it to have the properties of a liquid and a gas. This process is known as mechanical or solventless extraction and generally yields a cleaner, purer, and safer product.

Once extracted, the CO_2 oil can be added to a vaporizer pen to deliver high concentrations of THC. The cannabinoid concentration is over 90%, which is comparable to BHO dabs, shatter, and wax. Unlike BHO extraction, the supercritical fluid extraction method does not leave any contaminants, pesticides, or potentially harmful substances behind after extraction. Nonsolvent extraction methods include dry processing, water-based processing, and a combination of pressure and heat.

Methods to Extract Kief and Produce Hashish

Concentrates can also be made by compressing the marijuana plant's resin. The resin contains highly concentrated trichomes, which are crystal-like and translucent in appearance. When trichomes become dry and brittle, they fall off the plant and become **kief**. Kief can be pressed together to form **hashish.** This method of making hashish is done by using low heat and high pressure. Hashish is less potent than BHO concentrates. Street names for hashish include chocolate, shit, and hash. **Bubble hash** is a type of hash made using ice-water extraction. The process involves adding the cannabis flower to ice water, agitating it manually or with a machine, and retrieving the resin glands broken from the flower. The resin contains THC and CBD in their natural, unadulterated form.

Spice (Synthetic Cannabinoid)

Common Use, Method of Administration, Street Names, and Legal Status

Spice, or synthetic cannabinoid, is a human-made psychoactive substance sprayed on shredded plants to be smoked. Spice is intended to replicate the effects of marijuana, earning it the name "fake weed." It is often mixed with marijuana or dispensed as a liquid that can be vaporized or inhaled. It is known for its hallucinogenic properties. Street names for spice include K2, dawn, paradise, demon, bliss, black magic, black mamba, ninja, genie, zohai, Bombay blue smoke, skunk, crazy clown, and moon rocks.

Synthetic cannabinoids are the most prevalent new psychoactive substances that mimic the effects of illegal substances. Some cannabinoids are Schedule I substances because they are known to cause adverse effects and do not have an approved medical use. In addition, some cannabinoids are marketed as natural incense or air freshener, giving consumers the false impression that they are safe when instead they have harmful health consequences.

MECHANISM OF ACTION

Spice acts on the same neurotransmitters as THC, the active ingredient in marijuana. However, spice is much more potent than THC. This is because THC is a partial agonist at the CB1 receptor (CB1R), whereas spice is a full agonist of CB1R. Additionally, there is no cannabidiol in spice like there is in marijuana. It is hypothesized that cannabidiol may protect against psychosis. Compared to natural cannabis, the effects of spice are more powerful and longer lasting, and carry the potential for overdose and toxicity.

Because it is not regulated, using spice can lead to unpredictable and detrimental effects. This is particularly true for individuals who are predisposed to psychosis. The term *spiceophrenia* has been used to describe the more intense and persistent paranoid hallucinations associated with spice use. There is also emerging empirical support suggesting that the ease with which spice binds to the CB1R can contribute to other mental and cognitive issues, including depression, anxiety, and impairment of executive functioning.

SHORT-TERM EFFECTS AND SERIOUS HEALTH EFFECTS

The **short-term effects of spice** include the following:

- Nausea and vomiting
- Increased heart rate
- Altered perceptions of surroundings
- Seizures
- Euphoria
- Relaxation
- Losing touch with reality
- Confusion
- Agitation
- Suicidal ideation
- Irritability
- Hypertension
- Dizziness
- Dry mouth
- Delusional thinking
- Violent behavior
- Memory impairment
- Paranoia

Some effects of spice can lead to a serious condition known as **rhabdomyolysis,** which causes severe health conditions or even death. Rhabdomyolysis causes muscles to break down and release a protein known as myoglobin into the blood. Renal failure can occur because the kidneys cannot remove the excess waste.

Inhalants

There are hundreds of industrial, domestic, and medical inhalants misused by individuals wishing to experience their psychoactive effects. Although many substances can be inhaled, the category of inhalants refers to substances whose only route of administration is inhaling, huffing, or sniffing. **Categories of inhalants** include the following:

- **Volatile solvents** are liquid substances that change to gas (i.e., vaporize) at room temperature if left in unsealed cans or containers. Examples include gasoline, dry-cleaning fluid, paint thinner, degreasers, nail polish remover, felt-tip pens, magic markers, glue, correction fluid, and lighter fluid. Volatile solvents also include naphthalene, an ingredient found in mothballs.
- **Aerosols** are sprays containing solvents and propellants, such as fluorocarbon and butane. Examples include cooking products, hair spray, deodorants, spray paint, and keyboard cleaner (i.e., compressed air duster).
- **Gases** are medical anesthetics, some of which include nitrous oxide (i.e., laughing gas), halothane, and chloroform. Gases also include propane, butane, refrigerants, and helium. Nitrous oxide is found in propellant canisters (i.e., whippets) and in products used to raise octane levels in high-speed racing vehicles.
- **Nitrites** are compounds similar to those used in medications prescribed for chest pain. Examples include cyclohexyl nitrite (i.e., poppers), isoamyl (amyl) nitrite (i.e., snappers), and isobutyl (butyl) nitrite (i.e., quicksilver). Nitrites are also found in leather cleaner and room deodorizer.

Additional street names for inhalants include snotballs, Texas shoeshine, bullet bolt, and highball.

Prevalence and Methods of Administration

In 2020, the number of individuals between the ages of 12 and 17 who used inhalants in the prior year was 2.7%. This percentage was highest among preteens, with 3.4% of them reporting inhalant use in the past year, compared to 0.5% of adults aged 26 and older, according to data from the National Survey on Drug Use and Health conducted annually by the Substance Abuse and Mental Health Services Administration (SAMHSA). In 2021, an estimated 4.8% of 8th graders reported past-year use, according to the Monitoring the Future national survey results on drug use.

Methods for administering inhalants and their street names include the following:

- **Gladding** refers to inhaling aerosol contained in air fresheners.
- **Huffing** describes inhaling substances from a saturated cloth and then holding it to the face or stuffing it into the mouth.
- **Sniffing** or **snorting** refers to inhaling fumes directly through the nose.
- **Ballooning** involves inhaling nitrous oxide from a balloon.
- **Bagging** involves spraying a substance in a paper or plastic bag and then inhaling it.
- **Dusting** describes spraying aerosol substances into the nose or mouth.

Sudden Sniffing Death Syndrome (SSDS)

Sudden sniffing death syndrome (SSDS) is a fatal heart condition resulting from inhalant use. This effect can result from a single use or from multiple uses. Long-session use (i.e., inhaling the substance for a long duration) increases the risk of SSDS. SSDS is more likely to occur with chemicals contained in aerosols, propane, and butane. Heart failure and death can occur within minutes of inhalant use. Inhalant use can also cause death by asphyxiation, seizures, suffocation, or coma.

The **effects of inhalant use** include the following:

- Acute intoxication
- SSDS
- Paranoia
- Headache
- Sleep disturbance
- Nausea and vomiting
- Cravings
- Suffocation
- Lethargy
- Suicidality
- Hallucinations
- Apathy
- Slowed reflexes
- Mouth sores and rhinorrhea (i.e., nasal drainage)
- Loss of consciousness
- Irritability
- Weakened immunity (with nitrites)
- Euphoria
- Nystagmus
- Double vision (i.e., diplopia)
- Excessive thirst
- Loss of appetite
- Poor concentration
- Bloodshot eyes
- Dizziness
- Muscle weakness and spasms
- Unsteady gait
- Coma

Mechanism of Action, Solubility, and the Onset of Action

Except for nitrites, inhalants work by suppressing the CNS. Nitrites are inhalants that work as vasodilators. There is evidence that the chemical toluene—found in paint sprays, gasoline, and paint thinners—increases dopamine, contributing to psychological dependence.

Inhalants are fat-soluble, which means that they remain in fatty tissues for prolonged periods, which increases the risk of toxicity and long-term effects. The liver metabolizes up to 10% of inhalants. For most inhalants, 90% of the chemical is eliminated through respiratory expiration. The onset of action for inhalants varies, with most effects experienced within seconds and lasting up to 45 minutes. The effects of butane only last minutes, whereas toluene is longer acting. Chronic inhalant use causes toxicity to nearly every organ in the body. Some long-term effects may be permanent.

LONG-TERM EFFECTS, TOLERANCE, DEPENDENCE, AND WITHDRAWAL SYMPTOMS

The **long-term effects of inhalants** include the following:

- Cardiovascular effects (irregular heart rate, myocardial fibrosis)
- Hematologic effects (leukemia, bone marrow damage)
- Psychological effects (apathy, depression, psychosis)
- Renal effects (acute kidney failure, renal tubular acidosis)
- Dermatologic effects (contact dermatitis, burns)
- Gastrointestinal effects (ulcers)
- Neurologic effects (cerebral hypoxia, peripheral neuropathy, myelin sheath degeneration)
- Pulmonary effects (wheezing or coughing, emphysema)

Tolerance and dependence can develop with inhalant use. Fatalities can occur with a single use, and polydrug use increases the risk of overdose, particularly when inhalant use is combined with other CNS depressants (e.g., opioids, alcohol). Withdrawal symptoms generally occur within 24–48 hours and can last up to 5 days. **Withdrawal symptoms** include the following:

- Vomiting
- Headache
- Muscle cramps
- Stomach upset
- Visual hallucinations

NITRITES

The effects of the chemical amyl nitrite differ from those of other inhalants. Amyl nitrite is found in room deodorizers and prescription medications used to treat chest pain. As a vasodilator, amyl nitrite causes blood vessels to dilate and involuntary muscles to relax. The effects of amyl nitrite take place within 1 minute and can last up to 5 minutes. Overdose may occur in high dosages, characterized by severe face flushing, excessive heart activity, and severe headache. High dosages can also produce feelings of weakness and suffocation.

Amyl nitrites found in room deodorizers are known by the street name "locker room." Nitrites differ from other chemical inhalants in that they are vasodilators. Nitrites are often misused to enhance sexual activity, earning them the street names rush, hardware, and climax. Nitrite misuse is associated with polydrug use, which increases the risk of adverse effects. Nitrites are often taken in combination with Viagra or other erectile dysfunction medications. This combination results in a significant drop in blood pressure and can be fatal. When nitrites are combined with amphetamines, there is a risk of adverse cardiovascular effects.

Performance-Enhancing Drugs

ANABOLIC STEROID MISUSE

Anabolic-androgenic steroids are synthetic variations of the hormone testosterone. *Anabolic* refers to the effects of muscle building, and *androgenic* refers to masculine sex characteristics. Anabolic steroids can be obtained by a prescription to treat hormone-related issues, such as the delayed onset of puberty. Anabolic steroids are also prescribed to treat cancer or AIDS-related muscle loss, low red blood cell count, and certain forms of breast cancer.

Anabolic steroids can be injected into the muscle, taken orally, delivered subcutaneously, or used topically as a gel or cream. They are often misused as performance-enhancing drugs among competitive athletes seeking to boost performance and enhance muscular appearance. Common oral steroids include oxymetholone (Anadrol), oxandrolone (Oxandrin), methandrostenolone (Dianabol), and stanozolol (Winstrol). Street names for anabolic steroids include gym candy, Arnolds, pumpers, hype, 'roids, juice, and stackers.

There are several patterns of steroid misuse, including the following:

- **Cycling:** Taking steroids off and on, providing a rest period between cycles. Cycling periods are usually between 6 and 16 weeks.
- **Pyramiding:** Slowly increasing the steroid dosage, then titrating down after their maximum peak is reached.
- **Stacking:** Using several steroids at once, while mixing methods of administration.
- **Plateauing:** Overlapping the use of different steroids and methods of use. This is done to avoid developing tolerance.

Gender- and Age-Specific Effects

In **males,** the short-term effects of anabolic steroids include the following:

- Decreased sperm production and reduced sperm motility
- Testicular shrinkage
- Testicular tumors
- Breast enlargement
- Prostate enlargement
- Persistent erection
- Decreased libido

In **prepubescent males**, effects include the following:

- Precocious puberty
- Stunted growth
- Enlarged penis
- Painful and prolonged erections

For **females**, the short-term effects of anabolic steroids include the following:

- Facial hair growth
- Voice deepening
- Infertility
- Decreased breast size
- Decreased bone mass
- Irregular menses or amenorrhea
- Alopecia (hair loss)
- Clitoral enlargement

Psychological and Physiological Effects

The **psychological effects** of anabolic steroid misuse include the following:

- Psychosis
- Aggression ('roid rage)
- Impaired judgment

- Paranoia
- Mania
- Anxiety
- Depression and suicidality
- Delusional thinking
- Mood lability

The **physical effects** of anabolic steroid misuse include the following:

- Increased creatine concentrations in muscles
- Severe cardiac effects, including heart damage and heart attack
- Tendon rupture
- Decreased appetite and sleep loss
- Liver disease
- Fluid retention
- Infertility and sterility
- Acute kidney failure
- Blurred vision
- Severe acne
- Weakened immunity
- Rhabdomyolysis, resulting in damage to muscles and kidneys
- High blood pressure
- Jaundice
- High cholesterol and hyperglycemia

Mechanism of Action, Tolerance, Dependence, and Withdrawal

Anabolic steroids work by increasing the number of androgen receptors responsible for muscle size and strength. Activation of the androgen receptors causes a spike in calcium, creating effects in the brain, heart, and muscles. Anabolic steroids also activate CNS neurotransmitters, including stimulation of the growth hormone (GH)/insulin-like growth factor 1 (IGF-1) axis, or GH/IGF-1 axis. Anabolic steroids increase beta-endorphin levels and act on the same neuropathways affected by other substances, including dopamine and serotonin. These pathways are implicated in the development of tolerance and dependence. Dopamine encourages individuals to repeat pleasurable activities, and serotonin influences mood.

Symptoms of withdrawal from anabolic steroid misuse include the following:

- Weakness
- Diarrhea
- Loss of appetite
- Craving
- Difficulty sleeping
- Decreased libido
- Low energy
- Headaches
- Anxiety
- Depression
- Body dysmorphia (can also drive misuse)

Sympathomimetics, Stimulants, Diuretics, and Beta-Blockers

In addition to anabolic steroids, performance-enhancing drugs include the following:

- **Sympathomimetics** are endogenous agonists that mimic the action of hormones active in the sympathetic response, including epinephrine (adrenaline), norepinephrine (noradrenaline), and dobutamine (which mimics catecholamines), and ropinirole (dopamine). Epinephrine is a hormone produced in the adrenal gland and is a CNS neurotransmitter involved in the body's fight-or-flight response. Norepinephrine is a vasoconstrictor and neurotransmitter responsible for mental alertness and the regulation of stress. Dopamine is the neurotransmitter responsible for pleasurable experiences.
- **Stimulants** (e.g., nicotine, caffeine, adrafinil) are used to increase energy, endurance, and awake time.
- **Diuretics** are misused for rapid weight loss and to flush out banned performance-enhancing substances.
- **Beta-blockers** are misused for cardiovascular effects (i.e., to lower blood pressure), to promote smooth muscle relaxation, and to quell performance anxiety.
- **Erythropoietin** is used to enhance red blood cell production. This is used in blood doping, the process by which a person uses donor blood or their own previously harvested blood. A climb in red blood cells increases the availability of oxygen provided to muscles, which helps with endurance and stamina. Misuse of erythropoietin can damage immunity and may be fatal.
- **Synthetic oxygen carriers** are delivered via blood doping to decrease lactic acid, thus promoting increased aerobic fitness and endurance.
- **Xanthine** is an ergogenic/thermogenic aid that decreases body fat and aids in wakefulness. It is found naturally in chocolate and tea.
- **Narcotics and NSAIDs** are used to control pain to enable longer training sessions.
- **Nonsteroidal anabolic supplements** (e.g., insulin, human growth hormone, and insulin-like hormone) aid muscle recovery.
- **Thyroid hormones** are substances that regulate metabolism and increase energy.
- **Bee pollen** is a dietary supplement used to reduce stress and increase energy.

Co-Occurring Disorders

Individuals with co-occurring disorders have an SUD along with the diagnosis of a mental illness. For example, an individual can be diagnosed with AUD and major depressive disorder or panic disorder. This is very common in individuals with SUD. Often, the substance use/abuse originates as a method of self-medication for the mental illness, although mental disorders may also occur subsequently to SUD as well.

Treatment for co-occurring disorders must address the individual's comprehensive needs because each disorder can cause, exacerbate, maintain, imitate, or hide the other. For this reason, frequent screening and assessment for the presence of a co-occurring disorder are critical for maximizing treatment efficacy. Counselors recognize that poor detection often results in poor treatment. When critical signs are missed and diagnoses go unrecognized, the client's recovery is negatively impacted.

Addiction counselors must differentiate between a client's **primary** and **secondary diagnoses**, with the primary diagnosis detected first and the secondary diagnosis identified afterward. When a mental illness develops after an SUD, full detox is necessary to diagnose the mental disorder. When substance use develops after a mental illness is diagnosed, sometimes effective management of the mental illness (through pharmacotherapy, behavioral therapy, and/or cognitive therapy) may help reduce the individual's tendency to abuse substances. Effective treatment consists of treating the most problematic symptoms first, regardless of when they appeared in the client's life.

Mental Disorders That Commonly Occur Alongside SUD

Although the symptoms of several mental disorders can co-occur with SUD. A complete list of criteria for each diagnosis can be found in the DSM-5-TR, but common symptoms include:

- Depressive disorders
- ADHD (particularly untreated ADHD in adolescents)
- Bipolar I disorder
- PTSD
- Psychotic disorders
- Schizophrenia
- Eating/feeding disorders
- Anxiety disorders
- Personality disorders (primarily borderline personality disorder and antisocial personality disorder)

Although addiction counselors do not generally diagnose mental conditions, the client's treatment must include identification of any conditions present and, when necessary, a referral for a full psychiatric assessment. For efficacious treatment planning and clinical decision making, counselors discern whether symptoms exist independent of each other, or whether one is caused by the other.

Cross-Cutting Symptoms for SUD and Mental Disorders

Cross-cutting symptoms occur in SUD and in mental disorders. For example, individuals with a depressive disorder can experience sadness, anhedonia, and even psychotic symptoms—all conditions that can occur with psychoactive substance misuse or withdrawal. Addiction counselors must also understand that children and adolescents likely have a different clinical presentation than adults. Additionally, individuals with trauma and adverse childhood experiences are at a much higher risk for SUD, mental disorders, or both.

There are numerous cross-cutting symptoms with **co-occurring diagnoses**, including the following:

- Psychosis
- Delusions
- Hallucinations
- Suicidal ideation
- Emotional dysregulation
- Impulsivity
- Disorganized speech
- Compulsions
- Sleep disturbances
- Paranoia

Co-Occurring Disorder Treatment Models

Effective treatment for co-occurring disorders is geared toward holistically meeting the individual client's treatment needs. The following models can be used to treat co-occurring disorders:

- **Sequential treatment:** The client receives treatment for one condition followed by treatment for another.
- **Parallel treatment:** The client participates in two treatments concurrently, one for each condition.
- **Integrated treatment:** Clients are provided all-inclusive treatment for co-occurring disorders at one time.

Effective counseling services address all of the biopsychosocial-spiritual assessment elements for the SUD and the mental disorder.

Role of Psychotropic Medication

Many individuals receiving treatment for co-occurring disorders require **psychotropic medication** (e.g., antidepressants, antipsychotics, mood stabilizers) to help manage the symptoms of a mental disorder. Addiction counselors must remain knowledgeable of the psychoactive effects of psychotropic medications, and when necessary, they must **collaborate** with the client's medical provider or prescriber. When collaboration is neglected, there is the danger of providers conveying two separate messages, with one provider supporting psychotropic medication and another provider or treatment center advocating for the client to remain off all medications.

The role of the primary therapist is to coordinate care with all providers, assess the client's mental status, educate the client on medication compliance, and remain vigilant for confused bias in the recovery community. Confused bias occurs when individuals from mutual support groups encourage discontinuation of psychotropic medication because of fear that this may threaten the client's sobriety. Although such advice is generally well-meaning, it is misguided and can have dangerous consequences for the client, reinforcing the stigma of mental illness and engendering mistrust among individuals with co-occurring disorders.

Drug Paraphernalia

Cannabis or Marijuana

Paraphernalia used with cannabis or marijuana can be broken down into a few categories.

Bongs, bubblers, and pipes:

- Bongs are water pipes used to smoke marijuana. They work by filtering and cooling marijuana through water, which tends to give the user a more potent hit.
- Bubblers are a combination of pipes and bongs. They differ from bongs in that marijuana is not held in a bowl but is instead inhaled by letting go of a small hole near the chamber, known as a carb or carburetor.
- Marijuana pipes are small devices used to smoke cannabis. A pipe contains a bowl that holds the cannabis, a mouthpiece, a chamber, and a carburetor. The carburetor is used to control airflow.

Grinders, rolling papers, blunts, and roach clips:

- Grinders are small, round containers made of wood or metal; they are used to break up parts of the marijuana plant to be smoked in a joint or blunt.
- Rolling papers are used to smoke marijuana directly as a joint, blunt, or spliff. Cigarette paper or an emptied cigar can also be used.
- Joints contain marijuana, blunts are made from a hollowed-out cigar, and spliffs are blunts that combine tobacco and marijuana.
- Roach clips are metal clasps that hold the joint in a way that allows it to be smoked in its entirety. THC is more concentrated in the end, or butt, and the roach clip allows this portion to be smoked without burning the fingers.

Vaporizers, vape pens, and dabs:

- Vaporizers are used with various forms of cannabinoids, including oils or hash. They can also be used with nicotine.
- Vape pens frequently come with prefilled cartridges and are small vaporizers that use a battery and cartridge containing a heating element and cannabis oil.
- Dabs are cannabis oils and extracts vaporized off a hot surface and smoked. A dab rig uses a nail as a heating device.

Crack and Cocaine

Drug paraphernalia associated with crack and cocaine use include the following:

- **Glass pipes, light bulbs, and stems** slowly heat cocaine to produce crack. Light bulbs are used after the inner filament is removed. Stems are hollow glass tubes or tubes with rounded ends used to smoke crack.
- **Mirrors or flat, smooth surfaces** along with **razors** or **playing cards** are used to arrange cocaine into even lines, and dollar bills and straws are used for snorting.
- **Small spoons** are used to hold and heat crack cocaine to be used intravenously. **Plastic disposable needles and tourniquets** (e.g., belts, rubber ties) are used to inject cocaine.
- **Steel wool, faucet screens or aerators, and copper scouring pads** are often used as filters or screens to hold crack in place during use.
- **Aluminum cans and tinfoil** are used to freebase crack cocaine, along with a hollowed-out pen or straw.
- **Vials and transparent bags** are used to store cocaine.
- **Keys, tops of pens, or small compartments** are used to snort a smaller portion of cocaine known as a bump or one-hitter.

MDMA and Inhalants

Drug paraphernalia associated with MDMA (i.e., Molly or Ecstasy) include the following:

- **Club accessories**, which include pacifiers, neon glow sticks, and candy necklaces.
- In powdered form, MDMA can be snorted, which is associated with paraphernalia similar to what is used with cocaine (e.g., **rolled-up dollar bills, mirrors, razor blades**).
- **Menthol** or **mentholated rub** is used with Ecstasy to enhance the euphoric effects.
- **Painters' masks** or **surgical masks** are used to place mentholated rubs or oils to be inhaled directly in combination with Ecstasy to heighten euphoric effects.

Drug paraphernalia associated with inhalants include the following:

- Tubes of model glue
- Aerosol cans or containers, including deodorizers, compressed air dusters, spray paint, whipped cream, and hair spray
- Clothing, bandanas, and rags saturated with the inhalant
- Paper or plastic bags sprayed with the inhalant
- Balloons used to inhale nitrous oxide
- Volatile solvent cans or containers, including fingernail polish remover, gasoline, felt-tip markers, lighter fluid, and paint thinner
- Pill bottles, canisters, or containers used for nitrites

Heroin, Meth, and Crystal Meth

Drug paraphernalia associated with heroin, meth, and crystal meth include the following:

- **Glass pipes and stems** are used with steel wool to smoke crystal meth. The steel wool prevents burns on the mouth.
- **Flutes** are glass pipes used to smoke crystal meth.
- **Lighters and straws** can have a yellow tint caused by smoking the substances.
- Plastic **disposable needles and tourniquets** (e.g., belts, rubber ties) are used to inject heroin.
- **Tinfoil** or **gum wrappers** are used to smoke heroin or inhale meth.
- **Spoons** are used to heat heroin, which turns the bottom of the spoon black.
- **Bowls** are used for smoking meth or crystal.
- **Baggies, condoms,** or **balloons** are used to store or transport the substances.
- **Cotton balls** or **cigarette filters** are used to smoke the substances.

Drug Screening Tests

A **drug test** is conducted to determine the presence or absence of one or more substances. Drug tests may be conducted as part of a preemployment screening, athletic screening, or forensic evaluation, or to monitor past or present substance use. **Immunoassay (IA) drug tests**, also known as qualitative or presumptive drug screens, use antibodies to detect the presence of multiple substances and their metabolites.

When IA testing yields unexpected results, a confirmatory test should be performed. This is because IA drug tests lack **specificity and sensitivity**, meaning they can result in false positives and false negatives. A **confirmatory drug test**, also known as a definitive or quantitative drug test, is generally performed using gas chromatography/mass spectrometry or high-performance liquid chromatography. This method involves samples being sent to laboratories for analysis. Chromatography tests can detect small amounts of specific drugs more accurately than IA drug tests. They are generally not used during initial screenings because they are more expensive and less efficient than IA drug tests.

Factors Determining How Long a Substance Will Remain in a Person's System

Several factors determine how long a substance stays in a person's system. Different substances and classes of substances can stay in a person's system for varying periods. For example, alcohol can be detected in urine 10–12 hours after last use, whereas benzodiazepines remain for up to 1 week. The duration that a substance has been used and the frequency of use also influence detection windows. Marijuana can be detected in urine for up to 3 days for infrequent users, but it can remain detectable for 30 days with chronic, heavy users.

Other factors that influence how long a substance will remain in a person's system include:

- Polydrug use
- Race and ethnicity
- Metabolic rate
- Hydration level
- Body weight or body fat
- Physical activity

DETECTION WINDOWS FOR COMMON SUBSTANCES

Detection windows serve as general guidelines for the period of time that a substance can be detected. Detection windows by drug types include the following:

Substance	Blood	Urine	Hair	Oral Fluid (saliva)	Sweat
Alcohol	24 hours	10–12 hours (ethyl glucuronide [EtG]: up to 48 hours)	N/A	Up to 24 hours	N/A
Amphetamines	10–14 hours	2–4 days	Up to 90 days	1–48 hours	7–14 days
Methamphetamine	24 hours	2–5 days	Up to 90 days	1–48 hours	7–14 days
Barbiturates	1–2 days	Up to 7 days	Up to 90 days	N/A	N/A
Benzodiazepines	6–48 hours	Up to 7 days	Up to 90 days	N/A	N/A
Marijuana (cannabis)	6–24 hours	1–30 days	Up to 90 days	Up to 24 hours	7–14 days
Cocaine	12–24 hours	1–3 days	Up to 90 days	1–36 hours	7–14 days
Codeine (opiate)	6–12 hours	2–4 days	Up to 90 days	1–36 hours	7–14 days
Morphine (opiate)	Up to 3 days	2–5 days	Up to 90 days	1–36 hours	7–14 days
Heroin (opiate)	Up to 6 hours	2–3 days	Up to 90 days	1–36 hours	7–14 days
PCP	12–24 hours	5–6 days	Up to 90 days	N/A	7–14 days
MDMA (Molly)	1–2 days	1–3 days	Up to 90 days	1–2 days	7–14 days

National Institute on Drug Abuse (NIDA)

Since 1980, the **National Institute on Drug Abuse (NIDA)** has worked with SAMHSA to establish guidelines for drug screenings for federal employees. These guidelines can be used as a best practice for common drugs of abuse and each of their predetermined thresholds (i.e., cutoff levels).

The NIDA five-panel drug test, also called the SAMHSA-5, comprises the following five substances and two derivatives. Federally regulated industry standards include the following cutoff levels:

Drug Type	Initial Test Cutoff Level	Confirmatory Test Cutoff Level
Marijuana metabolites	50 ng/mL	15 ng/mL
Cocaine metabolites	150 ng/mL	100 ng/mL
Opiate metabolites	2,000 ng/mL	2,000 ng/mL
PCP	25 ng/mL	25 ng/mL
6-Acetylmorphine	10 ng/mL	10 ng/mL
MDMA	500 ng/mL	250 ng/mL
Amphetamines	500 ng/mL	250 ng/mL

False-Negative Immunoassay (IA) Drug Tests

A confirmatory drug test should follow an IA test that yields unexpected results. Confirmatory drug tests provide greater specificity and sensitivity and often have lower cutoff thresholds than IA tests. In addition to individualized factors, a false negative on a urine drug test can occur for one or more of the following reasons:

- The drug was used outside of the window of detection.
- Substances were used that were not detected; for example, cannabinoids and inhalants are challenging to detect with urine drug screens.
- The presence of a substance was detected, but it fell below the cutoff threshold.
- The substance has been altered or tampered with, including violations of specimen collection protocols. One indicator of adulterants is low creatinine levels, which may mean that the person diluted the specimen or consumed an excessive amount of water. Another method is to add enzymes that affect the urine's pH balance. Bleach and iodine are oxidizing agents used to change a specimen's pH balance.

FACTORS THAT MAY PRODUCE FALSE-POSITIVE RESULTS

Certain factors may produce a false-positive result on an IA drug test. IAs are more likely to indicate false positives for amphetamines and methamphetamines, alcohol, PCP, LSD, and benzodiazepines. Factors associated with **false positives** on IA drug tests include the following:

- The presence of **mouthwash or foods rich in yeast** is correlated with a positive screening for alcohol.
- Some **cold medications**, including pseudoephedrine, may produce false-positive results for amphetamines.
- **Stimulant medications prescribed for ADHD** may produce a false-positive result for amphetamine and methamphetamine.
- Foods containing **poppy seeds** may produce false-positive results for opioids.
- Certain **antidepressants** may produce false positives. For example, venlafaxine (Effexor XR) may produce a false-positive result for PCP, sertraline (Zoloft) may produce a false-positive result for benzodiazepines, and amitriptyline may produce a false-positive result for LSD.
- **NSAIDs** (e.g., ibuprofen) may produce a false-positive result for barbiturates, PCP, and THC.
- **Pain relievers** (e.g., tramadol) can produce a false-positive result for PCP.
- Certain **blood pressure medications**, including diltiazem (Cardizem), may produce false-positive results for LSD.
- **Secondary or passive inhalation of marijuana smoke** may produce a false-positive result for THC.

Evidence-Based Screening and Assessment

Initial Screening and Assessment

Screening to Determine If Client Meets the Criteria for SUD

An evaluation for SUD is performed in two phases. In the first phase, the counselor **screens** the client to determine if he or she meets the criteria for SUD and/or a co-occurring mental disorder. If the client meets criteria for substance use or a co-occurring mental disorder, then assessments specific to the substance or disorder are carried out. Counselors use screening to ensure that the client's specific needs are not beyond the scope of a particular treatment program. Careful consideration is also given to the therapeutic fit between the counselor and client—the counselor should have the knowledge, awareness, and skills necessary for the client to successfully engage in treatment.

During the screening phase, the counselor must review confidentiality and its limitations. Informed consent must be obtained, with the counselor outlining fees, third-party correspondence, the counselor's scope of practice, appointment scheduling, criteria for placement, and the counselor's theoretical orientation. These administrative practices should be reviewed while the counselor exhibits kindness, empathy, and compassion. The potential client should be treated with respect, and there is an emphasis on establishing rapport and developing a therapeutic alliance.

Tools for Substance Abuse

The **Michigan Alcohol Screening Test** was developed in 1971. The original assessment consisted of 25 yes-or-no questions with a complex grading system in which each question carried a different weight when scoring. In the most recently revised version of this screening tool, the client must answer yes or no to 22 questions, which are then scored with a 0 or 1 based on the answer. Clients who score 0–2 have no alcohol problem. Clients who score 3–5 are early to middle problem drinkers. Clients who score 6 or more are problem drinkers. This test is accurate with a 95% level of confidence, according to the National Council on Alcoholism and Drug Dependence. Some research indicates that the 6-point cutoff for labeling an alcoholic should be raised to 10 points.

The **Drug Abuse Screening Test** is the nonalcoholic counterpart to the Michigan Alcohol Screening Test. If either the Michigan Alcohol Screening Test or Drug Abuse Screening Test is positive for addiction, use the **Addiction Severity Index** to determine in what areas the drug use has been the most invasive. The areas assessed include medical, legal, familial, social, employment, psychological, and psychiatric. The Addiction Severity Index test is longer, covering 180 items.

The **Substance Abuse Subtle Screening Inventory (SASSI-4)** was first developed in 1988 to help identify covert abusers. Multiple revisions have occurred since. Typically, abusers hide their drug problems with lies, subterfuge, and defensive responses because they are:

- Unwilling to accept responsibility
- Hesitant to confront bad feelings and pain
- Afraid of the consequences (incarceration or rehabilitation programs)
- Conflicted (have mixed feelings) about quitting use of the chemical

The counselor uses the SASSI-4 to determine the truth, produce profiles useful for treatment planning, and understand the client. It can be administered as a one-page pencil-and-paper test, a computerized test with automated scoring, or an audio test. The SASSI-4 takes 15 minutes to complete and 5 minutes to score. The adult version has an overall accuracy of 93%. The Adolescent SASSI-A3 has an overall accuracy of 94%. They both contain "face-valid" and subtle items, which do not tackle drug abuse in a directly apparent way.

Dimensions of the ASAM Multidimensional Assessment

If the client meets the criteria for treatment, the counselor moves forward with scheduling an appointment. In instances in which the client is not a good fit for the counselor or facility, a referral is then made. Counselors use placement instruments such as the **American Society of Addiction Medicine (ASAM)** help make appropriate referrals. The **six ASAM dimensions** are:

- **Acute intoxication and withdrawal:** Is the client exhibiting signs of withdrawal? How serious is the risk? Is there a history of severe withdrawal symptoms or seizures? Is there significant risk given the substance, duration of use, or recent discontinuation?
- **Biomedical conditions and complications:** Are there any underlying medical conditions or chronic conditions that have the potential to complicate treatment? Has the client been compliant with treatment for underlying conditions?
- **Cognitive, behavioral, and emotional conditions:** Are there any underlying mental health conditions? What are the client's coping skills and level of distress? Does the client have the capacity to function independently, or does he or she require assistance with activities of daily living?
- **Readiness to change:** Are there internal or external motivating factors present? Does the client want this treatment, at this time, with this provider?
- **Relapse, continued use, or continued problem potential:** Is the client at imminent risk due to psychological distress associated with severe mental illness or substance use? Is the client at risk for harming themselves or others?
- **Recovery environment:** Does the client's current living situation place them at high risk for continued substance use? Are there supportive family members, friends, or work/school supports?

Addiction Severity Index

Developed by McLellan et al. in 1980 (with slight revisions in 1992), the **Addiction Severity Index** is a standardized assessment instrument that collects information on several aspects of the client's substance use. The Addiction Severity Index can also assist in developing the client's treatment plan. The **seven functional assessment domains** are as follows:

- Medical status (e.g., "Do you have any chronic medical problems that continue to interfere with your life?")
- Employment and support (e.g., "How long was your longest full-time job?")
- Drug use (e.g., "How many times have you overdosed on drugs?")
- Alcohol use (e.g., "How many times have you had alcohol delirium tremens?")
- Legal status (e.g., "How many months have you been incarcerated in your life?")
- Family/social status (e.g., "Have any of your blood-related relatives had what you would call a significant drinking, drug use, or psychiatric problem?")
- Psychiatric status (e.g., "How many times have you been treated for any psychological or emotional problems?")

As a semistructured interview, the Addiction Severity Index addresses major life events in each of the domains and the frequency, length, and duration of the client's substance use. A **problem severity index** is also assigned based on the client's substance use during the past 30 days. Examples of questions used for the severity index include the amount of money spent on substances or substance-related activities, how long the substance has been used, and how often substance-related consequences have occurred.

Formal Intake Process

If a client's situation is deemed appropriate for treatment, the counselor proceeds with a **formal intake** process. There are two phases of a formal intake process:

- The initial portion of the intake process is **administrative** in nature. This is the portion of time allocated to review informed consent, clarify fees, and explain services.
- During the second portion of the formal intake process, the counselor performs a **comprehensive biopsychosocial assessment**. When applicable, the counselor's next objective is to review the client's screening results. The counselor must then determine if the client has an SUD. If this is confirmed, the counselor must determine the severity of the client's substance use. During this time, the counselor also works to determine the presence of a co-occurring mental health disorder.

The formal intake assessment is also used to determine if the participation of family members or significant others is appropriate. If so, the counselor obtains a signed release of information permitting their involvement. The counselor must also obtain a signed release of information to provide or receive information from a third party (e.g., school, court, noncustodial guardians).

Initial Clinical Assessments

The primary purpose of an initial clinical assessment is to obtain relevant information useful for formulating a diagnosis. One method for obtaining this information is a biopsychosocial-spiritual assessment. A biopsychosocial-spiritual assessment is an integrative, holistic, comprehensive assessment used to collect information on the client's background and history by examining the influence of biological, psychological, social, and spiritual factors.

An initial intake assessment provides counselors with a complete picture of the client's substance use, coping skills, treatment needs, and recovery tools. Methods for obtaining this information include the use of screening and assessment instruments, the clinical interview, counselor observations, and/or drug and alcohol testing. In addition to obtaining accurate background information, there are several objectives of a clinical assessment. (The following list is non-exhaustive.)

- Providing a framework for treatment interventions
- Determining the appropriate level of care (i.e., the anticipated frequency, length, and duration of treatment) and treatment setting
- Identifying client strengths, supports, sociocultural influences, and contextual factors
- Creating the space to form a therapeutic alliance
- Assessing the client's motivation to change and helping the client begin to feel that change is possible

Biopsychosocial Assessments

Biopsychosocial assessments offer a collaborative, strengths-based, holistic approach to the diagnosis of SUD. Not all individuals who are tolerant of or dependent on a psychoactive substance meet the criteria for SUD. For example, individuals with chronic health conditions may develop tolerance to and dependence on medications that are taken as prescribed.

Addiction is shaped by biopsychosocial factors such as age, medical history, the presence of a co-occurring disorder, genetics, culture, socioeconomic status, and environmental conditions. A thorough assessment can help determine if the client engages in licit prescription drug use or has crossed the line into illicit drug use. Individuals at risk for substance misuse may use more than one prescribing doctor, use their medication for another purpose, or use a substance in order to experience euphoria.

A thorough assessment can help determine if the client engages in licit or illicit drug use. Individuals at risk for substance misuse include those who use more than one prescribing doctor or substance in order to experience euphoria.

Ongoing Screening and Assessment

Biopsychosocial-Spiritual Assessments

The biopsychosocial-spiritual assessment provides a holistic view of the client's needs by addressing all four assessment components (i.e., biological, psychological, social, and spiritual). Information collected in the assessment is used to help guide treatment planning. The counselor incorporates any co-occurring mental health disorders or physiological conditions related to substance use into the client's treatment plan. This approach allows counselors to integrate all factors contributing to the development and maintenance of an SUD. The causes and conditions of SUD are varied. SUD is likely attributed to a combination of factors, including the substance that is misused, the amount used, and the length of time that it was misused. The ASAM multidimensional assessment results are useful for guiding treatment planning and ensuring that clients are appropriately served across all levels of care.

Biological Factors Associated with SUD

Biological factors can increase an individual's susceptibility to SUD. **Genetics** and the interaction of **genetics and environmental factors** (i.e., epigenetics) account for nearly half of a person's risk of addiction. Counselors must carefully assess the client's **physical symptoms** throughout treatment. Counselors obtain a thorough **family history** and, when appropriate, include family members in the treatment planning process.

Biological factors that influence an individual's SUD include the following:

- The interaction or reaction of prescribed medications
- Sleep disturbances and sleep-related conditions
- Intellectual functioning
- How the substance is chemically processed
- Prenatal care (including nicotine use)
- Age or developmental level
- Intellectual functioning
- Diet and exercise
- Gender

In some instances, individuals with SUD experience neurological difficulties associated with long-term substance misuse (e.g., Wernicke-Korsakoff syndrome, or "wet brain"). Counselors use the ASAM criteria to accurately appraise physiological symptoms associated with long-term use, intoxication, and withdrawal. Dimension 1 (acute intoxication and withdrawal) and dimension 2 (biomedical conditions and complications) are particularly helpful for assessing physiological symptoms.

Psychological Factors Associated with SUD

Psychological components can contribute to the development and maintenance of SUD. The mental status exam guides treatment planning by exploring the client's level of functioning in several areas, including speech, appearance, behavior, perception, mood, insight, and cognitive factors. For clients with a history of psychological or psychiatric treatment, relevant aspects of prior episodes of care also help guide treatment planning. Elements from dimension 3 (emotions, behaviors, and cognitions) and dimension 4 (readiness to change) of the ASAM criteria address psychological components that are helpful in guiding treatment planning.

Psychological factors that influence an individual's SUD include the following:

- The client's subjective level of distress
- Decision making
- Psychological trauma and abuse
- Perception of condition
- Emotional dysregulation
- Suicidal or homicidal ideation
- Coping skills
- Depression and anxiety
- Executive functioning (e.g., impulsivity, self-control)
- Low self-esteem
- Positive and negative outcomes of substance use

Social Factors Associated with SUD

Social factors consist of any aspect of the client's thoughts and behaviors as they occur in the context of their social environment. Elements from dimension 3 (emotions, behaviors, and cognitions), dimension 5 (relapse or continued use), and dimension 6 (recovery/living environment) of the ASAM criteria address social components helpful in guiding treatment planning.

Social factors that influence an individual's SUD include the following:

- Interpersonal relationships; social supports
- Sexual and intimate relationships; marital status
- Relationships with coworkers or classmates
- Peer influences
- Disconnection from others
- Socioeconomic status
- Community attitudes regarding drug use
- Recreational activities and related interests
- Living situation
- Legal issues
- Military status

Cultural Factors Associated with SUD

Cultural components of an assessment are used to guide treatment planning and optimize long-term recovery from SUD. Counselors have an ethical responsibility to provide culturally responsive and culturally sensitive treatment to every individual served.

Cultural factors that influence an individual's SUD include the following:

- Race
- Ethnicity
- Sexual orientation
- Gender identity
- Language spoken
- Homelessness
- Cultural norms
- Acculturative stress
- Access to affordable health care
- Cultural implications related to disabilities (e.g., physical, mental, learning)
- Marginalized status

Religious or Spiritual Factors Associated with SUD

Clients with religious or spiritual practices often find comfort and support in their faith-based community. Twelve-step programs (e.g., Alcoholics Anonymous [AA] and Narcotics Anonymous) adhere to the belief that addiction is a spiritual disease with a spiritual solution. Members are encouraged to believe—or become willing to believe—in God or their conception of a higher power. Although religious or spiritual involvement can be a protective factor for some, it can be a risk factor for others. For some, religion and spirituality are associated with shame and rejection and include experiences of trauma and abuse. During the initial assessment, counselors assess for these factors and incorporate findings into the client's treatment plan whenever possible.

Relapse

Individuals experience a **relapse** when returning to substance misuse or problematic behaviors after a period of stopping. Relapse can involve any compulsion or addiction. For individuals with SUD, a relapse includes abuse of any mood-altering (i.e., psychoactive) substance. Individuals suffering from substance abuse and addiction should be educated on the **stages of relapse** so they can seek help.

- The first stage of relapse is **emotional relapse**. During this stage, the individual experiences emotions that signify the beginning of a possible relapse, such as anxiety, anger, isolation, and defensiveness. He or she may also become withdrawn, stop going to meetings, or develop poor eating and sleeping habits.
- The next stage of relapse is **mental relapse**, during which the individual starts to think about using the substance or reminisces about using in the past. The individual may begin to plan to relapse at this stage.
- The third, and final, stage of relapse is **physical relapse,** in which actions are taken to use the substance again. The earlier that relapse is addressed, the less likely it is that the individual will reach the stage of physical relapse.

Individuals must be empowered with a **relapse prevention plan** so they are prepared if they face early signs of relapse. This plan should identify triggers for use/abuse, detail a list of tools and coping mechanisms to use should the early stages of relapse occur, identify support systems (family, mentors, sponsors, etc.) to call in case of triggers/cravings, and identify the support group(s) that will provide consistent reinforcement and encouragement in the path to recovery.

Assessing the Conditions of a Client's Relapse

Research shows that although relapse is common for some individuals with SUD, evidence-based prevention strategies can be used to engage individuals in lifelong recovery. One such method is for counselors to use the **Situational Confidence Questionnaire**, which assesses the causes of relapse, including personal states (e.g., emotional, mental) as well as situational confidence, which is the degree of self-assurance in resisting using in tempting situations.

Counselors assessing relapse conditions may also consider answers to the following questions:

- Does the client have a clear understanding of their medical treatment plan?
- Does the client's current treatment plan require modifications?
- Are there co-occurring mental or physical disorders interfering with treatment compliance? If so, is the client receiving treatment addressing these needs?
- Is the client currently experiencing withdrawal? Are there appropriate, drug-specific treatment protocols in place to address withdrawal symptoms?
- Are there treatments in place to help prevent cravings?

Strategies Used to Address a Relapse

A relapse occurs when a person returns to substance use after a period of abstinence, either briefly or for a longer duration. Although relapses are not always a part of recovery, outcome studies show that between 40% and 80% of patients relapse within the first year of recovery. Using a strengths-based approach to treatment has proven to be effective for clients seeking post-relapse treatment. This approach emphasizes empathetic understanding, collaboration on agreed-upon treatment goals, and methods designed to improve self-efficacy.

Cognitive-behavioral strategies also improve treatment outcomes. These strategies include, but are not limited to, the following:

- **Evaluate the client's abstinence violation effect:** This occurs when a person believes there is no intermediate response to a lapse. The person may reason that if one drink ruins abstinence, he or she may try to "make the most of it."
- **Investigate the seemingly irrelevant decisions:** Whereas high-risk situations may be easy to identify, taking a step back and examining the seemingly irrelevant decisions made before exposure to high-risk situations may help fine-tune relapse prevention plans.
- **Recognize covert antecedents:** These include intrapersonal and interpersonal states. Examples of covert antecedents include temperament, emotional conditions (e.g., dysphoria), and relationship factors.
- **Create a decision grid accounting for the problem of immediate gratification:** The problem of immediate gratification is the tendency to accept a small reward now in place of a larger one later. For individuals who relapse, more pronounced and negative long-term consequences are ignored in favor of small, short-term rewards. The decision grid considers time frames when listing the pros and cons of substance use.

Strategies for Preventing Relapse

Strategies to prevent relapse include the following:

- Clients find it beneficial to get a reward when they have abstained from drugs or alcohol successfully, as a positive reinforcement. This strategy is known as **contingency management** or a **contractual agreement**. The reward should be one that the client wants; otherwise, it will be ineffective.
- **Cognitive therapy** is marked by replacing negative thought patterns with positive self-talk. Thought patterns that are automatically negative may trigger the client to relapse. When negative thought patterns happen, the client should replace them with a more functional action. Some techniques for reducing negative self-talk include free association, dream interpretation, and memory techniques. The client may rely on drugs to replace relationships.
- A new approach called **motivational enhancement therapy** uses role-playing to teach the client how to communicate goals and feelings.

Diseases Caused by Bloodborne Pathogens

The most common infectious diseases caused by bloodborne pathogens include, but are not limited to, the following:

- Human immunodeficiency virus infection/acquired immunodeficiency syndrome (HIV/AIDS)
- Hepatitis B
- Hepatitis C

Counselors must understand and abide by **state laws and ethical guidelines** protecting the **confidentiality** of individuals with an infectious (i.e., communicable) disease. In general, counselors are not authorized to disclose a client's medical information unless it poses an immediate risk to the safety of others. Counselors engage in ethical decision making by seeking outside consultation and client collaboration. **Confidentiality limitations** (e.g., duty to warn) are reviewed when obtaining informed consent.

The **ACA Code of Ethics (2014)** states, "When clients disclose that they have a disease commonly known to be both communicable and life threatening, counselors may be justified in disclosing information to identifiable third parties, if the parties are known to be at serious and foreseeable risk of contracting the disease." Counselors make this disclosure after determining the client's intention to inform third parties, as well as their intention to continue to engage in behaviors placing others at risk. Counselors also inform clients of any applicable laws related to mandatory disclosures.

HIV/AIDS

Human immunodeficiency virus (HIV) is a bloodborne pathogen that weakens an individual's immune system. If left untreated, it can lead to **acquired immunodeficiency syndrome (AIDS).** The progression of HIV can be controlled with appropriate medical care, including **antiretroviral therapy.** Although HIV is not curable, medical treatment can help individuals live longer and reduce the chances of sexually transmitting HIV to others. HIV can be transmitted intravenously, sexually, and perinatally. HIV transmission in blood donations is rare but less so in low-income countries.

Individuals with SUD are at higher risk of contracting HIV. Sharing needles with someone infected with the virus and having unprotected sex are contributing factors. Studies show that 10% of individuals diagnosed with HIV report using drugs intravenously. HIV/AIDS can also be spread through oral sex but to a lesser degree. Oral sex transmission rates are higher if the semen of an infected person comes into contact with oral ulcers, bleeding gums, or genital sores.

Mothers with HIV/AIDS can transmit the virus to their infants during pregnancy, birth, or breastfeeding. However, pregnant mothers with HIV can significantly reduce mother-to-child transmission by taking HIV medication through childbirth and providing postpartum antiretroviral therapy medication to their newborn babies.

At-Risk Populations for HIV Infection

Certain populations are at greater risk for HIV, including those who live in communities with higher rates of transmission and subpopulations engaging in high-risk behaviors. Substance use, impulsivity, high-risk behaviors, and exchanging sex for money are additional factors that amplify risk among all populations. In addition, certain cross sections of populations, including adolescents and young adults, are at greater risk for infection.

Men engaging in unprotected anal sex with other men are most affected by HIV. In 2018, the Centers for Disease Control and Prevention (CDC) reported that bisexual and gay men account for nearly 70% of newly diagnosed cases of HIV. African American males have the highest infection rates, followed by Hispanic males. Women engaging in unprotected sex with a male partner diagnosed with HIV are at greater risk than males who have unprotected sex with a female partner diagnosed with HIV.

Health-care disparities among socially and economically marginalized communities are associated with poorer health outcomes. Inequitable resources impact access to care, utilization of care, and the quality of care received. Additional factors contributing to higher infection rates among racial and ethnic minority populations include the stigma associated with male-to-male sex, homophobia, discrimination, and mistrust in the health-care system.

Hepatitis B

Hepatitis B virus (HBV) is a bloodborne pathogen transmissible through blood, semen, and other bodily fluids. Individuals who have unprotected anal and vaginal sex or who share needles and other drug paraphernalia (e.g., syringes) with someone infected with HBV are at an increased risk. Mothers with HBV can transmit the virus to their newborn babies.

Individuals newly infected with HBV may not have symptoms. For those who do, symptoms include lethargy, nausea, vomiting, stomach pain, joint pain, and dark urine. HBV is a short-term illness for many, but for those first diagnosed at an early age, HBV can be chronic and life-threatening. HBV can lead to cirrhosis of the liver or liver cancer, developing more quickly with alcohol consumption.

HBV is vaccine-preventable. The spread of HBV can be lessened by refraining from sharing razors or toothbrushes with those infected, as well as using pre- or postexposure prophylaxis (e.g., latex gloves, disinfecting contaminated surfaces).

Hepatitis C

Hepatitis C virus (HCV) is a bloodborne pathogen most commonly transmitted by sharing needles and other injectable drug paraphernalia with an infected person. HCV can become a chronic, long-term condition for over half of individuals infected. The progression of HCV is slow. Clinical symptomatology for HCV may not be noticed for 20–30 years. Long-term conditions include cirrhosis of the liver and liver cancer. Because of the slow progression of HCV, individuals generally do not seek medical care until the infection has caused advanced liver damage.

Unlike HBV, HCV is not vaccine-preventable. In response to HCV morbidity and mortality rates, the CDC now recommends a one-time screening for all individuals older than 18 and every pregnant woman during each pregnancy. Individuals residing in areas where HCV prevalence is less than 0.01% are exempt from testing recommendations.

Men are more at risk for contracting HCV than women. Alcohol consumption can exacerbate symptoms and worsen the infection. Additional risk factors for HCV include having an HIV coinfection, receiving immunosuppressive therapy, being diagnosed with HBV, and having fatty liver disease. For most, early detection and treatment can result in a virologic cure.

Treatment Recommendations for Bloodborne Infectious Disease and SUD

For counselors working with individuals diagnosed with a bloodborne infectious disease and SUD, treatment recommendations include the following:

- Provide access to **testing** for bloodborne infections and follow-up care.
- Supply clients with accurate, **up-to-date medical information** and resources.
- Assess for and address **health-care mistrust**.
- Help clients **reduce risk-taking behaviors** (e.g., engaging in unprotected sex).
- Provide periodic **risk assessments**, including an assessment for suicidal ideation.
- Obtain informed consent to collaborate with the client's medical team and behavioral health specialists to achieve **integrated treatment**.
- **Distinguish between symptoms** that are virus or substance induced and those caused by a mental disorder, including insomnia, mood swings, psychosis, depression, aggression, and cognitive changes.
- Offer **medication-assisted treatment** for opioid addiction, which reduces the risk of contracting an infectious disease.
- Support **public health policies**, such as needle and syringe exchange programs and medication-assisted treatment, that are proven to reduce HIV risk.

Treating SUD and Comorbid Virus-Induced Pain

Counselors understand that clients with SUD may be prescribed opioids for virus-induced pain. Recommendations for working with clients with SUD who take prescription medications for virus-induced pain include the following:

- Counselors must stay within their **scope of practice** and **collaborate** with the client and other medical providers. Counselors empower clients to review potential risks and harms with their medical team.
- Counselors show respect for the **client's autonomy** and decision making surrounding pain medication.
- Counselors may recommend **alternative therapies**, including cognitive behavioral therapy (CBT), nontraditional medications, and mindfulness-based stress reduction techniques **as coordinated adjunctive interventions** to complement pain medication. For example, recent studies indicate that buprenorphine has shown efficacy in treating pain caused by HIV.
- Counselors are aware of their own **biases** regarding pain management and recovery, and they avoid value-laden and absolute statements about complex, individualized client issues surrounding prescription medication and recovery from SUD.

Places Used to Conceal Substances

Abusers who misuse substances often devise clever places to conceal drugs. According to the United States Drug Enforcement Administration (DEA), adolescents commonly develop multiple methods for hiding illegal substances, some of which include **hiding substances inside the following**:

- Graphing calculators
- Marker tops
- Candy wrappers
- Tin mint containers
- Lipstick
- Heating vents
- Mattresses
- Wall hangings
- Battery compartments, including those found in alarm clocks, video game consoles, and television remote controls
- Heating vents
- Toilet tanks
- Hairbrushes
- Books
- Baseball caps
- Glove compartments
- Flashlights
- Shoes

Other means of hiding illicit substances include slicing a tennis ball and placing drugs inside before storing it in the original can. Substances can be hidden in decoy containers of everyday products such as potato chip canisters, behind wall hangings, or in draperies.

National Harm Reduction Coalition's Principles of Harm Reduction

With social justice as its foundation, the National Harm Reduction Coalition has established principles to minimize the consequences of substance use for people who use drugs (PWUD), their families, and their communities. The purpose of the principles is to promote awareness and incorporate safe and effective strategies for meeting PWUD where they are. This includes actively engaging with PWUD to prevent drug-related fatalities and minimize the negative effects of drug use. At its core is the advocacy for the respect, worth, and dignity of PWUD through fair and equitable treatment.

The **eight harm reduction principles set forth by the National Harm Reduction Coalition** are summarized below:

- To minimize the negative consequences of drug use through compassionate, therapeutic care rather than punitive coercion or condemnation
- To recognize that drug use is a "complex and multifaceted phenomenon"—with varying symptoms and levels of acuity—with some patterns of drug use being riskier than others
- To facilitate policies and practices aligned with reducing morbidity and mortality among PWUD, which may not always include total cessation of drug use as a pathway to treatment
- To provide services and interventions to PWUD, their families, and the surrounding communities, that reduce stigma, save lives, and decrease the negative health effects of substance use
- To ensure that PWUD or those with a history of drug use are provided the opportunity to actively engage in public policy discourse and participate in developing relevant and applicable programs, policies, and practices
- To foster the rights of PWUD to be their own agents of change, and in doing so, empower PWUD to voluntarily participate in peer-delivered recovery support
- To understand how oppression, trauma, racism, discrimination, and other social determinants of health influence a person's capacity to access and fully engage in drug-related harm reduction
- To fully acknowledge the acute risks and tragic consequences of substance use and dependency

Documentation

CLINICAL DOCUMENTATION

Clinical documentation provides a chronological account of the client's episode of care. Documentation must be clear, concise, and objective. Counselors understand that timely documentation is essential for **accuracy.** Additionally, counselors must provide documentation demonstrating **compliance** with applicable documentation regulations (e.g., agency, federal, state). There are many elements of clinical documentation, including, but not limited to, the following:

- Screening and assessment reports
- Signed copies of informed consent
- Signed release-of-information forms
- Intake reports
- Treatment outcome data
- Termination notifications
- Discharge summaries
- Documentation supporting the clinical diagnosis

Progress reviews are conducted at predetermined intervals, with short-term goals generally reviewed every 3 months and long-term goals every 6 months. A timely review of treatment goals and interventions is essential for accurately determining the client's level of care. In addition, counselors must establish medical necessity to justify diagnosis and treatment, which insurance companies often use to justify payment for services.

CLINICAL PROGRESS NOTES

Progress notes are included in the client's record and provide the counselor's account of each clinical interaction. Counselors create progress notes to provide a chronological and comprehensive narrative of the client's progress through each phase of counseling. In addition, individual progress notes reflect the client's response to the therapist's interventions.

Counselors must ensure that information in the progress note is **objective and nonbiased**. Direct quotes from the client help provide a factual account of the client's attitude, mood, or response to treatment. **Individual progress notes** detail the client's progress toward treatment plan goals, treatment interventions, response to the interventions, and post-session plans (e.g., referrals, follow-up meetings). Counselors also assign and document client homework, which maximizes progress by helping clients implement strategies learned in session.

Case Management

Multidisciplinary Approach to Treatment for Individuals with SUD

Multidisciplinary teams provide holistic care for clients with complex and comprehensive treatment needs. In the context of addiction counseling and treatment, multidisciplinary or interdisciplinary teams consist of professionals who use their expertise to establish an integrated approach to client care.

Multidisciplinary teams help the counselor or addiction specialist address each client's biopsychosocial-spiritual treatment needs. For clients in need of medical treatment, physicians, pharmacists, nurse practitioners, or other trained medical staff can assist with medication-assisted therapy and other forms of medication management. In addition, a pharmacist or pharmacy assistant can be used to dispense prescribed medications and alert the treatment team to any adverse medication interactions.

For clients requiring mental health assistance or psychoeducational services, team members can include psychiatrists, psychologists, case managers, family therapists, and other trained counseling professionals. Lastly, peer recovery support specialists and other members of the recovery community can be used to help the client achieve and maintain sobriety.

Making Client Referrals

Counselors make **referrals** to ensure that the client's complex and comprehensive needs are met. Client referrals provide assistance to clients whose treatment needs fall beyond the purview of the counselor or current treatment facility. Counselors must possess the knowledge and skills useful for providing appropriate referrals within a network of numerous community agencies and additional systems of care (e.g., crisis care, educational services).

Counselors making referrals ensure that the client understands the purpose of the referral and whether or not he or she is motivated to obtain the services. Counselors must actively participate in the coordination of care by assisting the client with any potential roadblocks or barriers, ensuring that the client receives culturally appropriate care, and evaluating the outcome of the referral. Collaboration among referral sources is essential for fostering integrated and holistic client care.

Successful Collaboration with Referral Sources

The referring counselor must ensure that the referral agency receives information outlining the reason for the referral, significant aspects of the client's case conceptualization, treatment needs, and current progress toward treatment plan goals. Counselors must follow state and local guidelines when exchanging information to ensure that privacy practices are followed and ethical standards (e.g., confidentiality) are upheld. Prompt communication is necessary for successful collaboration. In cases in which the addiction specialist is unfamiliar with or unsupportive of the referral source's actions, the expertise of the outside provider must be respected to keep successful client treatment at the forefront. In these circumstances, addiction counselors are encouraged to seek consultation and supervision to clarify the outside sources' unfamiliar roles, actions, or processes.

Referring to an Alternative Primary Service Provider

Counselor or client circumstances may warrant termination of services and a referral to an alternative primary provider.

A referral to an alternative provider is warranted on behalf of the **existing counselor** if:

- The treatment he or she provides is no longer benefiting the client.
- New client needs have developed, and the counselor lacks sufficient knowledge, skills, and experience necessary to assist.
- The counselor is absent for an extended period of time or has been terminated from employment.

A referral to an alternative provider may be warranted on behalf of **the client** if:

- The client has an insurance plan that no longer covers the primary provider's services, or the coverage has lapsed.
- The client has an outstanding bill and is unable to pay the fees agreed upon at intake.
- The client has been receiving services that are no longer supported by the referring counselor's agency.

Discharge and Continuing Education

Client Termination

When a client reaches the end of therapy, the addiction counselor prepares the client for discharge and termination. If a client achieves his or her treatment plan goals and the counselor believes the client has received the maximum benefit from services, then the client and counselor work together to proceed with termination.

Premature or **unexpected termination** occurs when the client or counselor unilaterally chooses to end treatment. For example, this can happen when several no-shows are followed by the counselor's inability to reach the client to reschedule. Premature termination also occurs when the counselor unexpectedly vacates their position.

When preparing the client for planned discharge, the counselor assesses the client's progress, including whether the client could benefit from a different level of care. The counselor then summarizes and documents these findings. Discharge planning also includes evaluating how well the client applies learned concepts and skills in their everyday lives. When discharge and termination are unexpected, it is good clinical practice to send the client a letter stating that services will end unless the client responds to the notification by a specific date, which is generally 10 working days. A copy of the letter should be placed in the client's chart. The client's discharge summary must also include the client's disposition at discharge (e.g., met treatment goals, withdrew against staff advice).

Discharge Planning and the Continuing Care Plan

During the initial counseling stage, the client and counselor create an individualized treatment plan and continuing care plan. The treatment plan goals and objectives help give counseling direction and focus. A continuing care plan is an offshoot of the treatment plan, providing direction and focus to post-discharge goals and objectives. Careful construction of the continuing plan of care is essential for its seamless implementation. This is best accomplished through client-counselor collaboration.

When possible, a recovery support specialist participates in the client's discharge planning to learn how to best support the client after completing treatment. This can be in the form of a peer and/or a certified specialist. The continuing care plan offers a summary of treatment conditions, including reasons for admission, significant findings identified during treatment, the client's primary and secondary diagnoses, response to treatment interventions, supports needed post-discharge, and directions on how to administer any prescribed medications. A well-crafted continuing plan of care highlights salient aspects of the beginning, middle, and end of the client's treatment, with an additional focus on recommended post-discharge treatment and support.

Client, Family, and Community Education for Substance Abuse and Recovery

The primary goal of client, family, and community education for substance abuse and recovery is prevention. The dissemination of information can be formal or informal, with formal dissemination included in psychoeducational programs or intentional conversations with the client, family member, or individuals in the community. The purpose of education is to equip all parties with an awareness of the risk factors and preventative factors for SUD and how to best support the recovery process.

Education must be culturally sensitive. Culturally relevant educational components include risk and preventative factors associated with cultural identity, race, ethnicity, beliefs, gender, sexual orientation, age, religion, and social groups. Counselors promote health and wellness by working with all communities in various settings (e.g., school, correctional facilities) to reinforce conditions amenable to recovery from psychoactive substance use.

Primary, Secondary, and Tertiary Prevention Strategies for SUD

Preventative strategies exist along a continuum and include primary, secondary, and tertiary prevention. Generally speaking, primary prevention aims at preventing disease before it occurs. Secondary prevention involves screening to identify those at risk for—or in the early stages of—disease so that long-term consequences can be avoided. Tertiary prevention involves treating those already diagnosed with a disease in order to minimize complications.

- **Primary prevention** strategies in the context of SUD include community-wide education regarding the risks of substance use and the consequences of substance misuse. These may target subpopulations that have higher risks for SUD.
- **Secondary prevention** strategies in the context of SUD include screening at-risk communities with regard to the use of substances (type, frequency), identifying those individuals who are misusing substances, and offering support and resources to prevent further deterioration.
- **Tertiary prevention** strategies include treatment facilities (inpatient and outpatient) that are directed at those with diagnosed SUD. They also include maintenance interventions for individuals who have been discharged and/or attained sobriety and need continued support.

Evidence-Based Treatment, Counseling, and Referral

Treatment Planning

Types of Treatment Modalities for Substance Use Disorder (SUD)

Counselors work to match each client with the treatment modality that best meets their unique needs. There are four primary treatment modalities:

- **Detoxification treatment programs**: Detoxification is offered as a means for medically treating withdrawal from psychoactive substances. Depending on the substance and the client's length of use, detoxification treatment can last between 2 and 14 days.
- **Inpatient (i.e., residential) treatment programs**: These programs are staffed with full-time medical practitioners and offer clients around-the-clock live-in care. Individual, family, and group counseling are offered, and clients are required to attend 12-step or similar mutual support groups.
- **Intensive outpatient programs (IOPs)**: Clients attending IOPs receive individual, family, and group counseling. IOPs can last up to 12 weeks, with structured activities lasting between 9 and 20 hours per week. The IOP allows clients to receive comprehensive, integrated services with minimal disruption to their normal schedules.
- **Outpatient treatment programs**: Less intensive than IOPs, outpatient services offer clients weekly or biweekly individual, family, psychoeducation, group, and/or medication management sessions to treat SUD as well as comorbid psychiatric or mental disorders.

Individualized Treatment Plans

Treatment plans give each counseling session focus, direction, and purpose. To specifically address each client's unique needs, each treatment plan must be individualized. The treatment plan is developed during the beginning phase of treatment and is reviewed and updated on an intentional and ongoing basis. Counselors work collaboratively with clients to establish agreed-upon treatment goals. During this process, the client and counselor determine the focus of treatment and carefully negotiate client-driven and counselor-directed goals. This collaborative process helps the client establish hope and provides a firm foundation for the therapeutic alliance.

A sound treatment plan includes actionable steps that the client and therapist can take to address salient aspects of the client's case conceptualization. Once the treatment plan goals are established, the client and counselor determine if collateral sources, such as family members or community supports, can be used to maximize the client's chance for success. It is essential to gauge the client's motivation to change and identify any roadblocks that would interfere with their success.

Goals and Individualized Treatment Plans

Treatment planning is an ongoing endeavor that includes evaluation and goal setting in order to determine what path the individual wants to take as part of recovery. The addiction counselor should develop short- and long-term goals with the client, determining where the person wants to be at a point in the future, such as in 5 years. One way to determine goals and establish a plan is to use the **SMART technique**, in which goals should take on the following characteristics:

- **Specific**: Identifies concrete actions and desired results
- **Measurable**: Can be objectively determined to be met or not met
- **Achievable**: Is appropriate for the person's abilities and situation
- **Relevant**: Pertains to a matter of importance to the patient
- **Time-based**: Has a clear time frame in view

Psychoanalytic Theory

Components of Sigmund Freud's Psychoanalytic Theory

Sigmund Freud, commonly known as the father of psychoanalysis, based his practice on **psychoanalytic and psychodynamic personality theories**. The foundations of these theories are based on the following concepts.

Levels of awareness:

- **Conscious**: Thoughts, feelings, and desires that a person is aware of and able to control
- **Preconscious**: Thoughts, feelings, and desires that are not in immediate awareness but can be recalled to consciousness
- **Unconscious**: Thoughts, feelings, and desires not available to the conscious mind

Components of the Psychoanalytic Model of Addiction

The psychoanalytic model of addiction states that the use of alcohol or drugs is the way a person has chosen to cope with anxiety or unconscious conflicts within his or her mind. The psychoanalytic model is directly related to the work of Sigmund Freud, who coined the term *id* to describe instinctual urgings. He believed that id instincts are seen in the libido and in aggressive acts. The superego tries to control the instinctive urges of the id. This is where internal conflict develops and is displayed in the ego, which exhibits states of anxiety. Defense mechanisms take the form of denial, projection, or redirecting the unacceptable impulses. Conflicted people use drugs and alcohol to disguise emotions that are too painful to confront. Addiction is a form of self-medication.

Review Video: Psychoanalytic Approach
Visit mometrix.com/academy and enter code: 162594

Freudian Psychiatric Terms

Common **Freudian psychiatric terms** include:

- **Oedipus complex** or **Electra complex**: At the age of 4 or 5, a child falls in love with the parent of the opposite sex and feels hostility toward the parent of the same sex.
- **Defense mechanisms**: These are conscious or unconscious actions or thoughts designed to protect the ego from anxiety.
- **Freudian slips**: Also known as parapraxes, these are overt actions with unconscious meanings.

- **Free association**: A method designed to discover the contents of the unconscious by associating words with other words or emotions.
- **Transference**: Transference takes place when feelings, attitudes, or wishes linked with a significant figure in one's early life are projected onto others in one's current life.
- **Countertransference**: This happens when the feelings and attitudes of the therapist are inappropriately projected onto the patient.
- **Resistance**: Resistance is anything that prohibits a person from retrieving information from the unconscious.
- **Fixation**: Someone who is bogged down in one stage of development has a fixation.

Review Video: Who Was Sigmund Freud?
Visit mometrix.com/academy and enter code: 473747

Freud's Stages of Development and the Components of the Personality

Stages of development: Each person passes through stages of psychosexual development (and can become trapped in any stage):

- **Oral**: Focus on sucking and swallowing
- **Anal**: Focus on spontaneous bowel movements or control over impulses
- **Phallic**: Focus on genital region and identification with parent of same gender
- **Latent**: Sexual impulses are dormant; focus on coping with the environment
- **Genital**: Focus on erotic and genital behavior, leading to development of mature sexual and emotional relationships

Personality structure: The personality has three main components:

- **Id**: Unconscious pleasure principle, manifested by a desire for immediate and complete satisfaction with disregard for others
- **Ego**: Rational and conscious reality principle, which weighs actions and consequences
- **Superego**: Conscious and unconscious censoring force of the personality, which evaluates and judges behavior

Freudian Defense Mechanisms Built Upon by Anna Freud

Freudian defense mechanisms applicable to SUD include the following:

Compensation	Protection against feelings of inferiority and inadequacy stemming from real or imagined personal defects or weaknesses.
Conversion	Somatic changes conveyed in symbolic body language; psychic pain is felt in a part of the body.
Denial	Avoidance of awareness of some painful aspect of reality.
Displacement	Investing repressed feelings in a substitute object.
Association	Altruism; acquiring gratification through connection with and helping another person who is satisfying the same instincts.
Introjection	Absorbing an idea or image so that it becomes part of oneself.
Isolation of affect	Separation of ideas from the feelings originally associated with them. The remaining idea is deprived of motivational force; action is impeded and guilt is avoided.
Intellectualization	Psychological binding of instinctual drives in intellectual activities; for example, the adolescent's preoccupation with philosophy and religion.
Projection	Ascribing a painful idea or impulse to the external world.
Rationalization	Effort to give a logical explanation for painful unconscious material to avoid guilt and shame.
Repression	The act of obliterating material from conscious awareness. This is capable of mastering powerful impulses.
Splitting	Seeing external objects as either all good or all bad. Feelings may rapidly shift from one category to the other.
Sublimation	Redirecting energies of instinctual drives to generally positive goals that are more acceptable to the ego and superego.

Examining defense mechanisms is helpful for those with SUD and co-occurring mental health disorders. Once insight has been established, the client learns to handle negative emotional states without using substances or engaging in maladaptive coping skills and defense mechanisms.

Adlerian Therapy

Also known as individual psychology, Adlerian therapy is a strengths-based, phenomenological approach to counseling based on the assumption that people are motivated by a purposeful desire to connect with others (i.e., social interest), overcome inferiority, and create a personal style of life. Alfred Adler believed that personality is influenced by birth order; however, his theory is future-minded and based on the premise that individuals have the capacity to create their own fate. Adlerian therapy is considered a precursor to CBT. There are four phases of Adlerian therapy:

- **Establishing a therapeutic alliance (i.e., engagement):** Practitioners use a collaborative approach to offer support and encouragement. Adlerians strive to understand each client's subjective and contextual experiences.
- **Examining psychological dynamics (i.e., assessment):** The assessment process includes exploring the client's early childhood history, biopsychosocial influences, and family constellation—each factor represents a component of a client's lifestyle.
- **Fostering insight:** Adlerians believe that insight is the impetus for change. Practitioners help promote insight and self-understanding by providing present-moment (i.e., here-and-now) interpretations of potential underlying motives and behavior.
- **Providing reorientation and reinforcement:** This final phase emphasizes movement from insight to change. Practitioners help clients move toward mastery (i.e., superiority) by offering encouragement, support, and a change in awareness (i.e., reorientation).

Using Adlerian Therapy for Individuals Diagnosed with SUD

Adlerian therapy helps individuals with SUD by providing insight into the distorted sense of **security and belonging** that accompanies substance use. Clients are instead encouraged to develop a lifestyle that is motivated by **social interest** and an authentic connection with others. Social interest emphasizes the common good over individualism. Twelve-step groups such as AA reinforce this principle in tradition 1, stating, "Our common welfare should come first; personal recovery depends upon AA unity."

Adlerian therapy empowers clients to establish **purposeful or central goals.** A central goal is known as a **fictional finalism**, and it can be positive or negative. The goal of an Adlerian therapist is to assist clients in overcoming negative fictional finalism in which relief is sought through mood-altering substance use. This is accomplished by identifying and correcting erroneous beliefs, altering the trajectory of negative fictional finalism, and empowering clients to attain a sober lifestyle.

The first step in addressing fictional finalism is to examine a person's **private logic**. Private logic includes the client's subjective, sociocultural, and contextual experiences and worldview, which influence their convictions, perceptions, and assumptions about themselves and others.

Gestalt Therapy

The removal of masks and facades is the goal of gestalt therapy, according to its founder, Fritz Perls. A creative interaction must be developed so the client can gain an ongoing awareness of what is being felt, sensed, and thought. **Boundary disturbances** (lack of awareness of the immediate environment) may occur in the following forms:

- **Projection**: Fantasy of what another person is experiencing
- **Introjection**: Accepting the beliefs and opinions of others without question
- **Retroflection**: Turning back on oneself that which is meant for someone else
- **Confluence**: Merging with the environment
- **Deflection**: Interfering with contact; used by receivers and senders of messages

The **goal of therapy** is integration of the self and world awareness. The **techniques** of therapy include:

- **Playing the projection**: Taking on and experiencing the role of another person.
- **Making the rounds**: Speaking to or doing something to other group members to experiment with new behavior.
- **Sentence completion**: For example, "I take responsibility for ____________."
- **Exaggeration** of a feeling or action to clarify the purpose or intent.
- **Empty-chair dialogue**: Having an interaction with an imaginary provocateur.
- **Dream world**: Explored by describing and playing parts of a dream.
- **Reminiscence**: Unfinished business is believed to originate in the past but must be addressed in the here and now to constructively process emotional reactions such as rage, resentment, shame, and fear.

Person-Centered Therapy

Carl Rogers is credited with developing person-centered therapy, a humanistic approach to nondirective and client-centered counseling. Person-centered therapy assumes that incongruence results from a discrepancy between one's self-image and ideal self. Conditions of worth are created when an individual takes on a significant other's condition of regard to the extent that self-experience is sacrificed. Addiction professionals (APs) use person-centered therapy to reduce client defensiveness and help reduce the stigma associated with having an SUD.

Rogerian therapists believe that client growth occurs in the presence of the following three counselor attitudes:

- **Congruence:** Inner feelings match outer actions.
- **Unconditional positive regard:** The therapist sees the patient as a person of intrinsic worth and treats the client nonjudgmentally.
- **Empathic understanding:** The therapist is a sensitive listener.

Behavioral Therapy

Classical Conditioning and Operant Conditioning as Behavioral Therapy

Classical conditioning and operant conditioning are two types of **behavioral therapy**, each with separate applications for treating SUD.

- **Classical conditioning theory** was developed by the Russian Ivan Pavlov in the 1890s. Pavlov's experiments were based on the reflexive reactions of dogs that had been conditioned to salivate (the conditioned response) at the sound of a bell (the conditioned stimulus) that meant they would be fed soon. Addicts have a conditioned response associated with circumstances in which drugs or alcohol were used. The conditioned response can be psychological (craving the drug or alcohol) or physical. The circumstance or environment is the conditioned stimulus.
- **Operant conditioning theory** was developed by the American B. F. Skinner in the 1930s using rats and pigeons. It describes responses of the conditioned individual to negative or positive reinforcers. Negative reinforcers are the addict's withdrawal signs and symptoms. The positive reinforcer is relieving the withdrawal symptoms by consuming the drug or alcohol. Addictive behaviors can be switched off by removing the reinforcers.

Social Learning Theory

In 1977, Albert Bandura developed social learning theory to describe the relationship of a person to his or her environment. Bandura theorized that people learn from watching other people. He believed people self-regulate and manage their behaviors based on their established principles and inner values (standards). Inner values are not influenced unduly by external rewards or retributions. An inner value that does not oppose drinking to excess contributes to a person's alcoholic behavior. An inner value that opposes drinking to excess means that the person has a restrictive view of drinking and will self-regulate by stopping before he or she is intoxicated. The person who experiences a distinct difference between values and behaviors finds it necessary to change one or the other so that the values win out over the undesired behavior. This leads to a change of behavior that befits the person's set of values.

Behavior Therapy Techniques and Interventions for SUD

Contingency Management, Motivational Interviewing (MI), and the Matrix Model

The overall goal of behavior therapy is to examine processes that initiate behavior, maintain it, or discontinue it. Methods of behavior therapy include classical conditioning, operant conditioning, and social learning. The following interventions use elements of behavior therapy:

- **Contingency management:** The client is rewarded with tokens, gift cards, or other positive reinforcements for meeting predetermined targeted behaviors (e.g., periods of abstinence, negative drug screens). In some inpatient treatment centers, community reinforcement (e.g., increased privileges, visits) is used to reinforce healthy behavior.
- **Motivational interviewing (MI):** MI is a strengths-based model using behavior therapy techniques to decrease ambivalence (i.e., negative behavior) by reinforcing and enhancing the client's motivation to change.
- **The matrix model:** The matrix model is a combination of multiple behavioral, cognitive, social, and emotional approaches, including mutual support groups, relapse prevention, and psychoeducation.

12-Step Facilitation Therapy, Assertiveness Training, Cue Exposure, and Counterconditioning

Behavior therapy uses principles of classical conditioning, operant conditioning, and social learning to modify targeted behaviors. Examples of behavior therapy techniques and interventions for SUD include the following:

- **Twelve-step facilitation therapy:** Mutual support groups (e.g., AA, NA) use social support to promote treatment engagement and sustained abstinence.
- **Assertiveness training:** Counselors use assertiveness training to teach drug-resistance skills and offer healthy ways for clients to get their needs met. The behavioral component of assertiveness training happens when new skills are correctly applied and positively reinforced by a sense of confidence and improved interpersonal relationships.
- **Cue exposure:** Cue exposure involves exposing clients to triggers that induce cravings while simultaneously introducing techniques that reduce this reaction.
- **Counterconditioning (aversive conditioning):** Counterconditioning, or aversive conditioning, uses overt and covert sensitization to address behaviors requiring change. This intervention, which is primarily used with AUD, is derived from the principles of operant conditioning. Overt sensitization involves pairing a negative behavior (i.e., stimulus) with an undesirable consequence (i.e., response). Overt conditioning is the process that occurs when an individual taking disulfiram becomes violently ill after drinking alcohol. Covert sensitization also pairs a negative behavior with an unpleasant consequence. However, instead of using external consequences (e.g., disulfiram), covert sensitization encourages clients to visualize harmful consequences to discourage negative behaviors (e.g., injuring the self or others, legal problems, hurting relationships).

Rational Emotive Behavior Therapy (REBT)

The central premise of rational emotive behavior therapy (REBT) is that **irrational thought patterns** must be changed (i.e., disputed) in order to change behaviors. Albert Ellis, who is credited with developing REBT, used the **ABC model** to examine the pathway of irrational thinking. This provides the client with an understanding that one's thinking—rather than the activating event—influences emotions and behaviors. Restructuring client thoughts actively promotes a change in negative self-talk and self-defeating behaviors. The elements of the ABC model are:

- A = **A**ctivating event
- B = **B**eliefs surrounding the event
- C = **C**onsequences, including healthy and unhealthy emotional and behavioral consequences

The counselor then introduces the next steps of **cognitive restructuring:**

- D = **D**isputing irrational thoughts
- E = The **E**ffect of "D"
- F = The new **F**eeling

Cognitive Behavioral Therapy (CBT)

Aaron Beck is credited with developing cognitive behavioral therapy (CBT). CBT is a collaborative, problem-focused, structured approach based on the premise that emotional distress results from **cognitive distortions** or self-defeating errors in thinking. CBT therapists believe that mental disorders such as depression result from dysfunctional thoughts about oneself, others, and the future (i.e., **the cognitive triad**).

Counselors help the client restructure thoughts that support sobriety and enable them to develop the skills required for relapse prevention. When clients learn to restructure automatic thoughts, they can begin to experience a decrease in problematic behaviors and psychological distress.

CBT is didactic in nature, using **psychoeducation** with homework assignments to reinforce recovery skills.

Dialectical Behavior Therapy (DBT)

Developed by Marsha Linehan, dialectical behavior therapy (DBT) is an evidence-based practice for SUD, borderline personality disorder, eating disorders, and PTSD. DBT is based on the premise that individuals with SUD and co-occurring disorders experience childhoods in which emotions were either dismissed or minimized. DBT emphasizes building a **therapeutic alliance** to create trust and counteract those invalidating experiences. Counselors using DBT convey **radical acceptance** to address poor impulse control, a lack of belonging, and emotional distress (i.e., frustration intolerance). DBT practitioners use **unconditional positive regard** and acceptance to enhance the client's willingness and commitment to change.

DBT teaches clients to recognize and accept two opposing viewpoints or **dialects.** One way this is achieved is by examining black-and-white or all-or-nothing dialects that accompany common thinking patterns of those with SUD and co-occurring mental health disorders. Clients are taught to accept and validate their experiences and emotions but also to acknowledge that successful recovery involves examining cognitive processes and managing overwhelming emotions. Thus, DBT is the synthesis of the dialectal polarities embedded in the concepts of **acceptance and change.**

Therapeutic Tasks for Counselors Using DBT

The therapeutic tasks for counselors using DBT with SUD include the following:

- **Integrate two opposing dialects:** The counselor helps the client integrate dialects by sitting with—and eventually integrating—the two opposing dialects of change and acceptance. Successful integration of dialects is enhanced by facilitating here-and-now experiences.
- **Foster distress tolerance and acceptance:** DBT techniques support the tolerance and acceptance of uncomfortable feelings. Clients learn to tolerate emotional distress without engaging in substance use. Counselors help clients accept the present situation by using cognitive and behavioral coping skills such as self-soothing and decision making.
- **Create substance-specific target behaviors:** Counselors help clients develop a hierarchy of behaviors requiring change. For individuals with SUD, this includes goals such as enhancing personal safety, increasing community support, decreasing substance misuse, and alleviating withdrawal symptoms.
- **Enhance treatment adherence:** Counselors actively commit to securing a therapeutic attachment with clients to maximize treatment adherence.
- **Help with emotional regulation:** Counselors help clients learn how to accurately label current feelings, decrease reactionary responses, and lessen the intensity of emotional experiences. Increasing positive emotions and taking opposite action (intentionally acting in the opposite of what a negative emotion would usually incite) are also used to help clients recover.
- **Teach assertiveness strategies:** Counselors teach assertiveness strategies and conflict resolution skills to help clients with interpersonal issues and set appropriate boundaries with others. Interpersonal effectiveness aims to keep the client's valued relationships intact while simultaneously honoring their own self-worth and dignity.

Stages of DBT

The four stages of DBT are as follows:

- **Stage 1:** Clients exhibit harmful behaviors (e.g., self-harm, substance use) and experience an overwhelming sense of emotional distress.
- **Stage 2:** Clients begin to make behavioral changes but remain emotionally inhibited.
- **Stage 3:** Clients have progressed through therapy and have learned to successfully apply coping skills as they navigate the world in their newly acquired sobriety.
- **Stage 4:** Clients begin to experience belonging and connectedness. Clients become willing to develop their concept of a higher power or experience peace and happiness associated with spiritual fulfillment.

Reality Theory

Developed by William Glasser, reality therapy (i.e., choice theory) assumes that reality is not based on actual events but on a person's perception of those events. The main goal of reality therapy is to help clients take responsibility for their present feelings, thinking, and behavior. Reality therapists work with clients to help transform **failure identities** into **success identities.** Success identities are attained when clients take personal responsibility for their actions. With personal responsibility comes the ability of a person to satisfy their individual needs without infringing on the rights of others.

Reality therapists help clients with SUD learn healthy ways of **connecting** with others, rather than turning to substances for the feeling of false connectedness and fulfillment. Glasser believed that meeting one's core needs of **love and belonging** leads to a greater sense of self-worth and fulfillment.

Core Principles of Reality Therapy/Choice Theory

Reality therapists use the following core principles to help clients adopt responsible behavior and a success identity. These eight principles are involvement, identifying current behaviors, evaluating those behaviors, planning for transitioning current behaviors to more appropriate behaviors, committing to change, taking a no-excuses approach, taking a no-punishment approach, and remaining steadfast in the pursuit of change. Examples of these as they apply to an individual with SUD are as follows:

- **Involvement:** Counselors understand that attachment, commitment, and the therapeutic alliance are critical for engaging the client in counseling and SUD treatment.
- **Identifying current behaviors:** Counselors help clients focus on how substance use affects their lives and interpersonal relationships. Clients begin to take personal responsibility for their choices and examine the consequences of their substance use.
- **Evaluating behavior:** This is accomplished by asking the client to take an honest appraisal of their behavior, specifically how their current behavior is meeting or interfering with their need for love and belonging.
- **Planning transition into responsible behavior:** Counselors help clients make reasonable plans to change irresponsible behavior. This may involve the client changing their involvement with people, places, and things tied to substance use.
- **Commitment to change:** Counselors obtain a commitment from clients to engage in counseling and follow the prescribed treatment plan. Clients commit to taking measurable steps toward a new life in sobriety.
- **No excuses:** Counselors discourage clients from making excuses or blaming others for their substance use.
- **No punishment:** Counselors rely on natural consequences instead of punishing clients for irresponsible behavior.
- **Remaining steadfast in the pursuit of change:** Counselors remain committed to helping clients attain sobriety and reevaluate treatment goals in the event of a relapse or setback.

Reality therapists focus on a client's **total behavior,** which includes aspects of thinking, doing, feeling, and physiology that make up a person's total functioning. Personal responsibility occurs when a client can control what he or she does and thinks.

Solution-Focused Therapy

Created by Insoo Kim Berg and Steve de Shazer, solution-focused therapy is a time-limited, future-oriented approach to counseling. **Solution-focused therapy** aims to differentiate methods that are effective from those that are not, and to identify areas of strength so they can be used in problem solving. The premise of solution-focused therapy is that change is possible, but that the individual must identify problems and deal with their problems in the real world. This therapy is based on using questioning to help the individual establish goals and find solutions to problems. Topics for questioning include the following:

- **Pre-session**: The patient is asked about any differences that he or she noted after making the appointment and coming to the first session.
- **Miracle**: The patient is asked if any "miracles" occurred or if any problems were solved, including what, if anything, was different and how this difference affected their relationships.
- **Exception**: The patient is asked if any small changes were noted. The patient is also asked if any of their problems no longer seem problematic, and if so, how that change manifested.
- **Scaling**: The patient is asked to evaluate the problem on a 1–10 scale and then to determine how to increase the rating.
- **Coping**: The patient is asked about how he or she is managing.

Solution-focused therapy is a social constructionist theory beneficial for treating SUD because of its affirming, optimistic, and respectful examination of a client's current strengths. Thus, solution-focused therapy does not use confrontation or forceful examination of one's past, which can be a source of shame for a client who is new in recovery or having difficulty remaining sober.

Brief Therapy

Brief therapy is a collaborative, time-sensitive, goal-oriented therapeutic model pioneered by Sigmund Freud. It is not a theoretical approach but a structure used across settings to narrow treatment focus and to reduce health-related risks associated with SUD. Although several theoretical approaches can be adapted for brief treatment, most models for SUD are grounded in motivational enhancement theory.

Brief therapy models have a defined and predetermined beginning, middle, and end, with the number of sessions contingent upon the client's treatment needs. The counselor's tasks during each **phase of brief treatment** include the following:

- **Phase I:** Counselors use the transtheoretical model of behavior change to determine the client's willingness and commitment to change. Motivational enhancement techniques are implemented as the counselor collaborates on treatment goals with the client. This collaborative effort helps refine the therapeutic focus and helps the client prepare to change.
- **Phase II:** The counselor's task is to move the client from the pre-contemplation stage of change to the action stage. Psychoeducation is used to teach recovery-related skills, and the client is assigned homework to reinforce those skills. The counselor continues to elicit change talk and is prepared to quickly address any roadblocks to recovery.
- **Phase III:** The counselor emphasizes the client's progress, refines relapse-prevention skills, and prepares the client for long-term recovery. The counselor and client identify social supports, community resources, and family members to assist the client after termination.
- **Phase IV:** The client attends prescheduled booster sessions to report on their progress and address any potential setbacks since termination.

Change Theory

The Transtheoretical Model of the Stages of Change

James Prochaska and Carlo DiClemente's **transtheoretical model of the stages of change** is based on theoretical models of motivation and behavioral change. Constructed on a biopsychosocial framework, the transtheoretical model of the stages of change comprises the following stages:

- **Pre-contemplation:** In this stage, individuals lack total or partial awareness of behaviors requiring change. Individuals in this stage are usually unwilling to consider making alternative choices in the near future.
- **Contemplation:** Individuals in this stage realize that there are behaviors in need of change, and they may seek help to do so, but there is a lack of readiness. This stage is marked by ambivalence as individuals weigh the pros and cons of changing.
- **Preparation:** Individuals in this stage determine that the pros outweigh the cons when considering what life will look like with the proposed changes. In the preparation stage, individuals commit to change. Individuals may still be engaging in behavior that requires change, but they are ready to stop in the near future.
- **Action:** Individuals in this stage commence modifying behaviors. They follow strategies that increase their likelihood of success and begin to make alternative lifestyle choices.
- **Maintenance:** This stage is characterized by the continuation of committed changes. Relapse-prevention strategies are beneficial in the maintenance stage.

In the event of a **relapse**, the client temporarily leaves the change cycle. Then, if the client is willing, the counselor helps them get back on course by reviewing relapse-prevention strategies and examining areas in which the client wishes to improve.

Early and Middle Phases of Change for a Client Entering Treatment for SUD

Clients who enter treatment for psychoactive substance dependency progress through identified stages. The transtheoretical model can be used to measure the client's progressive growth. Although no two clients are alike, progressive growth can be categorized into stages.

In the early phase of treatment, the client is in the **pre-contemplation stage**. The client lacks awareness or is partially aware of the need for treatment. Once the client presents for screening and assessment for an SUD, he or she is generally motivated by an emotional low point. Upon admission, the client may require detox to stabilize and recover from withdrawal. Once detox is complete, the client begins to weigh the pros and cons of continued treatment when entering the contemplation stage of change.

In the middle phase, the client begins to take personal responsibility for recovery as the implications of his or her addictive behavior are recognized. Despite an awareness of the problem, clients in the **contemplation stage** have not made a firm commitment to change. Clients often vacillate between accepting treatment and rationalizing or minimizing the consequences of their substance use. As the client begins to comprehend recovery-related concepts and seeks to resolve ambivalence, the **preparation stage** of change is entered. During this stage, the client expresses a readiness to change. The client begins to accept the consequences of their addiction and look for alternative solutions.

Final Phase of Change for a Client Entering Treatment for SUD

Clients who successfully progress through the pre-contemplation, contemplation, and preparation stages of treatment are in the final phase of recovery. The client is now in the **action stage** of change. In this stage, clients begin to take responsibility for their recovery and make positive lifestyle choices. They have acquired coping strategies; developed a relapse prevention plan; and worked to repair family, work, and interpersonal relationships. The client begins to resolve symptoms of any co-occurring diagnosis. Recovery has become part of the client's identity as independence from treatment begins.

The action stage is followed by the maintenance stage of change. In the **maintenance stage**, personal, emotional, and spiritual growth continues as the client recognizes that recovery is ongoing. Clients have now grasped the spiritual component of recovery and have integrated those principles as part of their day-to-day life. Recovery remains a part of the client's identity but is now balanced with other life pursuits.

Motivational Interviewing (MI)

Developed by William Miller and cofounder Stephen Rollnick, **motivational interviewing (MI)** is an evidence-based practice that uses a person-centered, strengths-based approach to reduce ambivalence and evoke lasting change. It is a nonauthoritarian method for creating change. Individuals with SUD are viewed as experts in their own recovery. Counselors using MI implement the following basic interaction techniques, which use the acronym *OARS*:

- **O: Open-ended questions** are used to encourage reflection and promote a back-and-forth dialogue between the counselor and client, thereby allowing the client to tell their story.
- **A: Affirmation** is the acknowledgement of the client's strengths and intrinsic motivation; showing genuine approval.
- **R: Reflective listening** and empathetic listening help the client stay engaged in self exploration.
- **S: Summarization** ties together certain concepts and themes or reflects several statements back to the client.

Counselors using MI de-emphasize confrontation and coercion and instead examine the client's resistance. **Rolling with resistance** is an MI strategy used to decrease "sustain talk" (i.e., what is keeping them in the problem) and is mainly used in the earlier stages of change. **Flexible pacing** is an MI strategy used to help the counselor stay with the client and resist the urge to jump ahead or push the client forward rather than move at their own pace.

Components of MI

Counselors using MI help individuals pass through the stages of change, emphasizing the following foundational components:

- **Collaboration:** Clients are viewed as partners as they work together with counselors to establish agreed-upon treatment goals. The partnership helps strengthen the therapeutic alliance, which results in higher levels of cooperation and self-disclosure.
- **Evoking:** Counselors use evoking to explore a client's intrinsic motivation to change. Ambivalence is investigated by examining the discrepancy between the client's behavior and values. Counselors are encouraged to help **tip the decisional balance** with the client, so he or she can successfully move from contemplation to preparation. **Commitment, activation, and taking steps** help move clients from preparation to action.
- **Autonomy:** Counselors emphasize the client's sense of responsibility and capacity for self-direction.
- **Compassion:** Counselors express warmth and support as the client begins to make positive life changes. Compassionate care prioritizes the client's welfare and sends the message that the counselor has the client's best interest at heart.

Family Therapy

Impact of SUD from a Family Systems Perspective

An individual's addiction does not occur in isolation. The individual who uses psychoactive substances and their family members are all uniquely affected. Healthy family systems successfully navigate conflict and thrive in environments with consistent love and care. Family systems shaped by addiction are challenged by a breakdown in communication as families adapt and change around the inconsistent actions of the family member with an addiction. Children who grow up in this environment often **lack the safety and security** required for healthy development. Children struggle to conform and adapt to inconsistent parenting, leading to unmet needs and **impaired attachment.**

General family systems theorists believe that families marked by chaos and inconsistency desperately attempt to adapt and change in an effort to maintain balance, or **homeostasis.** If one person's behavior improves, changes will likely occur elsewhere in the family. As a means of adapting to ever-changing boundaries, members take on roles such as the enabler, hero, scapegoat, mascot, and lost child. It is the family therapist's job to disrupt the family's equilibrium (which is maintained by homeostasis) in order to restore the family to healthy functioning.

Murray Bowen's Family Systems Theory

Bowen's family systems theory focuses on the following concepts:

- The role of **thinking versus feeling/reactivity** in relationship/family systems.
- The role of **emotional triangles:** The three-person system or triangle is viewed as the smallest stable relationship system. It forms when a two-person system experiences tension.
- **Generationally repeating family issues:** Parents transmit emotional problems to a child. (Example: The parents fear something is wrong with a child and treat the child as if something is wrong, interpreting the child's behavior as confirmation.)
- **Undifferentiated family ego mass:** This refers to a family's lack of separateness. There is a fixed cluster of egos of individual family members as if they all have a common ego boundary.
- **Emotional cutoff:** A way of managing emotional issues with family members (cutting off emotional contact).
- Consideration of thoughts and feelings of **each individual family member** as well as seeking to understand the family network.

Review Video: Bowen Family Systems Theory
Visit mometrix.com/academy and enter code: 591496

Assessment in family systems theory includes the following:

- Acknowledgement of **dysfunction** in the family system.
- **Family hierarchy**: Who is in charge? Who has responsibility? Who has authority? Who has power?
- Evaluation of **boundaries** (around subsystems, between family and the larger environment): Are they permeable or impermeable? Flexible or rigid?
- How does the **symptom** function in the family system?

Treatment planning is as follows:

- The therapist creates a mutually satisfactory contract with the family to establish service boundaries.
- Bowenian family therapy's goal is the differentiation of the individual from the strong influence of the family.

Virginia Satir's Experiential/Humanistic Approach

Virginia Satir and the Esalen Institute's experiential family therapy draws on sociology, ego concepts, and communication theory to form **role theory concepts**. Satir examined the roles of "rescuer" and "placater" that constrain relationships and interactions in families. This perspective seeks to increase intimacy in the family and improve the self-esteem of family members by using awareness and the communication of feelings. Emphasis is on individual growth in order to change family members' behavior and deal with developmental delays. Particular importance is given to marital partners and to changing verbal and nonverbal communication patterns that lower self-esteem.

Satir's Communication Impediments in the Family Dynamic

Satir described four issues that impede communication among family members under stress. Placating, blaming, irrelevance, and being overly reasonable are the **four issues that block family communication**, according to Virginia Satir:

- **Placating** is the role played by some people in reaction to threat or stress in the family. The placating person reacts to internal stresses by trying to please others, often in irrational ways. A mother might try to placate her disobedient and rude child by offering food, candy, or other presents on the condition that he or she stop a certain behavior.
- **Blaming** is the act of pointing outward when an issue creates stress. The blamer thinks, "I'm very angry, but it's your fault. If I've wrecked the car, it's because you made me upset when I left home this morning."
- **Irrelevance** is a behavior wherein a person displaces the potential problem and substitutes another unrelated activity. A mother who engages in too much social drinking frequently discusses her hair's split ends whenever the topic of alcoholism is brought up by her spouse.
- Being overly reasonable, also known as being a **responsible analyzer,** is when a person keeps his or her emotions in check and functions with the precision and monotony of a machine.

Structural Family Therapy

Salvador Minuchin's structural family therapy seeks to strengthen boundaries when family subsystems are enmeshed, or to increase flexibility when these systems are overly rigid. Minuchin emphasizes that the family structure should be hierarchical and that the parents should be at the top of the hierarchy.

Joining, enactment, boundary making, and mimesis are four techniques used by Minuchin in structural family counseling:

- **Joining** is the worker's attempt at greeting and bonding with members of the family. Bonding is important when obtaining cooperation and input.
- Minuchin often had his clients enact the various scenarios that led to disagreements and conflicts within families. The **enactment** of an unhealthy family dynamic would allow the therapist to better understand the behavior and allow the family members to gain insight.

- **Boundary making** is important to structural family therapies administered by Minuchin because many family conflicts arise from confusion about each person's role. Minuchin believed that family harmony was best achieved when people were free to be themselves, without becoming enmeshed in the emotional states of other family members.
- **Mimesis** is a process in which the therapist mimics the positive and negative behavior patterns of different family members.

STRATEGIC FAMILY THERAPY

Strategic family therapy (Jay Haley, 1976) is based on the following concepts:

- This therapy seeks to learn what **function** the symptom serves in the family. In other words, what payoff is there for the system in allowing the symptom to continue?
- This therapy **focuses** on problem-focused behavioral change, emphasis of parental power and hierarchical family relationships, and the role of symptoms as an attribute of the family's organization.
- Helplessness, incompetence, and illness all provide **power positions** within the family. The child uses symptoms to change the behavior of the parents.
- Strategic family therapists view maladaptive behavior as the result of circular communication. **Circular communication** occurs when a behaviorally reinforced feedback loop maintains the family's homeostasis and dysfunction.

Haley tried to develop a strategy for each issue faced by a client. Problems are isolated and treated in different ways. A family plagued by alcoholism might require a different treatment strategy than a family undermined by sexual infidelity. Haley's background was unusual in that he held degrees in the arts and communication rather than in psychology. Haley's strategies involved the use of directives (direct instructions). After outlining a problem, Haley would tell the family members exactly what to do.

JOHNSON MODEL OF INTERVENTION

The **Johnson model, pioneered by** Dr. Vernon Johnson, is a family intervention approach that is planful, strategic, and confrontational. The primary goal of the Johnson model is to help the person with SUD accept treatment. The Johnson model centers around an intervention team, which includes an intervention specialist or trained professional and friends, family, or spiritual advisors concerned for the individual's health and welfare. Planning is essential for determining how to persuade the person to receive treatment for substance use.

The Johnson model is addiction focused, with each person in the individual's social network commenting on how their loved one's addiction has impacted them, refraining from focusing on past resentments. The interventionist's role is to instruct team members to only express concerns backed by solid evidence. Although confrontational in nature, the Johnson method remains care focused by encouraging the individual's support group to express love and concern rather than blame and resentment.

UNILATERAL FAMILY THERAPY (UFT)

Unilateral family therapy (UFT) provides family members with support and guidance to motivate a family member with SUD to seek treatment. The goals of UFT are to repair broken family relationships, minimize conflict and stress, and ensure the safety of all family members.

UFT is based on the principles of **contingency management**, a form of operant conditioning used to provide motivational incentives to help individuals with SUD agree to treatment. Therapists using this approach support family members in the following ways:

- Respond to the ongoing need for psychoeducation on SUD.
- Help family members set appropriate boundaries with one another.
- Address the influence of substance-misusing relatives.
- Engage the family during all phases of the individual's treatment.

UFT is similar to **community reinforcement training (CRT)**, an evidence-based practice for AUD. CRT uses psychoeducation to teach families that AUD is a disease rather than a moral failing. CRT is used to empower family members to engage in enjoyable activities and lead purposeful lives independent of the individual family member's recovery status. Outcomes for UFT and CRT show an increase in treatment engagement and participation in 12-step programs, including Al-Anon for family members.

ARISE Intervention Approach

Developed by Judith Landau and James Garrett, ARISE is an acronym for **A Relational Intervention Sequence for Engagement**. This intervention approach is also referred to as an **invitational intervention** and is based on the **transitional family therapy** approach. The ARISE intervention approach refers to the person with the addiction as the **person of concern (PoC)**. A **concerned other (CO) or family link** steps forward to organize and carry out the intervention. The CO can be a family member, friend, or any significant person in the PoC's life. In addition to building an intervention team, the CO helps influence the family's health communication and decision making.

Stages

The ARISE intervention is based on the assumption that individuals with SUD do not have to reach rock bottom to benefit from treatment. Research shows that individuals who agree to treatment before experiencing adverse health consequences have higher success rates than those who do not. ARISE emphasizes the importance of treating the entire family, rather than treating the individual with SUD in isolation, and it regards SUD as a family disease.

The ARISE intervention model consists of up to three sequential stages. The goal of the initial stage is to help the addicted person, or PoC, recognize the need for treatment and motivate them to comply willingly. Once the PoC agrees to treatment, the ARISE team develops an action plan. If the PoC does not comply, the team identifies alternative solutions and outlines enforceable consequences to be carried out if the individual with addiction does not commit to treatment. Finally, if there is continued noncompliance, consequences for rejecting treatment are enforced.

The ARISE approach is different from other intervention models in that the PoC is aware of all steps in the intervention process—there is transparency from beginning to end. Like other family interventions, the ARISE approach supports all family members and partners with the family network to help the PoC attain lifelong sobriety. The intervention itself is a straightforward attempt to understand the impact that the PoC's substance use has had on the family and how a life of recovery is an achievable outcome.

Group Therapy

Irvin Yalom's Therapeutic Factors

Irvin Yalom is credited with developing the concept of therapeutic or curative factors experienced in group therapy. His here-and-now or process groups are characterized by the following:

- Yalom stressed using clients' **immediate reactions** and discussing members' **affective experiences** in the group.
- Process groups have relatively unstructured, spontaneous sessions.
- Process groups emphasize **therapeutic activities**, such as imparting information or instilling hope, universality, and altruism.
- The group can provide a **rehabilitative narrative** of primary family group development, offer socializing techniques, provide behavior models to imitate, offer interpersonal learning, and offer an example of group cohesiveness and catharsis.

Open and Closed Groups

Groups can be either closed or open, serving different functions and purposes:

Closed Groups	Open Groups
• Convened by social workers. • Members begin the experience together, navigate it together, and end it together at a predetermined time (with a set number of sessions). • Closed groups afford better opportunities than open groups for members to identify with each other. • Closed groups provide greater stability, and they allow the stages of group development to progress more powerfully. • Closed groups provide a greater amount and intensity of commitment due to the same participants being counted on for their presence.	• Open groups allow participants to enter and leave according to their preference. • A continuous group can exist, depending on the frequency and rate of membership changes. • The focus shifts somewhat from the whole-group process to individual members' processes. • With membership shifts, opportunities to use the group's social forces to help individuals may be reduced. The group will be less cohesive and therefore less available as a therapeutic instrument. • The social worker is kept in a highly central position throughout the life of the group; he or she provides continuity in an open structure.

Review Video: Group Work and Its Benefits
Visit mometrix.com/academy and enter code: 375134

Core Values of an Effective Counseling Group Leader

An effective group leader is theoretically grounded, with the ability to use therapeutic techniques and values to intervene and interact with group members effectively.

The underlying values of counseling with groups include the following:

- Every individual has dignity and worth.
- All people have a right and a need to realize their full potential.
- Every individual has basic rights and responsibilities.
- The counseling group acts out democratic values and promotes shared decision making.
- Every individual has the right to self-determination in setting and achieving goals.
- Positive change is made possible by honest, open, meaningful interaction.

Tasks for Constructing a Counseling Group

The key elements in the group construction process include the following:

- The counselor makes a clear and uncomplicated statement of purpose that includes the members' stakes in coming together and the agency's (and others') stakes in serving them.
- The counselor's part should be described in the simplest terms possible.
- Identify the members' reactions to the counselor's statement of purpose and how the counselor's statement connects to the members' expectations.
- The counselor helps members do the work necessary to develop a working consensus about the contract.
- Recognize goals and motivations: manifested and latent, stated and unstated.
- Recontract as needed.

Tasks for Facilitating a Counseling Group

The group leader's role in facilitating the group process is as follows:

- Effectively screen and select group members.
- Promote **member participation and interaction**.
- Bring up **real concerns** in order to begin the work.
- Display knowledge of cultural diversity and possess an awareness of one's own cultural biases.
- Help the group keep its **focus**.
- Match interventions with each stage of group development.
- Reinforce observance of the **rules** of the group.
- Use theoretical models and evidence-based practices for group therapy.
- **Facilitate cohesiveness** and additional therapeutic factors.
- **Identify emerging themes**.
- Understand when to allow flexibility and when to reinforce structure.
- Establish worker **identity** in relation to the group's readiness.
- **Listen empathically**, **support** the initial structure and rules of the group, and **evaluate** initial group achievements.
- Handle group conflict and manage group contagions.
- **Suggest ongoing tasks** or **themes** for subsequent meetings.

Pre-Group and Initial Stages of Group Development

Although there are multiple perspectives on group development, there is a consensus that successful psychotherapy groups begin with a pre-group stage—followed by a defined beginning, middle, and end.

In the **pre-group stage of development**, counselors determine the following:

- **The group's purpose:** Counselors conceptualize the group's purpose and determine logistics such as the setting, the number of group sessions, whether to include a co-therapist, and whether the group will be open or closed.
- **How members will be chosen:** Some group leaders preselect appropriate members, whereas others secure a commitment after conducting a pre-group meeting.
- **The compatibility of the members that are chosen:** Additional consideration is given to the compatibility of various individuals, interaction styles, and personalities. Counselors also consider the impact of cultural diversity issues and their potential influence on group dynamics.

In the **initial stage** of group development, members are unsure of one another as they tentatively evaluate the process and become acquainted. The group leader works to facilitate cohesiveness as the group takes shape amid uncertainty. The approach-avoidance dilemma further characterizes this stage; members are inclined to seek help when part of a group, but hesitate to disrupt the equilibrium of the group. Tasks for members include orientation and exploration as they tentatively determine their level of involvement.

Middle, Working, and End Stages of Group Development

During the **middle stage** of group development, conflict peaks as members attempt to establish rank among one another. Group leaders understand the competitive nature of this stage and work to reduce divisiveness and stabilize the group system. Once group norms and cohesion are established, the group moves from the conflict stage to the working stage.

During the **working stage**, the leader takes a less prominent role. Members are now less concerned about their rank in the group. Trust has developed as members experience a heightened sense of the group's purpose. The group recognizes the significance of interpersonal interactions. The members and the leader are aware of group dynamics and therapeutic processes. True affiliation and intimacy characterize this stage. The safety and security of the group allow members to share openly and focus on the group's goals and objectives.

During the **final stage** of group development, members generalize learned strategies outside the group setting and share these experiences. Although many feel satisfied with the group coming to an end, some are apprehensive. Members offer advice and emotional support to hesitant members. The leader generally arranges a goodbye ceremony to help provide closure.

Bruce Tuckman's Five Stages of Group Development

Bruce Tuckman's five stages of group development are as follows:

- **Forming:** During this stage, members become affiliated with one another and the goals of the group.
- **Storming:** The storming phase is characterized by conflict as members attempt to establish rank.
- **Norming:** The group becomes more functional and cohesive. The group identity is formed as members work cooperatively toward a common goal.
- **Performing:** Group functioning is at its peak during the performing stage. Members experience trust, a sense of purpose, and intimacy.
- **Adjourning:** Members prepare for termination as the group moves to disband.

Self-Help Groups

Depending on the nature and severity of an individual's SUD, **self-help groups** can serve as an alternative or an adjunct to traditional therapy. The most widely available groups are 12-step groups (e.g., AA, Narcotics Anonymous). There are also groups that offer assistance and support to families and significant others of those with SUD (e.g., Al-Anon, Alateen).

Among the dozens of 12-step programs, there are support groups for **substance-specific addictions** (e.g., Cocaine Anonymous, Marijuana Anonymous). Also, mutual support groups are not confined to psychoactive substance addiction (e.g., Shoplifters Anonymous, Domestic Violence Anonymous).

As an alternative to 12-step programs, there are two additional forms of mutual support: **secular groups** (e.g., Secular Organizations for Sobriety/Save Our Selves, SMART Recovery, LifeRing Secular Recovery) and **religious recovery groups** (e.g., Celebrate Recovery). There are also support groups for individuals with co-occurring disorders (e.g., Double Trouble in Recovery, Dual Recovery Anonymous).

History, Purpose, and Success Rate

Alcoholics Anonymous (AA) was the first mutual support group to gain popularity in the United States. Since AA's inception in the 1930s, dozens of mutual support groups have become available to provide social and emotional support for members seeking assistance for a wide range of issues. Support group members are in various stages of recovery, which can provide hope for those who are new in sobriety and/or struggling. Membership is open to individuals seeking help with substances or any problematic behavior. It is suggested that participants look for the similarities rather than the differences between themselves and other members, which helps each group to establish an identity and allows individuals to band together to support each other and encourage change.

Although mutual support groups have anecdotally helped millions, there is no empirical evidence proving their efficacy. This is due to several reasons, including the anonymous nature of membership, the fact that attendance is mainly voluntary, and the underrepresentation of culturally diverse members (i.e., members are overwhelmingly white and male). However, research has found that individuals who participate in mutual support groups have higher rates of sustained abstinence and that actively involved members maintain greater periods of sobriety.

ALCOHOLICS ANONYMOUS (AA)

AA, an **abstinence-based recovery program**, was started by **Bill Wilson** and **"Doctor Bob" Smith** in the mid-1930s. The fellowship of AA was born out of the Oxford Group, a similar but more conservative recovery movement. Published in the mid-1940s, the **AA preamble** outlines the purpose of AA. The preamble states, "Alcoholics Anonymous is a fellowship of people who share their experience, strength and hope with each other that they may solve their common problem and help others to recover from alcoholism. The only requirement for membership is a desire to stop drinking." In 2021, the preamble was revised from "a fellowship of men and women" to "a fellowship of people" to reflect gender-neutral language.

The overall philosophy of AA is that alcoholism is a progressive disease of the mind, body, and spirit. The 12 steps outline lifelong aspirational principles (e.g., honesty, integrity, humility, willingness). Members choose a sponsor to take them through the 12 steps and to serve as a mentor on an ongoing basis.

AA meetings are open to the public or closed, with closed meetings conducted with AA members only. In most cities and surrounding areas, AA meetings serve special populations, including those based on gender, sexual orientation, age, and language spoken. AA members are encouraged to develop a belief—or become willing to believe—in a Higher Power or a God of one's understanding.

Pharmacotherapy

Medication-assisted therapy combines psychopharmacotherapy with ongoing counseling and recovery support to provide comprehensive treatment for SUD. Prescribed medication can be used to treat withdrawal symptoms, prevent an overdose, lessen cravings, or decrease substance-specific dependency. **Pharmacotherapy medications** include the following:

- **Sensitizers:** Sensitizers are used to deter alcohol consumption. When this medication is consumed alongside alcohol or other substances, very unpleasant effects occur. An example of a sensitizer is disulfiram (Antabuse).
- **Antagonists:** Antagonists are used to prevent overdose or help a person maintain sobriety. Examples include naltrexone (ReVia, Depade) and extended-release naltrexone (Vivitrol), which are used to treat opioid and alcohol dependency. Naloxone (Narcan) is an antagonist used to treat opioid overdose. Flumazenil (Mazicon) is used to treat benzodiazepine overdose.
- Medications that treat symptoms of **withdrawal** include desipramine (Norpramin), imipramine (Tofranil), bromocriptine mesylate (Parlodel), amantadine (Symmetrel), and buprenorphine (Subutex/Suboxone).
- Drugs used as **maintenance therapy** for **opioid addiction** include buprenorphine (Subutex/Suboxone), methadone, naltrexone hydrochloride (ReVia, Depade), and extended-release naltrexone (Vivitrol).
- **Post-acute withdrawal** symptoms can be treated with naltrexone (ReVia, Depade) and acamprosate (Campral).
- **Psychotropic medications** (e.g., antidepressants and antipsychotics) are used for co-occurring mental health disorders.

Crisis Intervention

Crisis Counseling and Crisis-Related Stressors

A crisis is any event causing substantial distress and profound disruption to a person's normal day-to-day activities. Although there are significant events that have the potential to cause a person to experience a crisis, counselors must also investigate the individual's perception of the event and examine the role of any existing cognitive errors. In addition, when stressors impact the individual's level of functioning, it is essential to investigate the types of crisis-related stressors.

There are basically two different **types of crisis-related stressors**. These stressor types are developmental (or maturational) crises and situational crises. A **developmental crisis** can occur during **maturation**, when an individual must take on a new life role. This crisis can be a normal part of the developmental process. A youth may need to face a crisis and resolve this crisis to be able to move on to the next developmental stage. This may occur during the process of moving from adolescence to adulthood. Examples of situations that could lead to this type of crisis include graduating from school, going away to college, or moving out on one's own. These situations would cause the individual to face a maturing event that requires the development of new coping skills.

The second type of crisis is the **situational crisis**. This type of crisis can occur at any time in life. There is usually an event or problem that occurs, which leads to a **disruption in normal psychological functioning**. These types of events are often unplanned and can occur with or without warning. Some examples that may lead to a situational crisis include the death of a loved one, divorce, unplanned or unwanted pregnancy, onset or change of a physical disease process, job loss, or being the victim of a violent act. Events that affect an entire community can also cause individual and community situational crises. Terrorist attacks or weather-related disasters are examples of events that can affect an entire community.

Managing a Crisis at the Initial Point of Care

When a client or prospective client presents with a crisis, their initial contact with a counselor must be a safe and reassuring experience. The first step in managing a crisis is to assess the client for suicidal and homicidal ideation. Then, when possible, a counselor sets up an in-person clinical interview with the client and performs a detailed mental status exam.

Depending on the nature of the crisis and the therapeutic setting, counselors use **brief** or **time-limited interventions**. Plans for the client must be immediate, clear, and specific and can even be broken down into hourly or daily increments. Counselors must partner with clients to develop an action plan that attends to their individualized needs and to assess their level of commitment to carrying out the plan. Counselors also attend to their own safety needs and ensure that other individuals in the client's life are safe. Crisis plans should focus only on immediate events related to the crisis rather than irrelevant long-term stressors.

Managing a Crisis

Counselors understand that a client with SUD may be under the influence of a psychoactive substance when experiencing a crisis, leading to impaired judgment, increased impulsivity, and intensified symptoms of a mental disorder. Counselors ensure that the physical environment is safe for the client and themselves. Counselors using **verbal de-escalation skills** are careful to physically position themselves near an unblocked, immediately available exit at all times. De-escalation techniques include speaking calmly, providing low levels of sensory stimulation, giving the client personal space, and avoiding statements that may be construed as blaming or threatening.

It is critical that counselors follow up with clients to assess adherence to their **crisis action plans**. Counselors must strive to provide seamless care and help clients if they encounter roadblocks when attempting to resolve their crisis. Research suggests that having built-in check-in points increases the client's likelihood of following through with their action plan. It is also important to assist with outside referrals along the way, particularly if the client requires a higher level of care. Finally, if the client is successful in managing the crisis, counselors share words of encouragement and support, pointing out the client's ability to persevere in times of distress.

Assessing and Determining a Client's Phase of Suicidal Ideation

Individuals with SUD can become overwhelmed by feelings of sadness, isolation, anxiety, and despair. When this occurs, expressions of **suicidal ideation** are not unusual. Suicidality is substantially higher among persons misusing substances, particularly those diagnosed with a comorbid mental health disorder. Individuals with SUD have a 10–14 times greater risk of death by suicide. Individuals with alcohol or opioid dependence carry the greatest risk for suicidality. People who report using opioids have a 40–60% increased likelihood of suicidal ideation and a 75% increased likelihood of a suicide attempt.

Without proper intervention, suicidality can become **progressive.** If left untreated, suicidal ideation can worsen, leading to developing a suicide plan and carrying out the plan. Several effective screening and assessment instruments are helpful for determining the client's phase of suicidal ideation. One of these is the **Columbia Suicide Severity Rating Scale**, a test that measures suicidal risk in the following four domains: the severity of ideation, the intensity of ideation, suicidal behavior, and lethality. This test also assesses protective factors and self-evaluation measures of hopelessness and hostility.

Ways to Effectively Intervene with Clients in the Initial Phase of Suicidality

Counselor strategies used in the initial phase of suicidality include the following:

- Counselors listen without interruption, using calming techniques and verbal de-escalation skills to help create a calm and safe environment.
- Counselors refrain from using dismissive platitudes (e.g., saying "Loss is just a part of life" or "Surely, your situation is not that serious").
- Counselors explain the limitations of confidentiality when evaluating clients for suicidality.
- Counselors take every threat and expression of suicidal ideation seriously.
- Counselors seek supervision and efficiently refer to another provider when appropriate.
- Counselors conduct a **risk assessment** and examine factors that may increase risk, including the following:
    - Recent experiences of significant loss, including breakups, jobs, or the death of a loved one.
    - An intensification of feelings caused by reaching sobriety for the first time and no longer using substances as a primary means for coping.
    - Prior history of suicidality, including family history.
    - Increased impulsivity due to SUD or co-occurring mental disorder.
    - Beliefs that feelings of worthlessness and hopelessness are permanent and cannot be overcome.

Ways to Effectively Intervene with a Client Who Has Devised a Suicide Plan

When left untreated, persistent suicidal ideation can result in a suicide plan. Clients with suicidal ideation and a suicide plan are at high risk for attempting suicide. In this middle and late phase of client suicidality, addiction counselors use the following strategies:

- Assess for signs of increased suicidality, including giving away possessions, getting one's affairs in order, and saying goodbye.
- Assess any recent use of psychoactive substances.
- Determine if a specific suicide plan has been made, including how the client plans to commit suicide, when the client believes that the plan will be executed, and where the attempt will be carried out.
- Ascertain the safety of the client's environment, including access to firearms.
- Obtain consent to speak to a supportive loved one.
- When the client is in acute danger, counselors seek the assistance of another professional to help transport the client to a safe setting. Do not leave the client alone while these arrangements are being made.

Forms of Self-Harm

There are two forms of self-harm. There are **suicide-specific intentions and actions,** and there are actions that are categorized as **non-suicidal self-injury (NSSI).** NSSI involves direct, intentional, destructive harm to one's bodily tissue for reasons not otherwise socially sanctioned (e.g., tattoos, body piercings). NSSI may be life-threatening, but there is a lack of suicidal intention. Some examples of NSSI include cutting, head banging, burning, biting, and scratching. Research shows that individuals engaging in NSSI are at higher risk for suicide-specific behaviors.

Standards of practice instruct APs to assess for suicide risk at the onset of the therapeutic relationship and at frequent intervals thereafter. APs are ethically and legally responsible for explaining the limits of confidentiality during informed consent. APs assess the client's understanding of these limits by providing examples of what constitutes self-harm and reiterating the need to keep the client safe. APs determine a client's risk for harm by assessing the client's ideation, plan, and means. If the client endorses suicidal thoughts, the AP must follow up by asking if the client has a plan. If the client has a plan, the AP then determines the details of the plan and discerns whether the client has the means to carry out the plan.

Risk Factors for Suicide-Specific Intentions and Actions and NSSI

Factors that increase the risk for suicide-specific intentions and actions and NSSI include, but are not limited to, the following:

- Severe mental illness
- Borderline personality disorder
- Psychoactive substance misuse
- Intellectual and developmental disabilities
- Trauma and abuse
- Acute medical conditions
- Depression, hopelessness, and anhedonia
- Eating disorders
- Anxiety disorders

Clinical and subclinical adolescent populations are at an increased risk for NSSI, with the average age of onset being between ages 12 and 16. Among adolescents, interpersonal distress increases the risk of NSSI.

Populations at Higher Risk for Suicide

Populations at a higher risk for suicide include:

- Individuals with **co-occurring SUD and mental disorders.** They are at increased risk for suicide during their first year of sobriety, particularly when adjusting to psychotropic medication or experiencing grief and loss.
- Individuals who identify as **LGBT**.
- **Racial and ethnic minority** populations, with higher rates among American Indian/Alaska Natives.
- **Men aged 85 and older**.
- **Men and women** between the ages of **45 and 54**.

Therapeutic Considerations for Special Populations

Impact of Adolescent SUD

The impact of adolescent SUD is reflected in the following domains:

- **Family relationships:** Family relationships become strained as adolescents seek separation and independence from their primary caretakers. Substance use complicates this process because substance-related behaviors require increased parental involvement. However, for many, parental SUD is also present, leading to unmet emotional and psychological needs often stemming from impaired attachment, exposure to intimate partner violence, poor boundaries, and emotional reactivity.
- **Interpersonal relationships:** Socially competent adolescents possess self-efficacy, prosocial behavior, and reliance on social cues for decision making. Adolescents often use substances to manage social anxiety and help navigate complex interpersonal relationships. Rather than develop prosocial behaviors, teens with SUD tend to be self-centered, lack empathy, and display impaired moral development. Teens with SUD often report a sense of disconnection from peer groups and an impaired social identity.
- **Sexual relationships:** Healthy sexual relationships are associated with having a positive body image, a sense of identity, and the emotional capacity to form intimate relationships. SUD can lead to impulsive sexual behaviors, blocking teens from healthy sexual experiences. Teens who misuse substances are more likely to have sex at early ages and report higher incidences of sexual assault and sexual trauma.
- **Emotional health:** Adolescents with SUD avoid taking personal responsibility for their actions and blame others. Substances are used to numb uncomfortable emotions. Teens with SUD are at higher risk for developing co-occurring mental disorders, such as depression and anxiety. Poor coping skills can lead to self-injurious behaviors.
- **Physical health:** Studies indicate that adolescent SUD is associated with developing physical health issues as an adult, including heart disease, hypertension, delayed puberty, a weakened immune system, and sleep disturbances. Additionally, risky and impulsive behavior can lead to automobile accidents, drug overdose, and diseases from unprotected sex.
- **Academics:** Adolescents who succeed academically engage in complex cognitive processes, including abstract thinking and ethical decision making. Substance misuse can cause short-term memory deficits and distorted thinking that lead to academic failure. As a result, the teen begins to encounter rejection associated with failure, which only reinforces the cycle of addictive behaviors.

Older Adults

Physical and Cognitive Risk Factors

Older adults who develop SUD are at greater risk of **morbidity and mortality**. There are several physical and cognitive risk factors leading to SUD and severe complications from SUD among older adults, including:

- **Brain chemistry:** Older adults experience slower rates of drug metabolism. Changes in brain chemistry also contribute to increased drug sensitivity and rapid substance dependence.
- **Physical conditions:** Aging adults are more likely to have one or more underlying medical conditions (e.g., high blood pressure, sleep disturbance, and chronic pain), which can complicate the client's clinical picture and treatment protocol.
- **Greater access to medications:** Greater access to prescription pills increases the chance of harmful drug interactions and exposure to potentially addictive medications.
- **Reduced mobility:** Reduced mobility, chronic pain, and other disabling conditions often contribute to diminished quality of life and increased substance misuse and SUD rates.

Psychological and Social Risk Factors

There are several psychological and social risk factors leading to SUD and severe complications from SUD among older adults, including:

- **Grief and loss:** Losing loved ones and navigating age-related living transitions can contribute to **social isolation and loneliness**. Older adults are also more likely to report multiple losses in a short time frame.
- **Previous mental health diagnosis:** Older adults with a prior mental disorder are at an increased risk for SUD, and vice versa. SUD can exacerbate suicidality. **Mental disorders** that are common among older adults—including PTSD, anxiety, and depression—can negatively influence cognitive functioning.
- **Financial stress:** Forced retirement and rising health-care costs can contribute to financial anxiety.
- **Avoidant coping style:** Multiple stressors combined with an avoidant coping style contribute to higher rates of SUD.

Treatment Barriers and Recommendations

For older clients, effective treatment seeks to alleviate or lessen psychosocial-spiritual factors that place clients at increased risk for SUD. The main treatment barrier for aging adults with SUD is a lack of reporting substance use to healthcare providers. **Underreporting substance misuse** may be due to the following factors:

- The misconception that older adults do not misuse psychoactive substances
- Difficult detection stemming from similar age-related symptoms (e.g., falls, dementia)
- The shame and embarrassment associated with addiction in older populations
- The tendency to avoid help-seeking behaviors, opting instead for privacy
- Permissive beliefs and attitudes surrounding substance misuse in older clients

Treatment strategies include individual counseling to rebuild self-esteem and to process any feelings of shame, embarrassment, loneliness, and loss. Case managers and other professionals can be used to establish and coordinate comprehensive medical care and connect the client with community networks (e.g., mutual support groups). Psychoeducation is useful for helping family members and caregivers recognize overt signs of SUD. Doing volunteer work—through 12-step programs and in other community activities—can help clients develop a sense of purpose and combat loneliness and isolation.

Gender-Related Risk Factors

Men and women diagnosed with SUD have different gender-related risk factors, consequences, and treatment needs. Gender differences are seen in the following:

- **Disease progression:** Women are more likely than men to present with a more severe clinical profile upon admission to treatment, despite a shorter duration of substance use. This is particularly true for alcohol, cannabis, and opioid dependence. For women with AUD, biological differences account for increased sensitivity to alcohol, more significant health complications, premature death, and higher mortality rates.
- **Neuroendocrine adaptations:** Dysregulation of the hypothalamic-pituitary-adrenal (HPA) axis—which is responsible for regulating the stress and reward systems of the brain—is implicated in greater instances of SUD among women. A dysregulated HPA axis is associated with greater sensitivity to stress during drug or alcohol withdrawal, including irritability, agitation, and depressed mood. HPA dysregulation is also associated with increased cravings accompanied by more pronounced emotional and behavioral distress, making women more prone to relapse.
- **Alcohol use disorder (AUD):** For women with AUD, biological differences account for increased sensitivity to alcohol, more significant health complications from alcohol use, premature death, and higher mortality rates than men.
- **Co-occurring mental disorders:** Women with SUD are more likely to experience trauma and are more likely to have a co-occurring mental disorder than are men. Nearly three-quarters of women with SUD have experienced child abuse, making them more susceptible to higher rates of depression, anxiety, eating disorders, intimate partner violence, and PTSD.

Barriers to Treatment Engagement Among Women

The onset of SUD tends to occur more rapidly in women than men; however, women are less likely to seek treatment. **Barriers experienced by women with SUD** include the following:

- Unsupportive family members or male partners who themselves remain in active addiction
- Fear of losing child custody, particularly among pregnant women
- Greater societal stigma surrounding addiction than with men, including being characterized as morally lax, promiscuous, and abandoning their role as the family's caregiver
- Limited financial resources due to disparities in earned wages and lower pay rates
- Shame, guilt, and embarrassment regarding behaviors when using, which are complicated by greater instances of depression, anxiety, and experiences of trauma
- Believing they are unable to handle emotional stress, certain health issues, and symptoms of mental disorders without using substances to cope

Gender-Responsive Treatment Recommendations for Women

Gender-responsive treatment recommendations are comprehensive, holistic, culturally sensitive, and person centered. Counselors working with women with SUD must be sensitive to the shame, embarrassment, and guilt surrounding negative sociocultural stereotypes, some of which depict women with SUD as inferior, damaged, or morally lax.

Treatment recommendations for women with SUD include the following:

- Comprehensive screening, assessment, and treatment for SUD, co-occurring mental disorders, intimate partner violence, and trauma
- Multidisciplinary treatment programs that integrate concrete services (e.g., shelter, transportation, legal assistance, childcare) and supportive services (e.g., parental education, couples counseling, family therapy)
- Building a safe and supportive therapeutic relationship with the client to address interpersonal obstacles such as intimate relationships, family dynamics, and social supports
- Safe medical withdrawal for pregnant women, particularly for opioid dependency in which abrupt discontinuation could be fatal

Sexual Identity and Sexual Orientation Concepts and Terms

The following concepts and terms are associated with **sexual orientation** and **sexual identity**:

- **Sexual identity** is the inner belief one has about one's sexual experiences and attractions. Sexual identity is usually expressed by one's sexual orientation.
- **Sexual behavior** refers to sexual activity with oneself or others and is distinct from sexual orientation.
- **Sexual orientation** is an enduring pattern of sexual, emotional, mental, and/or romantic attraction toward a particular sex or gender. Sexual orientations include the following:
  - Heterosexual: Opposite-sex sexual orientation
  - Homosexual: Same-sex sexual orientation
  - Lesbian: Same-sex sexual orientation or behaviors among women
  - Gay: Same-sex sexual orientation or behaviors among males and females
  - Bisexual: Same-sex and opposite-sex orientation or behaviors
  - Asexual: Very little or no sexual attraction to either sex or gender

Gender and Gender Identity Concepts and Terms

Key concepts and terms associated with **gender** and **gender identity** include the following:

- **Sex** refers to the gender one is assigned at birth (i.e., natal sex).
- **Intersex** refers to a person born with male and female sex characteristics.
- **Gender** is a sociocultural construct determined by norms, beliefs, and attitudes associated with being a male or female. Gender is fluid and varies in different societies and cultures.
- **Gender roles** develop from sociocultural expectations associated with one's natal sex (e.g., physical appearance, occupation).
- **Gender expression** is a person's outward presentation, in terms of behavior, dress, or mannerisms, in reference to gender sociocultural stereotypes.
- **Gender nonconforming** refers to those people whose gender identity or gender expression is not associated with stereotypical gender roles or gender norms.
- **Gender identity** is one's personal and deeply felt concept of what it means to be male, female, or neither gender.
- **Transgender** individuals are those whose gender identity and gender role conflict with the gender they were assigned at birth.
- **Cisgender** individuals are those whose gender identity and expression align with their natal gender.

Sexual Behavior, Sexual Orientation, Natal Sex, and Gender Identity

Sexual behavior is not the same as sexual orientation. **Sexual orientation** can include sexual behavior, but it also includes erotic fantasy, romantic attraction, and the desire for emotional connection with a particular gender or neither gender (i.e., asexuality).

Natal sex refers to the sex that one is assigned at birth, which can be male, female, or intersex (i.e., a combination of both). Natal sex is determined by chromosomal patterns, external genitalia, hormones, and primary reproductive organs. **Gender identity**, gender expression, natal sex, and sexual orientation are all separate concepts. For example, the deeply felt self-conception of one's gender identity is independent of one's natal sex and sexual orientation. Transgender is an umbrella term used to describe a person whose gender identity and natal sex do not align. Individuals who are transgender are in the process of shifting their gender roles. This can occur in various ways, including social changes (e.g., clothing, name) or medical changes (e.g., hormones, surgery).

Treatment Considerations Unique to LGBT Individuals

Research shows that individuals who identify as LGBT have higher instances of SUD and comorbid mental disorders than their heterosexual and cisgender counterparts. Behavioral health disparities among LGBT men and women include the following:

- Individuals who identify as gay and bisexual report increased instances of depression.
- Children and adolescents who identify as transgender or gender nonconforming are more likely to experience severe symptoms of depression, including suicidality and self-harm.
- LGBT individuals disproportionally experience eating disorders, social isolation, and trauma.
- Compared to the general public, smoking rates are higher among sexual-minority populations—specifically bisexual men and women.
- Significant disparities exist regarding marijuana use, with nearly 38% of sexual minorities reporting marijuana use, compared to 16% of the general public.

Treatment of Comorbid Behavioral Health Disorders Among Sexual-Minority Populations

Counselors working with LGBT individuals must provide LGBT-affirmative, nonjudgmental, supportive treatment in a safe environment. Many in the LGBT community have experienced homophobia, transphobia, and heterosexism. Additionally, **intersectional components** of each client's identity, including race, ethnicity, economic status, religion, age, disability, and other contextual factors impact each individual's experiences and treatment needs.

Counselors must assess for trauma; interpersonal violence; and the associated symptoms of shame, fear, and isolation. When episodes of prejudice and discrimination become internalized, it can significantly impact how clients relate to the outside world and the initialization and exacerbation of their substance misuse. Research shows that individuals who identify as LGBT have **higher rates of SUD and comorbid mental disorders** than their heterosexual and cisgender counterparts.

Finally, counselors understand that LGBT individuals are not mentally ill, nor is sexual identity pathological. Many LGBT individuals have experienced various degrees of religious trauma, ranging from judgment and rejection to outward condemnation for their sexual orientation. This trauma may also include attempts to change an individual's sexual or gender identity (e.g., so-called "conversion therapy"). Counselors recognize that coming out is not a singular event and may be reexperienced during sobriety.

Recovery-Oriented Principles

Counselors who adhere to **recovery-oriented principles** provide care that is respectful, holistic, and integrated. Respect is critical in protecting clients' rights, including the right to receive treatment in a safe environment—one that is free of discrimination. Culturally responsive counselors value diverse backgrounds and support each client's cultural values, roles, beliefs, and traditions.

Cultural assessments used for clients with SUD can be used to identify the following:

- The **sociocultural factors** contributing to the client's SUD and recovery
- The influence of the client's **religion** and **spirituality** on their substance use and recovery
- Challenges within one's **home environment** and **community**, including languages spoken in and out of the home, employment status, educational level, and family history of SUD
- Experiences of **trauma**, including historical trauma, racism, and discrimination
- **Systemic oppression** resulting from one's marginalized status
- **Disparities** in access, utilization, and quality of health-care services
- Individual, community, and family **protective factors**

Development of Racial Identity

Racial identity development is complex, multifaceted, individualized, and ever evolving. Culturally sensitive counselors understand factors contributing to **racial identity**, including the client's view of their **racial group membership**, how connected the client is to that group, how the client thinks others perceive the group, and how their cultural identity is tied to their overall sense of self.

There are various **models of racial identity development.** Acculturation models, such as the one presented by Peter Bell's *Chemical Dependency and the African American* (2002), measure the integration of minority and majority populations in terms of the minority culture's modified worldviews, social relationships, beliefs, customs, or language. Bell specifically examines the impact of race on the treatment of SUD, stressing the importance of approaching the treatment of minorities with SUD from a holistic perspective, with an acute understanding of the ways in which race may impact an individual's internalization, access, motivation, and response to treatment. The developmental stages of racial identity for minority-culture individuals—ranging from full integration with the majority culture to least integrated—include accultured, bicultural, culturally immersed, and traditional-interpersonal. Counselors work to match treatment services to the client's stage of racial identity development and make every effort to honor principles of diversity and inclusion.

John Berry's Model of Acculturation

Researchers suggest that an integrated strategy for acculturation yields favorable therapeutic outcomes. Rather than a developmental model of acculturation, Berry (1992) bases four strategies of acculturation on **two fundamental questions**:

- Does the person want to retain or reject their native culture as part of their identity?
- Does the person feel that it is important to reject or adopt the cultural values and norms of the majority culture (i.e., host culture, dominant culture)?

The **strategies of acculturation** are:

- **Assimilation:** A person accepts the cultural values and norms of the majority culture over their culture of origin.
- **Separation:** A person completely rejects the majority culture and instead keeps the values and norms of their culture of origin.
- **Integration:** A person keeps their culture of origin while also adopting the majority culture's values and norms.
- **Marginalization:** A person rejects their culture of origin and the majority culture.

Elements of Multicultural Counseling

In 1990, Don C. Locke defined these **four elements** of the ever-changing role of multicultural counseling:

- Multicultural counseling is aware of the cultural background, values, and worldview of the client and the therapist.
- Multicultural counseling makes note of socialization aspects in regard to the race, ethnicity, and culture of the client.
- Multicultural counseling makes every effort to see the individual within the group of people that they belong to.
- Multicultural counseling does not label the person as deficient and acknowledges that there can be a difference between the person as an individual and their group.

The unique characteristics in a person may need to be addressed to help the person come to terms with their own self-identity. The individual is also encouraged to value the racial or ethnic group of which they are a member.

Review Video: Multicultural Counseling
Visit mometrix.com/academy and enter code: 965442

Professional, Ethical, and Legal Responsibilities

Quality Control

Continuous Quality Improvement Plan

Continuous quality improvement is a multidisciplinary management philosophy that can be applied to all aspects of an organization, including such varied areas as the inpatient rehabilitation facility, outpatient programs, purchasing, or human resources. The skills of data collection, analysis, outcomes, and action plans) are all applicable to the analysis of multiple types of events, because they are based on solid scientific methods. Multidisciplinary planning can bring valuable insights from various perspectives, and strategies used in one context can often be applied to another. All staff must be alert not only to problems but also to opportunities for improvement. Increasingly, departments must be concerned with cost-effectiveness as the costs of medical care continue to rise, so the addiction counselor is not in an isolated position in an institution but is just one part of the whole, facing concerns similar to those in other disciplines. Disciplines are often interrelated in their functions.

Juran's Quality Improvement Process

Joseph Juran's quality improvement process is a four-step method of change (focusing on quality control), which is based on a trilogy of concepts: quality planning, control, and improvement. The steps to the quality improvement process are the following:

- **Defining** the project and organizing includes listing and prioritizing problems and identifying a team.
- **Diagnosing** includes analyzing problems, formulating theories related to the cause by root cause analysis, and then testing the theories.
- **Remediating** includes considering various alternative solutions and then designing and implementing specific solutions and controls while addressing institutional resistance to change. As causes of problems are identified and remediation is instituted to remove the problems, the processes should improve.
- **Holding** involves evaluating performance and monitoring the control system in order to maintain gains.

Legal and Regulatory Considerations

Regulation of Psychoactive Substances and Designer Drugs

Through **Title II of the Controlled Substances Act of 1970 (CSA),** the DEA aggressively monitors substances with the highest potential for abuse. The CSA regulates **controlled substances** by scheduling them on a continuum. Schedule I represents substances with the highest abuse potential, and Schedule V represents those with the lowest abuse potential.

The CSA considers a drug's abuse potential based on its ability to alter CNS activity and have the potential to cause physical or psychological dependence. Intentional and recreational use of substances designed to produce a high or an alteration in perception are said to have abuse potential. Scheduled drugs are also assessed for their therapeutic use and are placed on Schedule I if there is a high potential for abuse and the drug has no medical value.

Synthetic, or designer, drugs are created to mimic controlled substances but are structured by chemists with the intent to avoid being classified as illegal. To address this issue, the **Federal Analogue Act of 1986** was enacted to treat substance analogues, or any substance with chemical structures substantially similar to controlled substances, as Schedule I or Schedule II, provided that the substances are intended for human consumption. **In 2012, the Synthetic Drug Abuse Prevention Act** was signed into law; this act classified certain synthetic, or designer, drugs as Schedule I.

DEA Schedules for Controlled Substances

The DEA is a federal agency responsible for enforcing legal provisions regarding controlled substances within the United States. The DEA provides the following schedules for controlled substances:

- **Schedule I:** This category includes drugs with the highest abuse potential and drugs that can cause severe dependence. Drugs in this category have not been accepted for medical use (e.g., heroin, LSD, marijuana, Ecstasy).
- **Schedule II:** These drugs have higher abuse potential than Schedule III and lower abuse potential than Schedule I (e.g., cocaine, methamphetamine, oxycodone, fentanyl).
- **Schedule III:** These drugs have moderate to low abuse potential (e.g., anabolic steroids, codeine, ketamine, testosterone).
- **Schedule IV:** These drugs have a low potential for dependency (e.g., Xanax, Ativan, Ambien, Darvocet, Valium, Tramadol).
- **Schedule V:** These drugs have the lowest potential for abuse or dependency (e.g., Robitussin AC, Lomotil, Lyrica, Parepectolin).

Omnibus Transportation Employee Testing Act

In 1991, the **Omnibus Transportation Employee Testing Act** was passed, requiring mandatory drug and alcohol testing for all employees in safety-sensitive job positions. This includes all commercial truck drivers, ferry operators, airline pilots, bus drivers, train operators, and other employees conducting safety-sensitive duties.

Department of Transportation (DOT) testing is also mandated for employees who provide maintenance and mechanical work on safety-sensitive modes of transportation. In 1998, the DOT expanded the scope of testing to encompass any commercial vehicle entering the United States from Mexico or Canada. The DOT is monitored by the Office of Drug and Alcohol Policy and Compliance, which specifies and monitors conditions for testing and outlines how the results will be reported. The DOT screens employees for the following substances:

- Marijuana/THC
- Cocaine
- Amphetamines (including methamphetamine)
- Opiates (including heroin, codeine, and morphine)
- PCP

Substances not listed may also be screened at the employer's request.

Drug-Testing Conditions

Drug testing by the DOT for all employees in safety-sensitive job positions may be conducted in any of the following conditions:

- **Preemployment screening:** Preemployment drug screening is issued for individuals who have received a job offer or transferred into a new safety-sensitive job position.
- **Post-accident:** Drug screening is conducted on employees who receive a moving violation ticket (e.g., speeding, running a traffic light) or are involved in accidents requiring off-site medical attention or accidents resulting in a fatality.
- **Reasonable cause:** If an employer suspects that an individual in a safety-sensitive job position is under the influence, then the individual must submit to a drug screen. Reasonable cause must go beyond a simple hunch. Employers must observe notable signs and symptoms of impairment (e.g., slurred speech, unsteady gait) to establish reasonable cause.
- **Random:** An employee may be selected at random and must comply with the screening. Consequences for noncompliance are the same as those issued for a positive screening.
- **Return to duty:** Employees who have received an infraction related to psychoactive substance use must submit to a drug screen prior to their return to work.
- **Follow-up:** If an employee fails a random drug test, the employer may continue random drug testing up to 5 years after the initial positive drug screen.

Role and Duties of a DOT Substance Abuse Professional (SAP)

The DOT ensures that employees in safety-sensitive job positions are drug- and alcohol-free. Transportation employees who test positive for a psychoactive substance are referred to an SAP for assessment, evaluation, education, and follow-up care. The DOT requires that a separate entity provide counseling and treatment services to the employee to avoid a potential conflict of interest. The role of the SAP is to protect the general public; thus, the SAP is not a counselor but a keeper of public safety.

The **duties of the DOT SAP** may include, but are not limited to, the following:

- Providing a face-to-face drug and alcohol **assessment** to employees who violate the DOT rules and regulations for a drug-free work environment. SAPs use valid and reliable assessment instruments, including the SASSI, Mortimer-Filkins, or ASAM.
- Conducting an initial face-to-face comprehensive **clinical evaluation**, providing **treatment recommendations** (e.g., inpatient treatment, education programs), and providing the employee with **outside referrals when warranted.**
- Developing treatment **goals and objectives** that the employee must achieve before returning to work and performing safety-sensitive job tasks.
- Conducting a **face-to-face follow-up evaluation** with the employee to **review progress** toward treatment goals and objectives.
- Determining the employee's **overall compliance** with their employer's recommendations as outlined in the DOT rules and regulations.

Providing Return-to-Work Recommendations

The DOT SAP is responsible for assessing an **employee's readiness to return to work** after violating a DOT drug and alcohol regulation. As gatekeepers for public safety, SAPs shoulder an enormous responsibility when determining the employee's ability to return to work. A **final recommendation** for the employee to return to work is made after the following steps have been taken:

- Collaboration with the employer's medical review officer
- Confirmation that the employee has completed treatment
- A thorough review of current documentation from the employer's treatment provider(s), including progress reviews and discharge summaries
- Utilization of supervision, consultation, and information from outside resources familiar with the DOT SAP's duties
- An assessment of the employee's level of rehabilitation

The last part of the return-to-work process includes **synthesizing all data.** A return-to-work recommendation is made, and the SAP provides a plan for **follow-up and continued care**, including recommendations for testing and other conditions required to maintain employment.

Informed Consent

Informed consent is the process of fully informing clients about the inherent risks, limitations, and benefits of treatment, including the rationale for selecting a specific treatment, other treatment options, and cost. Additionally, counselors must disclose policies for **nonpayment** of services. Clients must also be provided information about the purpose, goals, and techniques of the provider's selected **theoretical approach** and orientations. Clients must understand that **treatment is voluntary**—that consent can be revoked at any time. Providers must obtain both **verbal and written consent** from the client. Providers must obtain informed consent to disclose confidential and privileged information for clients who are mandated to receive treatment. Providers take appropriate steps to prohibit harmful disclosures or limit disclosures in scope by providing limited information (e.g., compliance with treatment, treatment progress). Informed consent can be revoked at any time; however, for court-ordered and other mandated clients, the consequences of withdrawing consent must be made clear at the onset of treatment.

The client must be able to clearly articulate an understanding of the signed document in terms of the time frame in which the consent is valid and the associated **rights and responsibilities of the provider and client** (e.g., to receive respectful treatment, ask questions about therapy, and terminate counseling services at any time). The provider must inform the client that he or she has the right to refuse treatment at any given time without fear of retribution. Other mandatory disclosures include the addiction provider's education, background, experience, and approach, as well as the specifics about clinical supervision and consultation. Finally, practitioners explain **confidentiality**, its limitations, and situations in which practitioners have **the duty to warn.**

Legally Mandated Exceptions to Confidentiality

Limitations to confidentiality and privacy are determined by state and federal laws and the provider's credentialing or licensing board. Confidential limitations occur with some forms of legal communication. For example, when the provider receives a **subpoena,** standards of practice dictate that the provider consults with an attorney. In more states than not, a subpoena does not require testimony or the release of records unless the client consents. However, a judge may issue a court order, at which time records may be admissible in court and testimony may be required.

Counselors are legally mandated to protect the **safety and welfare** of their clients. When a counselor suspects that a client is a danger to themselves and others, or when the AP suspects elder abuse or child abuse, counselors must report such suspicions to the proper authorities. In a medical emergency, counselors may disclose confidential information (e.g., the nature of the client/counselor relationship). When a client reveals their intention to commit a crime posing a serious threat to public safety, confidentiality must be breached to protect those in imminent danger. Lastly, if a client brings **charges against a counselor**, the client waives privilege and protection of confidential information.

Title 42 of the Code of Federal Regulations (CFR), Part 2

US Department of Health and Human Services' Confidentiality of Substance Use Disorder Patient Records (42 CFR Part 2) pertains to the **patient records** of those treated for **SUD in federally assisted programs**. With some exceptions, **42 CFR Part 2** requires written consent to disclose protected health information. **Written consent** is required for information generated and exchanged with others for the purposes of payment, treatment, or health-care facility operations.

Updates included in the Part 2 Amendments (effective August 2020) permit individuals with SUD to provide written consent to disclose treatment records **to any entity** (e.g., the Social Security Administration) without naming a specific person as the one receiving the disclosure.

The most common exclusions to the 42 CFR Part 2 regulations (i.e., instances in which consent is not required) include the following:

- Medical emergencies or emergencies caused by natural disasters.
- Audits or program evaluations.
- Information exchanged for scientific research.
- Reports of child abuse or neglect.
- Reports of crimes on the premises of treatment programs or against treatment staff. In this case, limited information may be provided, with a court order required to disclose additional details. In criminal prosecutions, patient records are protected unless the client gives consent or there is a court order.
- Additional limited circumstances requiring a court order as outlined in 42 CFR 2.61-2.67.

Health Insurance Portability and Accountability Act of 1996 (HIPAA)

The **Health Insurance Portability and Accountability Act of 1996 (HIPAA)** protects personal and identifiable health information and confidential records. Under HIPAA, consumers have the right to control how their health information is handled and by whom (e.g., health plans, health-care clearinghouses, and health-care providers). In addition, state and federal guidelines prohibit electronic records from being **tampered with, destroyed,** or **disclosed** to unsanctioned persons.

To promote risk management, it is recommended that providers consider doing the following:

- Protecting information contained in **electronic records**, including those **stored in the cloud** or on other online storage mediums. With the advent and continued expansion of electronic health records, HIPAA has a set of specific standards of practice applicable to electronic health records.
- Ensuring that **paper records** are double locked, maintained in a confidential setting, and accessed only by appropriate personnel.
- Ensuring that **email platforms** are established with secure, encrypted servers.

- Sending a **facsimile (fax)** through a secure means and confirming that measures are in place in offices and with persons receiving the fax. The sender determines if the fax machine is in a secure location, the intended person receives the fax, and the fax includes a cover sheet specifying confidentiality.
- Establishing procedures for **appropriately disposing** of electronic and paper records (e.g., using crosscut shredders, performing a factory reset on mobile devices).

Review Video: HIPAA
Visit mometrix.com/academy and enter code: 412009

Ensuring the Secure Transmission, Storage, and Disposal of Electronic Client Data

APs and associated substance abuse treatment centers aim to ensure the secure transmission of electronic data to meet the requirements established by HIPAA and 42 Code of Federal Regulations (CFR) Part 2. Various methods used to help ensure the secure transmission of data include the following:

- **Virtual private network:** This method protects private data sent through public platforms. Two-factor identification methods enhance protections.
- **Encrypted platforms:** To help keep web browsing secure and help prevent unauthorized individuals from accessing client information, data are converted into an encrypted code to keep information secure and protected.
- **Media sanitation:** Media sanitation is the disposal of client information. When electronic information is sanitized, it is permanently destroyed through an irreversible process. Private information can also be sanitized by destroying the device used to store client data. Media sanitation includes processes for clearing (e.g., overwriting), purging (e.g., block erasing, degaussing), and destroying (e.g., pulverizing, incinerating).

Core Counseling Attributes

Relationship to Treatment Outcomes

Research indicates that the therapeutic alliance profoundly affects the counseling process. **Core counseling attributes** are counselor qualities that serve as the building blocks for the therapeutic alliance. When established and maintained, the client-counselor alliance positively influences treatment outcomes.

Several core counseling attributes enhance client growth; these attributes include flexibility, collaboration, respect, self-awareness, inclusivity, and conflict tolerance. Core counseling attributes are **interconnected, culturally sensitive**, and demonstrated with **empathy** throughout all phases of treatment.

Core counseling attributes also include the foundational skills of listening, reflecting, and attending to the client's expressed needs. Five essential qualities that enhance the therapeutic alliance are **genuineness, immediacy, personal ability, warmth,** and **unconditional positive regard**.

Genuineness and Immediacy

Genuineness consists of the following two elements:

- **Intrapersonal:** Counselors attend to intrapersonal facets by mindfully examining their own internal processes and experiences with a present awareness.
- **Interpersonal:** Once the intrapersonal elements are examined, the counselor can then attend to the interpersonal aspect of the relationship. This occurs when the counselor shares this process with the client.

Genuineness is about responding openly, transparently, and authentically. Genuineness is demonstrated in the present moment and reflects verbal and emotional congruency (i.e., there is consistency between the person's words and actions).

The skill of **immediacy** is used to reflect a parallel experience or to address what is going on between the counselor and client in the present moment. Once an alliance is formed, immediacy is furthered by the counselor's use of properly timed self-disclosure. Approving of or validating a particular behavior can be a form of self-disclosure. Immediacy is connected to listening and attending.

Personal Ability and Unconditional Positive Regard

Personal ability is reflected by a counselor's clinical competency in addiction-related concepts and practices. Effective addiction counselors are equipped with foundational knowledge, but they must also be attuned to their own psychological health. Counselors demonstrate personal ability by having the confidence to talk to clients about various issues but also recognize their own professional limitations. Counselors understand that supervision is intricately linked to self-awareness, the enhancement of clinical knowledge and skills, and the motivation to address professional limitations.

Unconditional positive regard is a core counseling attribute used to transmit respect, understanding, and trust. Effective counselors demonstrate unconditional positive regard by suspending judgment and providing clients with acceptance and care. Empathy and understanding are facets of unconditional positive regard. In addition, counselors seek to remain open minded and objective and refrain from active confrontation.

Therapeutic Relationship

Role of Verbal Communication

Verbal communication is achieved through spoken or written words. This form of communication represents a very small fraction of communication as a whole. Much information conveyed verbally may be **factual** in nature. Communication occurs along a two-way path between the addiction counselor and the client. One limitation of verbal communication can be **different meanings of words** in different ethnic and cultural populations. The meanings of words may differ in their denotation (the plain or explicit meaning) and connotation (the implied meaning). The use of words may differ depending upon personal experiences. The client may assume that the counselor understands their particular meaning of a word, and misunderstandings may occur.

Using Congruence

Congruence in communication is consistently communicating the same message verbally and nonverbally to convey authenticity on the part of the counselor. The addiction counselor's words, body language, and tone of voice should all convey the same message. If they do not, then the communication is incongruent, and the receiver cannot trust the communication/communicator. For example, if a person says, "I really want to help you," in a harsh tone of voice and with an angry affect, the communication is incongruent, and the message may actually be perceived as the exact opposite of the words spoken.

Communication is also incongruent if the individual gives a series of conflicting messages: "I'm going to stop drinking." "Why should I stop drinking?" "I know I need to stop drinking." "There's no point in stopping drinking completely." The addiction counselor must be alert to the congruence of client communication in order to more accurately assess the client, and to be aware of personal congruence of communication when interacting with the client. This helps to ensure that the counselor can cultivate a relationship built on trust.

Using Active Listening

Active listening techniques include the use of paraphrasing in response, clarifying what was said by the client, and offering encouragement (e.g., saying "tell me more"). Key **overarching guidelines of active listening** include the following:

- Don't become preoccupied with specific active listening strategies; rather, concentrate on reducing client resistance to sharing, building trust, aiding the client in expanding his or her thoughts, and ensuring mutual understanding.
- The greatest success occurs when a variety of active listening techniques are used during any given client meeting.
- Focus on listening and finding ways to help the client to keep talking. Active listening skills will aid the client in expanding and clarifying his or her thoughts.
- Remember that asking questions can often mean interrupting. Avoid questioning the client when he or she is midstream in thought and is sharing, unless the questions will further expand the sharing process.

Conveying Empathy

Empathy is one of the most important concepts in establishing a therapeutic relationship with a client, and it is associated with **positive outcomes.** It is the ability of one person to put themselves in the shoes of another. Empathy is more than just knowing what the other person means. The counselor should seek to imagine the **feelings** associated with the other person's experience (without having had this experience themselves) and then communicate this understanding to the client. Empathy should not be confused with sympathy, which is feeling sorry for someone. The counselor should also be aware of any social or cultural differences that could inhibit the conveyance of empathy. Due to the guilt and shame associated with individuals seeking help for SUD, empathy from the counselor is critical. By demonstrating empathy, the addiction counselor will build rapport and trust with the client, both of which are foundational elements of the successful counselor-client relationship.

Using Open-Ended Statements and Reflection

Broad **open-ended statements** allow the client the opportunity to expand on an idea or select a topic for discussion. This type of communication allows the client to feel like the counselor is actually listening and interested in what he or she has to say. It also helps the client gain insight into his or her emotions or life situations.

Reflection conveys interest and understanding to the client. It can also allow for a time of validation so the counselor can show that he or she is actually listening and understanding the shared information. It involves some minimal repetition of ideas or summing up a situation. These ideas or summaries are directed back to the client—often in the form of a question.

Using Restating and Clarification

Restating and clarification are verbal communication techniques that the addiction counselor may use as part of therapeutic communication. **Restating** involves the repetition of the main points expressed by the client. Many times, the counselor will not restate everything but will narrow the focus to the main point. This technique can achieve clarification of a point and confirmation that what the client said was heard.

Clarification involves the addiction counselor attempting to understand and verbalize an unclear description or situation presented by the client. Many times, a client's emotional explanations can be difficult to clearly understand, and the counselor must try to narrow down what the client is trying to say through the use of clarification.

Rapport and Validation

Communication between the addiction counselor and the client can be improved by establishing rapport and validating certain information. **Establishing rapport** with a client involves achieving a certain level of harmony between the counselor and the client. This is often gained through the establishment of trust by conveying respect, nonbiased views, and understanding. By establishing rapport, the counselor helps the client feel more comfortable about sharing information.

Validation requires the counselor to use the word "I" when talking with the client. It evaluates one's own thoughts or observations against another person's and often requires feedback in the form of confirmation.

Using Therapeutic Communication Within the Group Environment

A **group** is a gathering of interactive individuals who share commonalities. Interventions through **group sessions** can provide an effective treatment opportunity to allow for growth and self-development of the client. This setting allows the clients to interact with each other. This allows clients to see the emotions of others, such as joy, sorrow, or anger, and to receive as well as participate in feedback from others in the group. The group can be very supportive and thrive in inpatient and outpatient settings. The one thing that the group cannot lack is definite **leadership and guidance** from the leader/counselor. The counselor must guide the members of the group in facilitating therapeutic communication.

Using Nonverbal Communication

Nonverbal communication occurs in the form of expressions, gestures, body positioning or movement, voice levels, and information gathered from the five senses. The **nonverbal message** is usually more accurate in conveying the client's feeling than the **verbal message**. Many clients struggling with SUD will say something quite different than what their nonverbal communication indicates. Nonverbal communication may also vary because of different cultural influences. The counselor must be aware of these cultural differences and respect their place in the therapy setting. The counselor should use positive, respectful, nonthreatening body language. A relaxed, slightly forward posture with uncrossed arms and legs may encourage communication.

Different Forms of Nonverbal Behaviors

There are many different types of nonverbal behaviors. There are five main areas of **nonverbal communication**: vocal cues, action cues, object cues, space, and touch.

- **Vocal cues** can involve the qualities of speech, such as tone and rate. Laughing, groaning, or sounds of hesitation can also convey important communication.
- **Action cues** involve bodily movements. They can include things such as mannerisms, gestures, facial expressions, or body movements. These types of movements can be good indicators of mood or emotion.
- **Object cues** include the use of objects. The client may not even be aware that he or she is moving these objects (for example, jewelry). Other times, the client may choose a particular object to indicate a specific communication. This intentional use of an object can be less valuable than other forms of nonverbal communication.

Space and touch as nonverbal forms of communication can vary greatly depending upon social or cultural norms.

- **Space** can provide information about a relationship between the client and someone else. Most people living in the United States have four different areas of space. **Intimate space** is less than 1.5 feet, **personal space** is 1.5–4 feet, **social-consultative space** is 4–12 feet, and **public space** is 12 feet or more. Observations concerning space and the client's physical placement in a setting can give a great deal of insight into different interpersonal relationships.
- **Touch** includes personal or intimate space with an action involved. This fundamental form of communication can send very personal information and communicate feelings such as concern or caring, but it must be used with discretion and cultural awareness.

Appropriate Use of Counselor Self-Disclosure

When used appropriately, counselor self-disclosure can build and enhance the therapeutic alliance. Self-disclosure is used when counselors reveal personal information about themselves to the client. Counselors who effectively use self-disclosure must ensure that it is delivered in the spirit of authenticity and reflects professionalism and competency. Counselors must also ensure that self-disclosure is viewed by the client as helpful and productive.

Counselors must remain mindful of professional boundaries and are cautioned against oversharing or using the exchange to fulfill unmet personal needs. The counseling skill of self-disclosure should never be self-serving. When used effectively, self-disclosure evokes the desire for the client to also self-disclose. Unconditional positive regard enhances the reciprocal nature of self-disclosure and can be used to model empathy and acceptance. Before using self-disclosure, counselors must engage in an effective decision-making process to minimize risk and maximize benefits.

INFLUENCE OF TRANSFERENCE AND COUNTERTRANSFERENCE

The counseling process requires counselors to attend to transference and countertransference issues and monitor their influence on the counseling relationship. Clients engage in **transference** when unconsciously projecting displaced attitudes and feelings associated with impactful past relationships onto the counselor. Freudians encourage counselors to evoke transference by serving as a blank screen; however, it can negatively affect the client-counselor relationship when this encounter goes unaddressed.

Countertransference is when the counselor projects their unconscious thoughts and feelings onto the client. Like transference, not all countertransference is problematic; however, when unrecognized and unexamined, it, too, can negatively influence the client-counselor relationship. Counselors strive to address countertransference through increased self-awareness and frequent monitoring as part of clinical supervision.

Ethical Considerations

Counselors engage in ethical decision making by considering the following:

- **Autonomy:** The freedom of a person to control the direction of their life without force or coercion; each individual has the right to make decisions for themselves.
- **Obedience:** The obligation to follow legal and ethical directives and mandates, including federal and state laws and the regulations of the counseling profession.
- **Conscientious refusal:** The obligation to refuse illegal and unethical directives; to act in a manner that prevents maltreatment of oneself and others.
- **Beneficence:** The desire to help others by promoting the well-being of those served; to act in the best interest of others.
- **Gratitude:** The need to show appreciation by passing along the good that was freely received from others; the duty to give back.
- **Competence:** The requirement to practice in a manner that reflects an understanding and application of the current treatment modalities, theories, and key addiction treatment philosophies.
- **Justice:** The obligation to treat others with fairness, to show equitable treatment by supporting equal access to services, behaving impartially toward others.
- **Stewardship:** The responsibility to appropriately, effectively, and judicially allocate available resources to those in need of help.

Additional considerations useful for ethical decision making include:

- **Honesty and candor:** The need for veracity or truthfulness in all personal, social, and professional settings.
- **Fidelity:** The need to honor promises and keep commitments.
- **Loyalty:** The responsibility to remain faithful to others and not abandon clients or other professionals.
- **Diligence:** The obligation to provide services that are efficient, prompt, and thorough; to possess the mindful awareness required for careful service delivery.
- **Discretion:** The ability to sense what needs to be provided in a particular situation; to carefully honor client confidentiality and provide appropriate privacy authorizations.
- **Self-improvement:** The need to strive to be the best version of oneself; to actively pursue personal and professional growth opportunities.
- **Nonmaleficence:** The need to "do no harm" in personal and professional relationships.
- **Restitution:** The responsibility to make amends when necessary, except when doing so would create additional injury to oneself or others.
- **Self-interest:** The need to consciously invest in and protect one's own interests and personal well-being.

Personal Ethics, Organizational Ethics, and Professional Ethics

Guided by morals and values, **personal ethics** determines how a person thinks, feels, and is motivated to act. Personal ethics helps a person discern what is acceptable behavior and what is not. Personal ethical principles are created through **self-reflection and self-awareness**. Ethical principles and values are influenced by societal norms, religious or spiritual beliefs, applicable laws, family-of-origin issues, cultural affiliations, and professional associations.

Philosophically, ethics refers to existential knowledge, values, and reasoning used to guide personal and professional conduct. An organization's mission statement, values, and principles dictate organizational ethics. **Organizational ethics** helps providers determine acceptable practices, ensure universal accountability, and monitor compliance with identified standards of care. **Professional ethics** is similar to organizational ethics. The function of professional ethics is to provide rules of conduct designed to protect the general public, create accountability, enhance treatment practices, mitigate risk, and minimize internal discord. Professional ethics differs from organizational ethics in that organizational ethics may not always conform to governmental or regulatory laws. The NAADAC Code of Ethics reflects applicable governmental laws and is designed to regulate itself without direct government intervention.

Principle Ethics, Virtue Ethics, and Mandatory Ethics

Principle ethics is rational, intuitive, objective, fair, and impartial, whereas **virtue ethics** is defined by one's character, internal motivations, and intentions. When applying principle ethics to ethical dilemmas, one uses morals and values to help answer the philosophical question "What 'should' I do?" When using virtue ethics to help solve ethical dilemmas, one seeks to respond with integrity by answering the philosophical question "How do I behave and who am I when no one is watching?" **Mandatory ethics** is dictated by minimal standards of conduct and guided by regulatory laws and practices, which include, but are not limited to, confidentiality, privacy, and mandatory reporting. The philosophical question associated with mandatory ethics is: What does the Code of Ethics dictate and require in terms of applicable laws and rules?

Aspirational Ethics, Positive Ethics, and Values Ethics

Aspirational ethics is used when applying the highest standards of practice to an ethical dilemma, answering the philosophical question "Am I using the highest quality of care available at this time, in this circumstance, with this particular client?" **Positive ethics** is a form of aspirational ethics used to guide practitioners in going above and beyond the call of duty to maximize client benefits and minimize client risk. The philosophical question that helps define positive ethics is "How can I be the best support or resource for this client?" Finally, **values ethics** is a form of personal ethics guided by one's morals, core beliefs, and actions. Values ethics is guided by the philosophical questions "What do I personally believe to be the best option in this situation? What are my unwavering beliefs?"

Compassion and Empathy

Compassion is the ability to help another person or oneself in times of physical, mental, or emotional pain. It is healing-centered and motivates APs to help others. Compassion is guided by the ethical values of justice, stewardship, fairness, and interdependence. Compassion requires sound judgment, an awareness of others' needs, and the motivation to help.

Empathy is the ability to put oneself in the shoes of another—to experience things from the other's perspective. Empathetic practitioners develop a true desire to help through nonjudgmental acceptance and solidarity, rather than pity or emotional contagion, and are guided by the principles of beneficence, kindness, and generosity. When expressing empathy, ethically sound practitioners work to keep their perceptions free from bias and prejudice, particularly with culturally different clients.

Components of Principle I, Sections 1–9

The Association for Addiction Professionals (NAADAC) and the National Certification Commission for Addiction Professionals (NCC AP) have compiled a Code of Ethics that is expected to be upheld by all practicing APs. The Code of Ethics (2021) is broken down into nine principles.

Principle I, sections 1–9, state the following. The counseling relationship emphasizes the importance of **treating clients with respect and dignity**, including protection from harm; the promotion of and respect for cultural diversity; and never engaging in or condoning **discrimination** based on race, ethnicity, sexual orientation, age, gender, economic status, physical or mental ability and condition, political party, military status, or religious or spiritual practices and beliefs.

APs support the client's **right to privacy** and work to foster self-determination and autonomy. Professionals help with autonomy by clearly explaining **informed consent**, **the limits of confidentiality**, mandatory disclosures, truthfulness with third-party payers, and the need to balance ethical and legal rights when a client's capacity to provide informed consent is limited.

Professionals working with **mandated clients** review the distinct aspects of confidentiality, including information released to third parties, the use of information with supervisors and consultants, and the consequences of treatment refusal, while continuing to foster autonomy. **A release of information** must be signed when communicating and collaborating with other professionals, systems of care, and any other specified or requested individual.

According to the NAADAC/NCC AP Code of Ethics (2021), boundaries inherent in the client-counselor relationship must be established, as well as "the risks and benefits associated with moving the boundaries of a counseling **relationship beyond the standard parameters**." Relationships "beyond the standard parameters" must be approached with caution and discretion, and the professional must seek **consultation and supervision** when considering multiple or dual relationships. The **risks and benefits** of such relationships are discussed and **documented**. **Multiple relationships** may include relationships with a client's family member or business associate, and professional or other social relationships. The AP makes every effort to avoid these relationships. However, when this is impossible, all efforts are made to minimize risk and avoid exploitation.

Similar stipulations apply to individuals with whom the professional has had a **prior relationship**. APs take precautions when accepting as a client a person with whom the counselor had a prior relationship. Professionals must weigh the risks and benefits of this relationship, seek consultation and supervision, document the recommendations, and proceed in a manner that would avoid harm and exploitation. The same care, consideration, and recommendations are given to a professional considering **entering into a personal relationship with a former client**.

Termination and Abandonment

Counselors adhere to the NAADAC/NCC AP Ethical Standards (2021) for termination and abandonment. Counselors **terminate** services when the client no longer needs or wants services. Termination is also recommended in cases in which the counselor cannot remain objective. Counselors provide pre-termination counseling and make client referrals when warranted. Counselors make referrals for clients or individuals associated with the client who pose a risk to the counselor's safety. Careful considerations are made in such cases, and referrals are provided only after obtaining and documenting discussions with a supervisor or consultant.

Counselors refrain from **abandoning** clients. When counselors anticipate short-term or permanent service suspension, they promptly notify clients. Counselors follow up with clients and make arrangements for the client to be transferred or referred, or to continue services based on the client's needs and desires.

Referring Clients to an Alternative Primary Service Provider

Counselors provide ethically sound **alternative primary service referrals** by doing all of the following:

- Ensuring that the client understands the reason for termination and can change conditions when applicable.
- Providing the client with written documentation citing the grounds for terminating the counseling relationship.
- Providing the client with up to three termination sessions to help ensure a smooth transition to another provider.
- Supplying the client with up to three alternative referral sources and allowing the client adequate time to follow up with the referral.
- Promptly facilitating the transfer of client records to the alternative referral source once the initial contact is made and the appropriate consent and release forms are signed.

Billing, Payment, and Fees

APs are mandated to disclose fees and billing, including fees for nonpayment, and they must specify policies for the collection of unpaid balances. Fees must be fair and reasonable, consistent with the services provided, and considerate of the client's ability to pay.

Additional ethical standards for **billing, payment, and fees** include the following:

- APs disclose all payment fees before the client's initial session and clearly explain charges for all services, including cancellations and missed sessions (i.e., no-shows).
- APs are responsible for disclosing policies for nonpayment, including use of collection agencies. APs provide timely written notice to clients if services are suspended and/or collection agencies will be contacted.
- APs cannot withhold records or reports (e.g., legal court reports, mandated counseling reports) solely based on nonpayment for services.
- APs provide third-party payers with accurate, factual, and timely information regarding the services provided and their costs. APs are responsible for explaining procedures that will go into effect if third-party payers deny payment.
- APs provide the same quality of services, regardless of the compensation received.
- APs must maintain accurate financial records.

Ethically Engaging in Bartering

APs may ethically engage in **bartering** in the following circumstances:

- If the client requests it.
- If it does not cause the client harm or exploitation.
- If it does not compromise the counseling relationship in any way, particularly when bartered services (e.g., house cleaning, repairs) are exchanged for counseling sessions. APs must adhere to guidelines for multiple/dual relationships.
- If state and federal laws allow it.
- If a written contract is provided that stipulates the fair market value of the items and the number of sessions provided through the exchange.

Self-Referrals, Commissions, Enterprises, and Gifts

The NAADAC Code of Ethics stipulates circumstances disallowing APs from endeavors leading to personal profit. Applicable standards for ethical practice include the following:

- **Self-referrals:** Unless permitted by agency or organizational practices, APs are prohibited from referring clients to their private practice.
- **Commissions:** APs are prohibited from offering or accepting any form of monetary remuneration for client referrals, including fee-splitting, rebates, kickbacks, or one-time payments.
- **Enterprises:** APs are prohibited from using client relationships for personal or monetary gain.
- **Gifts:** Before accepting a gift from a client, APs must consider the therapeutic relationship, the cost of the gift, the client's reason for giving the gift, and the AP's reason for accepting or declining the gift. Before making the decision to accept or decline the gift, APs must obtain consultation or supervision and document recommendations.

Communication, Treatment Planning, and Level of Care

Applicable NAADAC/NCC AP Ethical Standards (2021) for communication, treatment planning, and level of care include the following:

- **Communication:** APs must communicate in a culturally and developmentally appropriate manner, particularly when obtaining informed consent. Any cultural considerations or concerns related to the client's ability to grant informed consent must be documented.
- **Treatment planning:** APs must collaborate with clients when creating an individualized treatment plan. Treatment plans must be updated and revised at regular intervals to ensure successful provision of services.
- **Level of care:** APs must make every effort to provide clients with effective and appropriate treatment interventions. The level of care for each client must be determined using ASAM standards or an equivalent placement criterion.

NAADAC 10-Step Ethical Decision-Making Model

In addition to the Decision-Making Model outlined in Section VIII-3 of the NAADAC Code of Ethics, NAADAC also endorses a 10-Step Ethical Decision-Making Model:

- **Step 1: Identify** the problem. APs must first determine if the problem is an ethical problem, legal problem, and/or clinical situation. APs should have a foundational understanding of the NAADAC Code of Ethics (2021) and the decision-making process. Whenever possible, APs seek to understand and resolve initial concerns through direct, intentional, and open discussions with those involved.
- **Step 2: Apply** the NAADAC/NCC AP Code of Ethics and relevant laws. APs must engage in professional development emphasizing ethical and legal issues. Failure to acquire knowledge of applicable standards and laws does not indemnify the AP from their obligation.
- **Step 3: Consult** with supervisors, consultants, or subject matter experts. APs consult with NAADAC committee members, legal experts, and authorities when necessary.
- **Step 4: Generate** potential and reasonable courses of action that reflect all legal and ethical perspectives.

- **Step 5: Evaluate** each generated option. APs identify significant benefits and detriments of each option, stressing the ethical mandate to do no harm. Next, APs determine what is in the client's best interest, whether the AP's personal values are in question, and whether the course of action could be defended in front of an ethics committee.
- **Step 6: Implement** a viable course of action.
- **Step 7: Document** each step of the decision-making process and the chosen course of action. With nonmaleficence guiding the process, the AP must best determine how to protect the client. Secondary considerations apply to actions that protect the provider and actions that protect the agency. When situations apply to an identified client, the documentation becomes part of the client's records.
- **Step 8: Analyze** the implemented course of action. APs determine whether the course of action had the intended consequences and, when applicable, whether the client involved remained safe and protected from harm.
- **Step 9: Reflect** on the outcome. APs determine if the outcome was successful and whether adjustments to the decision are required.
- **Step 10: Reassess** the decision-making process. This step is crucial for determining if the selected course of action was effective and if the decision-making model itself was effective. APs must identify any additional data, such as potential legal or ethical issues, that may have been missed, and reactivate the process when necessary. Step 10 also helps target an AP's professional development and training needs.

Ethical Relativism and Ethical Absolutism

Determining what constitutes ethical and moral behavior is unique to each individual. The application and implementation of ethical codes is also unique. There is no one method that is better than the others. When evaluating dilemmas and solutions, there are two schools of thought: ethical relativism and ethical absolutism.

- **Ethical relativism** is the belief that there are no fixed principles of right or wrong—that decision making considers context and consequences and that it varies from person to person.
- **Ethical absolutism** is the belief that there are fixed moral and ethical standards—that ethical codes are to be taken literally, with little consideration of contextual factors.

Clinical Pragmatism

Grounded in relativism, **clinical pragmatism** is a consensus-oriented approach that combines clinical and ethical decision-making processes. Clinical pragmatism considers the practical and moral consequences of decision making and establishes such grounding through interpersonal assessment rather than absolute truths. Critics of clinical pragmatism believe that it relies too much on empirical evidence to determine what is right and wrong. Proponents argue that clinical pragmatists make necessary considerations of cultural diversity and situational complexity to determine what is right and wrong.

Humanistic Ethics

Humanistic ethics uses critical thinking skills and evidence to resolve ethical dilemmas and help individuals reach their highest potential. Values emphasized by humanistic ethics include self-efficacy, free will, integrity, autonomy, and self-actualization. Ethical humanists seek to find meaning in life and focus on the importance of treating others with respect and dignity. Humanistic ethics is criticized and embraced for fostering free religious thought through progressive, nontheistic relativism.

Situational Ethics

Situational ethics is based on relativism and embraces the notion that there are no universal doctrines for what is right or wrong; instead, solutions are reached through an intentional evaluation of each situation on a case-by-case basis. Rigid absolutist theories are rejected in favor of flexible standards based on the promotion of the greater good. Love and justice are the ethical principles that guide situational ethics. Love is understood in terms of a broad and unconditional love for all human beings. Overall moral principles may be sacrificed if the end justifies the means and love prevails.

Religious Ethics

Religious ethics consists of moral principles based on religious teachings. The Golden Rule (i.e., treat others how you would like to be treated) is the universal principle that guides religious ethics. Fair and equitable treatment of others is the cornerstone of religious ethics, which is grounded in a belief in God or a higher power and is expressed through humility, gratitude, empathy, and compassion.

Influence of Personal Values and Ethics on Clinical Practice

One of the most salient elements of ethical decision making is one's personal values. **Personal values** are influenced by numerous factors, including the following:

- Early childhood experiences
- Sociocultural norms
- Peer groups
- Religious or spiritual values and affiliations
- Political viewpoints
- Interpersonal relationships

Personal ethics shapes an AP's **theoretical orientation**, which is refined through experience, education, clinical setting, and supervision. Ethical conduct is shaped by positive and negative life and work experiences, including professional burnout, inadequate supervision, poverty, and trauma. Ethical conduct may shift or adapt, depending on the treatment setting or the clinical population being treated. The implicit values embedded in therapeutic interventions influence an AP's decision-making process: whether they accept best practices, the method of delivery they choose, and the techniques they select.

William Van Hoose and Louis Paradise's Conditions for Ethically Responsive Behavior

Van Hoose and Paradise (1979) state that a counselor may be behaving in an ethically appropriate fashion if "(1) he or she has maintained personal and professional honesty, coupled with (2) the best interests of the client, (3) without malice or personal gain, and (4) can justify his or her actions as the best judgment of what should be done based upon the current state of the profession."

Successful application of these core conditions and the **foundational principles** of autonomy, justice, fidelity, beneficence, and nonmaleficence can help resolve ethical dilemmas. However, providers must apply an ethical decision-making model when dealing with more complex clinical matters. APs adopt a systemic ethical decision-making model to minimize risk and help ensure client safety. An effective model considers not only situational ambiguities, but also the complex nature of individuals (e.g., clients, counselors), who hold varying worldviews, morals, and motivations.

Being Dually Licensed in Another Discipline

Addiction counselors holding additional licensures must follow the ethical code with the strictest mandate. Dually licensed or certified providers are under the jurisdiction of more than one ethical code. For example, the National Board for Certified Counselors Code of Ethics (2016) stipulates that an NCC "shall not engage in any form of sexual or romantic intimacy with clients or former clients for **2 years** from the date of service termination." Principle I-23 of the NAADAC Code of Ethics states that it is **not acceptable, under any circumstance or timeframe,** to date a current or previous client. Principle I-42 extends this restriction to virtual e-relationships with current clients. These principles are in place to minimize the potential for risk resulting from the **power differential** inherent in the counseling relationship, the possibility for **exploitation,** and the shift from a professional to a personal relationship, thereby **restricting access** to the counselor if future treatment needs arise for the client.

Attributes Associated with the Process of Ethical Decision Making

The three key attributes associated with the process of ethical decision making are:

- **Commitment:** APs remain steadfast in the process of ethical decision making and remain resolute in this purpose no matter the personal cost.
- **Competency:** APs have the capacity to gather and evaluate relevant information, generate alternative solutions, understand potential risks and benefits, and select an appropriate course of action.
- **Consciousness:** APs approach ethical dilemmas with intentionality and mindfulness, and they consistently apply moral principles to ethically responsive actions.

Determining the Effectiveness of an Ethical Decision-Making Process

There are several ethical principles and decision-making models, each with several criteria consistent with an effective decision-making process. However, what remains clear is that, above all, the AP's primary obligation is to **protect the client's safety** while simultaneously promoting the **mental and emotional well-being** of those served (i.e., beneficence). APs are responsible for choosing a research-driven clinical model and applying it with integrity, compassion, and skill.

Effective models of ethical decision making promote the following:

- Professionalism and trust in the provider
- Consistent application of ethical standards of practice
- Realistic and attainable steps for all persons involved in the decision-making process
- Consideration of the short- and long-term implications of the decision

Ethical Maturity

Ethical maturity is the capacity for a counselor to act in an ethically responsible manner. Ethically mature counselors possess knowledge of applicable laws, ethical codes, and standards of practice. Ethical maturity also includes having the skill set to purposefully apply ethical knowledge and the awareness to intentionally reflect and retrospectively assess the outcome of an ethical decision. Finally, ethical maturity is reflected in the ability to match an ethical action with moral standards and beliefs. Michael Carroll and Elisabeth Shaw (2013) cite the following **six components of ethical maturity:**

- The possession of moral character and watchfulness
- The ability to match an ethically oriented action with internalized ethical principles
- The courage to implement ethical decisions
- The avoidance of wrongdoing and the capacity to justify, defend, or explain actions to stakeholders
- The ability to live with the outcome of a decision—to be at peace with the consequences
- The capacity for rational and intentional self-reflection, leading to the integration of ethical concepts into one's moral character

Principles Associated with the Counseling Relationship

Principle I-1 of the NAADAC Code of Ethics states, "Addiction professionals shall accept their responsibility to ensure the safety and welfare of their client, and shall act for the good of each client while exercising respect, sensitivity, and compassion. Providers shall treat each client with dignity, honor, and respect, and act in the best interest of each client." The ethics principles applicable to the counseling relationship are autonomy and fidelity.

APs foster **autonomy** by empowering clients with the freedom to make their own decisions and, when appropriate, respect each client's choice and their capacity to act independently. The role of an AP is to help clients understand the impact that their decisions may have on themselves and others. **Fidelity** is the ability to remain faithful, committed, and loyal. A trusting therapeutic relationship is the foundation for client growth. APs nurture the virtue ethic of **loyalty** by fulfilling their obligations and commitments. APs remain open and transparent about all elements of the therapeutic process.

Informed Consent Process

Informed consent is the process of fully informing clients about the inherent risks, limitations, and benefits of treatment services, as well as the available alternatives, so they can voluntarily decide whether they wish to participate. Mandatory disclosures are detailed in Principle I, "The Counseling Relationship," of the NAADAC/NCC AP Code of Ethics (2021).

APs must review mandatory disclosures **before initiating services**. A **written copy** of an informed consent document must be provided to the client, and APs must also **verbally review** the consent form with the client. Informed consent procedures must comply with all **state and federal laws**, including, but not limited to, laws concerning the duty to warn, privileged information, and limits to confidentiality. APs must use **clear and understandable language** when reviewing the consent, with particular consideration toward the client's developmental stage, level of competency, and state of mind. For clients whose **primary language is not English**, or those who use another communication medium (e.g., sign language), **linguistically appropriate** services must be provided (e.g., an interpreter). The informed consent process must be reviewed with clients who enter treatment in an altered state (e.g., in crisis, under the influence of a psychoactive substance).

Ethical Aspects of the Therapeutic Relationship

APs collaborate with clients in a manner that honors the principles of benevolence and autonomy, using caution when the client's values and decisions vary from their own. APs remain aware of **transference/countertransference** and refrain from practices that foster client dependency or an overreliance on the AP to solve their problems.

APs are responsible for clarifying their role when working with more than one person. **Professional loyalty** helps define who the client is and in what capacity the AP will serve when encountering the client. The AP's role, for example, must remain clear when working with the client in group counseling, with family members, in couples counseling, and so forth. Identifying the actual client, and what information he or she is entitled to, must be addressed on an ongoing basis. Once the client is identified, the AP can then detail aspects of **advocacy.** Clients have a right to ask questions about their treatment, and APs are responsible for being attentive to those concerns. APs are ethically obligated to disclose intended advocacy efforts, how this information will be disclosed, and how the outcome may affect the client.

Ethical Obligations Regarding Dual or Multiple Relationships

Ethical obligations for **dual** or **multiple relationships**, or those in which multiple roles exist (e.g., friend, student, family member), are discussed openly with the client. APs make every effort to avoid the pitfalls of dual relationships. APs ensure that they are behaving in an ethically responsive manner by seeking supervision or consultation on these matters and by documenting the process. APs must not provide treatment services to their coworkers, current or former friends, or family members. APs clarify that the boundaries for a personal relationship extend to virtual relationships, including social media or their personal online presence. The onus is always on the provider to determine whether or not the relationship is permissible.

Confidentiality and Privileged Communication

As part of informed consent, APs review confidentiality with a client before initiating treatment and on an ongoing basis throughout treatment. APs agree to keep the client's personal information private except in conditions otherwise specified. APs have an ethical responsibility to obtain the client's **written authorization** when information is requested or exchanged with an outside party. Written authorization outlines how confidential information will be disclosed, with whom, and the purpose of the disclosure.

APs must abide by **regulatory laws and practices** outlining exceptions to confidentiality. **Legal and ethical limits** include situations in which the client is deemed to be a harm to themselves or others. APs must disclose to the client the types of information exchanged for the purpose of supervision and consultation. APs are transparent with clients and remain guided by the ethical principle of beneficence and the virtue ethics of discretion and loyalty.

Privilege applies to protecting confidential information in legal proceedings. State and legal mandates dictate the information that can be used in court, and they vary from state to state. APs must obtain **written consent** from the client to release personal information to the court and they must limit or prevent full disclosure from causing any potential harm to the client.

Client's Right to Privacy

Principle II-6 of the NAADAC Code of Ethics states, "Addiction professionals and the organizations they work for shall ensure that confidentiality and privacy of clients shall be protected by providers, employees, supervisees, students, office personnel, other staff, and volunteers."

Steps that APs use to keep information private include, but are not limited to, the following:

- APs refrain from seeking information that is neither beneficial to the counseling relationship nor necessary for treatment. APs obtain information on a **need-to-know basis** rather than requesting information out of curiosity.
- APs obtain written consent in the form of a signed **release of information**. The client has the right to agree or refuse the release of private information.
- APs debrief the client on the type of information exchanged with **shared providers, treatment teams, supervisors, and consultants**. During these interactions, limited information is exchanged (e.g., only using the client's first name and last initial) in person, and in all electronic communication. Debriefing consists of disclosing what information will be discussed, who will partake in the discussion, the limits of confidentiality, and the goals of collaboration and consultation. APs disclose to clients any information requested by any **third-party payer source**.
- APs withhold information contained in the client's file that could **cause harm** to the client.
- APs refrain from discussing the client's private information in a public place or **within earshot** of another person (e.g., in waiting rooms).
- APs explain the limits of confidentiality and privacy in **group therapy**. Although the group leader always stresses confidentiality, the client must understand the inherent risk of self-disclosure.
- APs disclose **the limits of confidentiality** when working with couples, families, children, and those who cannot voluntarily give consent to disclose information.

Ethical Documentation Standards

Ethically responsible APs adopt documentation standards in compliance with ethical and organizational standards to mitigate provider risk and enhance client safety. APs are responsible for following specific federal, state, and organizational standards, procedures, and regulations. **Suggested documentation standards** include the following:

- Documentation should reflect objective rather than subjective data unless otherwise specified.
- For paper records, entries must be legible and written in ink.
- Documentation should be composed in a timely, complete, and clear fashion.
- Case notes include the provider's credentials, signature, date, and the type of service provided.
- Conversations with supervisors, colleagues, consultants, and outside providers are documented. APs must include a signed release of information for any collateral services rendered.
- Documentation should include the client's progress toward treatment plan goals, with each case note providing evidence of clinical interventions and treatment compliance.
- Specific formats for case notes must be followed. Examples include SOAP (subjective, objective, assessment, and plan) notes or the DART (description, assessment, response, and treatment plan) approach to progress notes.

Principle Ethics and Virtue Ethics Associated with Principle III

Principle III of the NAADAC Code of Ethics is based on the principle ethics of beneficence and nonmaleficence and the virtue ethics of justice and loyalty. Promotion of the well-being of all, regardless of varying beliefs, attitudes, and worldviews, in conjunction with empathy and respect, is a foundational aspect of the therapeutic relationship. APs acknowledge the client's **right to**

competent treatment, including having a provider who is **loyal, respectful**, and **free from discrimination and bias.**

APs promote the overall well-being of clients and seek spiritual, mental, emotional, and social connection with all stakeholders through frequent self-monitoring and self-care. APs honor diversity, serve with integrity, and understand the impact of their personal and professional behaviors. APs seek justice for marginalized individuals while understanding their own positionality (e.g., marginalized, privileged) and the impact that intersecting identities have on the therapeutic relationship. APs seek supervision and/or consultation to help resolve issues stemming from multicultural differences and work to use their positions to appropriately advocate for those in need. Lastly, APs understand that the promotion of beneficence and nonmaleficence includes practicing within the scope of their personal and professional competence and acknowledging boundaries of competence.

Ethical Guidelines Associated with Professional and Personal Competence

APs are ethically obligated to practice according to standards aligned with ethical, professional, and personal competence.

APs' standards of ethical competence include the following:

- An accurate representation of professional memberships, differentiating between current and former membership status
- An accurate representation of educational degrees, credentials, certifications, and licensures
- Adherence to evidence-based practices that are science-based and outcomes-driven
- Adherence to boundaries of competence, which includes providing services commensurate with their level of experience, training, and education.
- Attainment of proficiency and competency through an active pursuit of the highest levels of education; APs keep abreast of current developments in the field of addiction and apply empirically grounded interventions and innovative techniques
- An accurate representation of techniques, modalities, and procedures, including providing informed consent on the intended benefits as well as the potential for associated risks, harm, and any additional ethical considerations

Ethical Guidelines Associated with Financial Arrangements

APs honor the ethical guidelines associated with financial arrangements with clients by doing the following:

- Refraining from any fraudulent, wrongful, or criminal conduct for financial gain
- Using a sliding scale or providing pro bono services to clients who otherwise cannot access or afford treatment
- Providing clients with community resources without accepting any form of monetary remuneration
- Refraining from monetarily profiting from client relationships, including receiving gifts from clients without first seeking supervision or consultation
- Correcting any misrepresentations of personal credentials or biographies shared with others through advertisements or endorsements

Ethical Components of Self-Care and Professional Impairment

APs have an ethical obligation to continuously **self-monitor** and engage in **self-care**. **Professional impairment** is a loss of functioning that would likely cause harm to the client or others. According to the NAADAC/NCC AP Ethical Standards (2021), Principle III-37: "Addiction professionals shall recognize the effect of impairment on professional performance and shall seek appropriate professional assistance for any personal problems or conflicts that may impair work performance or clinical judgment. Providers shall continuously monitor themselves for signs of physical, psychological, social, and emotional impairment."

APs are responsible for seeking supervision to address professional and personal issues and attend to any signs of impairment. Effective supervisors lead by the ethical principles of loyalty, integrity, and beneficence when partnering with APs to determine the impact of any personal problems or conflicts. It is expected that the **AP will cease or limit client responsibilities when impaired** until he or she can safely return to work. In tandem with **statutory mandates**, additional considerations must be given toward reporting and addressing prohibited actions, including sexual harassment, exploitation, fraud, or any criminal activity. **Failing to disclose criminal charges or continuing to practice when knowingly impaired** violates ethical standards and is subject to appropriate sanctions (e.g., probation, permanent loss of certification).

Ethical Responsibilities when Collaborating with Multidisciplinary Team Members

When working with **multidisciplinary care teams**, APs are responsible for the following:

- Educating medical professionals on the need to provide primary treatment strategies for SUD and to avoid, limit, or closely monitor forms of mind-altering prescription medication.
- Collaborating with a client's multidisciplinary team members to coordinate and integrate client care.
- Clarifying professional and ethical obligations among multiple providers. If a resolution is not attained, ethical dilemmas are presented to the care team first and then to the AP's supervisor.
- Providing collaborative care that is collegial, professional, fair, and respectful. APs should not offer counseling services to clients who are currently receiving services elsewhere unless the current counselor approves and the client's case is terminated.
- Recognizing the need for clients to be prescribed mood-altering chemicals and providing a supportive atmosphere for those who receive them.

Ethical Responsibility to Advocate for Individuals with SUD

APs have an ethical responsibility to **engage in advocacy efforts** for individuals with SUD. APs are aware of the **stigma** surrounding individuals with SUD and willingly support activities that dispel myths, misperceptions, and disinformation associated with addictions and the treatment of SUD. Advocacy efforts are provided through engagement in the **legislative process, public forums,** and **academic settings**. APs advocate for equitable access to health care, resources, and services used to treat SUD. APs promote each client's right to be treated with dignity and respect, and they make public statements within the scope and limits of their present knowledge.

APs refrain from **public comments** disparaging NAADAC, other APs, treatment providers, or individuals with addiction. APs carefully distinguish public communication they make as private citizens from statements they make on behalf of an organization, other APs, or other public groups. Lastly, APs are obligated to **support public policy and legislative action** concerning addiction, the addiction profession, and the lives of those affected by addiction.

Ethical Responsibility for Accurate and Honest Professional Representation

APs avoid false representations of themselves, their professional memberships, and their organizational relationships. APs remain accurate and honest in their professional representations when providing the following:

- **Trainings, workshops, and seminars.** For example, APs refrain from misrepresenting their NAADAC active provider status and their ability to provide NAADAC-approved personal development training.
- **Promotional advertisements** for professional training and related activities. APs ensure that all of their advertisements are free from deception and provide ample information for recipients to make informed decisions.
- **Testimonials.** APs ensure that written permission is granted before publishing testimonials and that testimonials do not misrepresent the provider's professional capacity. APs also discuss with former clients any potential implications or concerns regarding the use of their testimonials.
- **Reports to third parties.** APs provide honest, accurate, and objective reports to appropriate third parties, including individuals associated with courts, insurance providers, regulatory boards and agencies, recipients of evaluations, and referral sources.
- **Professional advice.** APs who offer advice or provide comments to the media (e.g., presentations, television) ensure that the information provided reflects solid scientific research, accurate academic findings, and best practices, and that it aligns with ethical standards.
- **Input into judicial or administrative proceedings.** APs serving in multiple roles during judicial or administrative proceedings disclose their roles and clarify ethical expectations.

Ethical Responsibility for Client Termination Planning and Referral

APs are responsible for providing a written plan for client accommodations in the event of the AP's **death, retirement, termination of practice, or professional impairment.** APs establish provider wills detailing arrangements for client records, including the name and phone number of a predetermined records custodian. APs conducting research are responsible for creating a written plan to transfer research data.

APs avoid recruiting **coworkers, supervisors, or colleagues** from places of employment to their private practice unless authorized to do so. APs ensure that client care is not compromised when **referring clients** from places of employment to private practice, and that they do not make such referrals unless permission is granted with written authorization.

APs seek supervision or make additional provisions when referring clients to other providers to **eliminate conflicts of interest.** Providers offer multiple referral options (i.e., three or more) to clients when necessary. APs have an ethical duty to **intervene to help clients** served by professionally impaired clinicians. Providers report professional impairment according to state laws and **provide assistance and consultation** to peers, colleagues, or supervisors demonstrating professional impairment.

Cultural Competency, Cultural Humility, and Cultural Sensitivity

Multicultural ethical standards of practice include components of the following:

- **Cultural competency:** APs intentionally seek **knowledge and understanding** of diverse cultural beliefs, attitudes, norms, traditions, and behaviors. APs understand how each client's individualized cultural differences **influence their experiences** within an organization, institution, and community, as well as the therapeutic relationship.
- **Cultural humility:** APs engage in the **lifelong aspiration** of cultural humility. This is attained through intentional focus, reflection, and awareness of one's own cultural biases, values, and assumptions. Cultural humility is other-oriented and accepting, and it lacks superiority. Cultural humility is practiced by remaining **teachable, open, self-critical, and receptive to new and challenging ideas and perspectives**. APs maintain this stance with all professional contacts (e.g., clients, supervisors, volunteers).
- **Cultural sensitivity:** APs adapt communication and behaviors in a manner that is accommodating and accepting of each client's cultural heritage, customs, norms, and values. APs are committed to providing culturally relevant interventions, techniques, and assessment instruments, and understanding the cultural limitations inherent in each. APs ensure that **linguistically appropriate** services are provided (e.g., interpreters).

Ethical Responsibilities for Developing and Maintaining Multicultural Competency

APs are professionally and ethically responsible for developing and maintaining multicultural competencies. **Components of multicultural competency** include the following:

- Obtaining multicultural knowledge
- Possessing awareness of each client's intersecting identities (e.g., Hispanic, LGBT) and the impact of these identities within the therapeutic relationship and within the client's family and the community
- Growing in cultural humility; this includes possessing an other-oriented stance, seeking cross-cultural encounters, engaging in intentional self-appraisal, and engaging with openness and curiosity
- Increasing skills required for being a culturally competent provider
- Refraining from engaging in behaviors indicative of underlying racial and discriminatory biases, whether overt or covert

Microaggressions are forms of covert discrimination and racism that evolve from underlying biases. These biases can harm the therapeutic relationship and manifest in transference and countertransference. APs are ethically responsible for seeking supervision to decrease microaggressions, biases, and impaired judgment.

Ethical Responsibility for Understanding Culturally Bound Personal and Professional Values, Beliefs, and Assumptions

APs have an ethical responsibility to **understand** their personal and professional **culturally bound influences** to decrease biases, judgment, discrimination, and microaggressions.

APs do not condone or participate in **discriminatory practices**. Instead, APs are committed to the practice of **cultural humility** by honoring and accepting the diverse cultural identities of all people. Therefore, APs must refrain from imposing their personal beliefs and values.

NAADAC asserts that **personal and professional ethics** must not be viewed as separate entities—that ethically responsive APs are motivated by their concern for all individuals. When an AP's culturally bound conditions oppose the client's, the AP seeks supervision and/or consultation to help provide services respectful of each client's **fundamental rights, dignity, and value.** APs document any recommendations received from supervisors and/or consultants.

Finally, APs are equipped with an awareness that cultural identity is **not limited to race and ethnicity** but may include sexual orientation, religious and/or spiritual practices, social status, age, physical abilities, and neurological functioning.

Ethical Multicultural Practice Within the Process of Informed Consent

APs incorporate **ethical components of multicultural practice** within the process of informed consent by doing the following:

- Provide information in a culturally sensitive and developmentally appropriate fashion. APs provide professional interpreters or translators to clients who have difficulty understanding the provider's language.
- Provide information about the counseling process in a manner that reflects credibility, capability, dependability, and trustworthiness.
- Explain confidentiality and privacy in a culturally sensitive manner, understanding that there are differing cultural views on disclosing personal information.
- Establish a collaborative relationship with clients, and, when necessary, adjust the procedures of informed consent to reflect diverse cultural implications (e.g., individual autonomy vs. communal decision making).

Qualities of an Ethical Multicultural Practitioner

Ethical multicultural practitioners possess the following **qualities**:

- The willingness and capacity to integrate evidence-based practices and interventions appropriate for use with a culturally diverse clientele
- The lifelong practice of cultural humility, including an openness to cultural differences and the ability to acknowledge professional limitations
- The ability to successfully engage with clients and comfortably discuss ways the provider can best respond to the client's culturally driven needs
- The active pursuit of professional development training applicable to the groups served
- The willingness to provide and/or advocate for diversity-inclusive services, including recruiting culturally diverse professionals, supervisors, and subject matter experts
- The willingness to understand and respect culturally specific structures and hierarchies, including an awareness of how systems of oppression, power, and privilege manifest in the lives of APs and the clients that they serve
- The understanding that client treatment and referrals are not based on the AP's personal values, attitudes, and beliefs

Behavior Requiring Modification to Meet Culturally Driven Client Needs

AP behaviors that may require **modification to meet culturally driven client needs** include the following:

- Nonverbal mannerisms, including professional distancing, that may send the message that the AP is uninterested
- Use of self-disclosure
- Handshakes, hugs, and eye contact
- Accepting or rejecting client gifts
- Incorporating aspects of the client's faith and spirituality in the treatment process, which may include healing practices and inviting the client's spiritual advisor to participate
- Conducting meetings at the client's home or school or at courtrooms, hospitals, and other settings outside of the AP's office

Principle V Terms

The following terms are included in Principle V of the NAADAC Code of Ethics:

- An **instrument** is a measuring device or tool used for assessment purposes. Assessment instruments can be formal or informal, with formal assessments offering standardized means for scoring, making them more objective than informal assessment instruments.
- **Usability** is determined by the level of ease associated with the administration and interpretation of an assessment tool.
- **Validity** refers to an assessment instrument's accuracy. Valid instruments accurately measure variables identified by the clinician. Content validity refers to the level of accuracy attained when measuring a specific, targeted construct.
- **Reliability** is the ability of an instrument to consistently measure what it intends to measure.

Test Instrument Usability

To determine an instrument's usability, consider the following questions:

- How long does the instrument take to administer?
- How easy and clear are the instrument's directions for administration?
- Have there been any problems associated with its use?
- Are there other similar instruments?
- Is it easy to score?

Conducting Culturally Sensitive Assessments and Evaluations

Ethical considerations for conducting **culturally sensitive assessments** and evaluations include the following:

- APs are obligated to use valid and reliable assessment instruments for individuals with SUD and co-occurring mental disorders. APs consider individual and cultural contexts and understand that assessment tools are only one component of the clinical evaluation. APs use multiple instruments to help provide a diagnosis, synthesize findings, or provide recommendations.
- APs exercise caution when selecting and using assessment instruments and practices in which the standardization group differs from that of the client. Supervision and/or consultation must be sought when assessment instruments are not normed on the client's cultural group. APs document the instrument's limitations and include other salient factors when interpreting assessment results.
- APs consider cultural contexts during the intake, assessment, and diagnosis process of treatment. APs understand that the client's culture influences how he or she processes, conceptualizes, and forms his or her experiences, beliefs, values, and attitudes.
- APs are ethically responsible for recognizing the adverse implications of historical trauma and discrimination, including consequential medical mistrust, stereotyping, and the pathologizing of specific individuals and groups.
- APs consider the client's cultural identities when treating clients and referring them for mental health and SUD treatment.
- APs use linguistically appropriate and culturally fair assessment instruments to provide contextually driven interpretations and explanations.

Ethical Values Related to Assessment, Evaluation, and Interpretation

The following ethical values are associated with assessment, evaluation, and interpretation:

- **Competency:** APs have the training and skills necessary for appropriately providing assessment, evaluation, and interpretation techniques.
- **Integrity:** APs remain honest and transparent when explaining the purpose of the assessment and how the results will be used. This explanation takes place before beginning the assessment and evaluation process.
- **Confidentiality:** APs are responsible for administering assessments in a confidential environment free from distraction. All assessment data are kept confidential unless a signed release of information is provided.
- **Objectivity:** APs remain objective when interpreting test results and provide accurate and honest reports to appropriate third parties.
- **Candor:** APs are forthcoming about how assessment results will be used, and they refrain from misusing the findings.
- **Beneficence:** APs understand that clients have the right to hear the results of an assessment, and the provider must present the results in a manner that does not cause harm to the client.

Ethical Components of Informed Consent When Providing Forensic Evaluations

The ethical components of informed consent when conducting forensic evaluations include the following:

- APs must inform the client—verbally and in writing—of the nature, purpose, and conditions of the forensic evaluation.
- APs inform clients on the nature of the relationship between the evaluator and client, including an understanding that the evaluation is not intended to be therapeutic.
- Before administering the evaluation, APs are obligated to disclose which persons or entities will receive the findings. APs secure appropriate releases when providing results to courts unless there is a court order waiving this requirement.
- Before administering the evaluation, APs are obligated to obtain written consent from a guardian to evaluate a child or an adult who lacks the capacity to voluntarily agree to the evaluation.
- APs do not conduct forensic evaluations on family members, coworkers, current or former clients, friends, spouses, or partners.
- APs report objective findings and use aggregate data to form conclusions. APs refrain from offering unsubstantiated and biased personal opinions when interpreting the evaluation results.

Selecting a Valid and Reliable Assessment Instrument

APs' ethical responsibilities for selecting a valid and reliable assessment instrument include the following:

- APs make every effort to use valid and reliable assessment instruments. Sound psychometric assessments are normed on the population being tested. When a client's cultural differences are not represented in the normed population, APs document the instrument's limitations, seek supervision and/or consultation, and document their recommendations.
- APs only administer assessment instruments and interpret findings if they have received the proper training. This also applies to technological assessments. APs receive specific training to ensure that the chosen technological assessments function correctly and measure the construct that they intend to measure.
- APs consider the validity and reliability of chosen instruments, including the instrument's limitations. Multiple assessment modalities must be chosen when providing a diagnosis, recommendations, or conclusions.

Distance Counseling, and Synchronous and Asynchronous Forms of E-Therapy and E-Supervision

E-therapy and e-supervision, also known as **distance counseling**, use telephones and computers to provide synchronous and asynchronous counseling, supervision, and consultation in separate or remote settings. APs ensure that the technology being used is compliant with all agency, organization, and **HIPAA standards of practice.**

Synchronous services take place in real time and involve interactive communication. **Asynchronous services** do not take place in real time; instead, they involve alternative modes of distance counseling. E-therapy and e-supervision use synchronous, asynchronous, or both platforms to deliver services. Text and instant messaging are mediums that are considered both synchronous and asynchronous, since it can be a rapid exchange or a staggered series of messages with more substantial gaps between them.

Examples of **synchronous services** include:

- Texting
- Instant messaging
- Online chatting
- Real-time, video-based services; webcams
- Land-line telephone services
- Mobile phone services

Examples of **asynchronous services** include:

- Emailing
- Faxing
- Texting
- Instant messaging
- Intranet services
- Discussion forums

Benefits Associated with Distance Counseling

Benefits of distance counseling include the following:

- The ability to bring services to individuals residing in underserved locations where access to traditional services is limited or obsolete
- The chance to provide psychoeducation and group services to culturally diverse individuals
- The ability to offer accessible services for individuals with physical disorders (e.g., mobility restrictions) or psychological disorders (e.g., agoraphobia)
- The elimination of travel costs and parking costs; less time spent away from work
- The chance to offer services to those who would otherwise not ordinarily seek traditional counseling due to factors such as stigma
- The ability to cut down on wait times for initial intake appointments
- Greater flexibility for the client and the AP
- The chance to strengthen continuity of care in the event of possible service disruptions, including client or AP relocation

Limitations Associated with Distance Counseling

Limitations associated with distance counseling include the following:

- Concerns over confidentiality due to parameters and procedures that differ from those associated with traditional counseling
- Difficulty creating and maintaining a solid client-counselor working relationship
- Difficulty assessing nonverbal cues when using specific platforms
- Rapidly evolving licensure jurisdiction and practices, including interstate practices for distance counseling
- Considerations associated with crisis and emergency situations, particularly when the AP is inaccessible

Technology-Assisted Care (TAC)

Technology-assisted care (TAC) offers delivery options across the entire continuum of client care, beginning with an initial intake and extending through termination. Common settings, methods, modalities, and options for the ethical provision of distance counseling and TAC include the following:

- **Settings:** TAC can be offered in a variety of settings, including inpatient and outpatient SUD and mental health treatment centers, private practices, schools, and correctional facilities.
- **Modality:** TAC can be delivered to individuals, groups, couples, and family systems. Electronic communication can also be used for case management services.
- **Methods** for providing e-therapy include telephone-based services, email, text messages, chat-based services, video-based services, social networking, self-directed technology-based services, and video tutorials.
- **Client service options:** APs can help clients access secure online apps used to learn coping skills, access 12-step meetings, track behaviors (e.g., diet, sleep), obtain published information from trusted sources, or check medication interactions.
- **Counselor service options:** Counselors can use technology to obtain education, training, consultation, and/or supervision.

Ethical Use of Technology, Social Media, and Distance Counseling

Methods used to provide relevant knowledge and skills include professional development, seminars, webinars, trainings, classes, and/or supervision. Learning objectives for APs' ethical use of technology, social media, and distance counseling include the following:

- Demonstrate knowledge of the proper and effective use of technology.
- Understand and abide by the ethical and legal factors unique to distance counseling and the use of technology. APs are subject to federal and state laws on interstate practices and must follow mandates applicable to APs' and their clients' state of residency.
- Demonstrate knowledge of evidence-based TAC.
- Understand the need to document distance counseling regulations and standards of care in clients' charts to mitigate provider risk and enhance client safety.
- Demonstrate knowledge of the legal and ethical regulatory guidelines for accessing, storing, maintaining, transmitting, and disposing of confidential and secure client information and records. This can be accomplished, in part, by using encrypted, cloud-based, or virtual private network services.
- Demonstrate compliance with HIPAA and other federal, state, organizational, and regulatory provisions regarding confidentiality and privileged communication.

INFORMED CONSENT UNIQUE TO E-THERAPY

There are several **elements unique to an electronic informed consent** (i.e., technology-inclusive disclosures) for clients, including, but not limited to, the following:

- Procedures for emergency and crisis services
- Service delivery in the event of technology failure
- Response time for asynchronous communication
- AP boundaries established for technology-based communication
- Cultural or language accommodations
- Secured methods for providing services (text or email-based therapy services are not considered secure); APs discourage clients from sharing passwords and other online accounts or email services with other family members
- Insurance coverage for e-services
- The effect of missed cues on the counseling process
- AP availability times
- Social media policies, including friend-request denials
- Confidentiality, privacy, and security limitations with electronic communication
- Identity verification
- The use of HIPAA-compliant servers
- The right to refuse electronic delivery of services
- Links to the AP's license and certification boards

CLIENT/SUPERVISEE CONSIDERATIONS FOR THE ETHICAL USE OF DISTANCE COUNSELING

APs and supervisors must determine whether the client/supervisee can use technology and if technological services are appropriate. Considerations for the client/supervisee's **capacity to receive distance counseling** include the following:

- The recipient's intellectual and developmental functioning
- The client's past or current mental health issues, including a history of violence, diagnosis, previous treatment, the potential for self-injurious behavior, and past or present substance misuse
- The recipient's communication skills
- The recipient's technological competency, including the ability to appropriately access and use selected electronic platforms
- The recipient's ability to access necessary technology, including accessibility for clients with disabilities; when appropriate, APs comply with Section 508 of the Rehabilitation Act (29 USC 794d) and make technology accessible to clients and supervisees with disabilities
- The recipient's support system, community supports, and closest emergency facility or hospital

STATE AND FEDERAL LAWS APPLICABLE TO DISTANCE COUNSELING

APs must comply with state and federal laws applicable to distance counseling. According to the NAADAC/NCC AP Ethical Standards (2021), "Addiction professionals comply with relevant licensing laws in the jurisdiction where the provider/clinical supervisor is physically located when providing care and where the client/supervisee is located when receiving care."

Emergency management protocols shall depend entirely on the location at which the client/supervisee receives services. During the informed consent process, providers shall notify their clients/supervisees of the legal rights and limitations governing the practice of counseling/supervision across state lines or international boundaries. Providers shall advise clients that mandatory reporting and related ethical requirements, such as the duty to warn/notify, shall be governed by the jurisdiction in which the client/supervisee is receiving services.

Ethical Components of Informed Consent for the Supervisor/Supervisee Relationship

Ethical components of **informed consent for the supervisor/supervisee relationship and supervision contract** include, but are not limited to, the following:

- The nature, duration, and conditions for obtaining, maintaining, and terminating the supervisor/supervisee relationship
- Selected supervision techniques, formats, types, methods, and approaches
- Supervisor and supervisee expectations and responsibilities, the benefits of carrying liability insurance, no-show fees, procedures for clinical emergencies, and conflict resolution
- Formal and informal means for evaluation, including the supervisor's responsibility for providing timely, accurate, and constructive feedback
- Means for monitoring the supervisee's professional development and the welfare of the supervisee's clients
- Client disclosure forms identifying students in training and how this status affects client confidentiality

Ethical Processes and Procedures Associated with Supervisory Oversight

Supervisors are ethically obligated to provide appropriate oversight for disclosures, boundaries, impairment, and multicultural practices, including, but not limited to, the following:

- Supervisors receive clinical supervision training before supervising APs.
- Supervisees must notify supervisors before disclosing personal addiction and recovery information with a client and must document any recommendations. Self-disclosures must benefit the AP-client relationship rather than the supervisee.
- Supervisors clearly outline professional, personal, and social boundaries with supervisees, students, and interns. Supervisors do not enter into romantic/sexual relationships or friendships with current or past supervisees, students, or interns.
- Supervisors monitor themselves and their supervisees for signs of physical, mental, or emotional impairment and take necessary steps to protect clients from resultant harm.
- Supervisors closely monitor and document the ongoing evaluation of supervisees whose limitations interfere with client care, including corrective actions and/or referrals for counseling. Supervisors provide honest and accurate supervisee appraisals based on clearly stated criteria.
- Supervisors are responsible for helping supervisees provide ethical, evidence-based services with individuals from multicultural populations and in diverse settings. Clinical supervisors model cultural humility and address the role of multiculturalism within the supervisor-supervisee relationship.

Encountering Another's Unethical Behavior

APs have an ethical obligation to have **open and honest conversations** with other professionals displaying unethical conduct. The recommended course of action differs when encountering violations with harm and violations without harm.

Considerations for the unethical behavior of another AP resulting in client harm include the following:

- The AP must treat violations involving harm and violations involving threats of harm equally.
- The AP must act quickly and professionally, beginning with an open dialogue with the other AP.
- The AP must obtain consultation and/or supervision and document the recommended course of action, including whether or not to file an official complaint.
- The AP must report all violations of harm to the appropriate licensing or certification authorities, federal and/or state governing authorities, and NAADAC.

For ethical violations that do not result in client harm, the AP informally discusses the behavior with the other professional unless doing so would violate client confidentiality.

Addressing Complaints of Alleged Ethical Misconduct

The **NAADAC and NCC AP committees** have jurisdiction and authority to investigate reports of **unethical misconduct** on behalf of APs applying for NAADAC membership, APs with a current NAADAC membership, and APs with an NCC AP certification. NAADAC also has the authority to issue rulings and to take disciplinary action when necessary. Relevant principles include the following:

- **Principle VIII-6:** APs are required to **participate** in implementing the NAADAC/NCC AP Code of Ethics. APs must also abide by any disciplinary action associated with noncompliance. Failure to participate is an ethical violation.
- **Principle VIII-7:** APs must help enforce the NAADAC Code of Ethics and **cooperate** with any actions of ethics committees of NAADAC and NCC AP or other professional organizations or boards of certification.
- **Principle VIII-14:** APs help enforce the NAADAC Code of Ethics by refraining from initiating a complaint or grievance as a form of **retaliation** against another person.

Role of Clinical Supervisors in the Ethical Decision-Making Process

Clinical supervisors play a vital role in the ethical decision-making process. Clinical supervisors serve as **gatekeepers** for ethical and legal issues, act as **role models**, and partake in professional development and ongoing training to maintain **clinical competence**. When an AP is faced with an ethical dilemma that he or she cannot resolve informally, the supervisee is obligated to discuss the issue with a supervisor and/or consultant. The supervisor and/or consultant considers **ethical standards of practice** and the **AP's scope of practice** during ethical decision making.

Clinical supervisors must avoid direct liability and vicarious liability.

- Direct liability results from the supervisor neglecting their role in the decision-making process as evidenced by "not making a reasonable effort to supervise."
- Vicarious liability results from the supervisee's dereliction of duty. The supervisor is responsible for the clinical work of the supervisee as well as the overall welfare and safety of the supervisee's clients. Therefore, supervisors must remain vigilant for any potential acts of violence by each supervisee's clients and understand the duty-to-warn process.

Responding to an Ethics, Licensing/Certification, or Malpractice Complaint

The process of responding to an ethics, licensing/certification, or malpractice complaint begins with prevention. APs can avoid costly pitfalls by carrying professional liability insurance. Professional liability insurance may also include access to an experienced malpractice attorney. It is important to seek representation from an attorney well versed in federal and state malpractice laws in the state in which the complaint originated.

When an AP is the recipient of a grievance or complaint, the first step is to seek clinical supervision. Establishing an initial supervisory relationship based on trust helps the provider conduct an honest self-appraisal of the ethical concern. APs receiving a complaint may experience shock, self-doubt, or anxiety. An appropriate response is thoughtful, informed, intentional, and effective.

Additional considerations for responding to a grievance or complaint include the following:

- Refrain from responding hastily—immediately contact a supervisor, consultant, and/or attorney for guidance.
- Do not ignore the investigation or take it lightly.
- Refrain from contacting the client or person filing the complaint.
- Do not turn over records before seeking legal counsel.
- Understand that the process may take time to resolve.
- Seek support and engage in self-care.
- Help the attorney understand any underlying thoughts or reasoning behind the actions under scrutiny.

Ethical Considerations Outlined in Principle IX

APs are encouraged to conduct research and publish "evidence-based and outcome-driven practices that guide the profession" (NAADAC/NCC AP Code of Ethics, 2021). The ethical standards for research and publication also apply to **e-publishing**, including professional and social media posts. APs promote **optimal functioning** for **diverse populations** in addiction and recovery. Researchers pledge to **accurately report data** in a manner consistent with ethical standards, federal and state board expectations, and internal review board standards, including disclosing any **potential conflicts of interest** and ensuring that the data reported are **free from distortion, bias, or manipulation**.

APs who publish research material must give **direct and indirect credit** to individuals contributing to the publication. APs refrain from **plagiarism** and do not **withhold data** required to substantiate and **verify** research claims. Using copyrighted materials without the original publisher's consent is considered **theft.** APs create a **written plan to transfer** research data in the event of their own death, incapacitation, or job departure. Lastly, it is the researcher's responsibility to ensure that his or her material is advertised truthfully and that manuscripts are submitted to one journal or publication at a time.

RIGHTS OF RESEARCH PARTICIPANTS

Researchers seek to protect and safeguard the rights of participants, especially in situations that deviate from ordinary standards of practice. Researchers uphold ethical standards and practices by honoring the rights of research participants, including, but not limited to, the following:

- **Confidentiality:** Participants have the right for their data and research contributions to remain confidential.
- **Welfare:** Researchers honor the ethical principles of fidelity and nonmaleficence to promote the safety and welfare of participants.
- **Informed consent:** Researchers ensure that participants have not been coerced and have the right to decline requests or terminate involvement at any time. When **students, supervisees, or clients** wish to become participants, researchers ensure that their participation does not jeopardize their academic standing and/or professional relationship.
- **Explanation:** Researchers must provide participants with an explanation of their findings.
- **Data abstraction:** Researchers intentionally disguise participants' identifying data unless consent grants the researchers permission to do otherwise.

ADC Practice Test

Want to take this practice test in an online interactive format?
Check out the bonus page, which includes interactive practice questions and much more: **https://www.mometrix.com/bonus948/adc**

Refer to the following for questions 1-4:

Samuel attends individual therapy at a substance use treatment facility as part of his aftercare plan. He has a long history of methamphetamine (MA) use, which initially required medically supervised withdrawal. During his initial interview, Samuel reported experiencing hallucinations in which demons in the form of shapes would taunt him whenever he left the house. He told the intake counselor that he had become paranoid, depressed, and suicidal.

Samuel has used alcohol, cocaine, and stimulants in the past but primarily desires the effects of smoking MA. Prior to admission, he had engaged in heavy MA use for several months, which involved continuous use of MA for approximately 1 week, causing him to go several nights without sleep. Once the substance was stopped, he experienced an unpleasant crash. During those times, his partner described him as a real Dr. Jekyll and Mr. Hyde because he "goes from being a decent guy to someone who is unpredictable and explosive." During this phase, Samuel craved more and more MA when he was unable to attain the high that he desired.

Today, he meets with his counselor and reports that he continues to experience psychosis after abstinence. They review his treatment plan and assess his ongoing needs. Samuel would like to take steps to repair his relationship with his partner. He is concerned about his sexual health and requests additional services to address those needs. Samuel is committed to ongoing therapy and would like to learn how to manage persistent symptoms of psychosis. He is connected with a case manager to help him find specialized behavioral health treatment.

1. Compared to cocaine, MAs:

a. Are metabolized at a much faster rate
b. Are metabolized at a much slower rate
c. Have plasma concentration levels that peak and decline more rapidly
d. Have plasma concentration levels that remain steady

2. Samuel's symptoms of psychosis have persisted after a period of abstinence. These symptoms have the potential to last a maximum period of:

a. Days
b. Weeks
c. Months
d. Years

3. After Samuel goes several days without sleep, Samuel's partner describes him as "unpredictable and explosive," and he requires more MA to attain a desired high and avoid withdrawal. This physical and physiological state is commonly referred to as:

a. Delirium
b. Tweaking
c. Pharming
d. A bender

4. Recreational MA use is correlated with increased rates of sexually transmitted infections (e.g., human immunodeficiency virus [HIV]):

a. Only when injected
b. Only when smoked
c. Only when snorted
d. Through any route of administration

5. Compared to females, which is true of male drinking patterns?

a. Males are less likely to report excessive alcohol use.
b. Males are less likely to die as a consequence of alcohol use.
c. Males aged 12–17 are less likely to have alcohol use disorder.
d. Males have lower instances of alcohol-related hospitalizations.

6. An addiction counselor with 6 months of sobriety actively attends Narcotics Anonymous (NA) meetings and is eager to share his success. During an initial intake, the counselor meets a client with SUD with the same ethnicity and gender as the counselor. The client has been hesitant to attend NA. The counselor should:

a. Self-disclose as a way to offer hope to a culturally similar client
b. Support the client in his own pathway of recovery
c. Provide information on NA and allow the client to make an informed decision
d. Self-disclose and offer to meet the client at a local NA meeting

7. Individuals with opioid use disorder (OUD) wishing to attain a longer-lasting heroin high engage in which one of the following methods of heroin administration?

a. Injecting
b. Smoking
c. Snorting
d. Oral ingestion

8. In motivational interviewing (MI), what is the role of the counselor?

a. An expert, providing unilateral direction and guidance
b. A subordinate, primarily listening and reflecting
c. A coach or consultant, asking key questions for learning
d. An authority figure, creating a professional treatment plan

Refer to the following for questions 9-12:

The client is a 26-year-old female who presents for an initial assessment with reports of depression, isolation, anhedonia, and a history of drug and alcohol use. She is accompanied by her mother, who expresses a concern that the client has been misusing opioids after a period of abstinence and fears that the client will overdose. The client was previously in two separate treatment programs for opioid use disorder. The client received methadone as part of a detox program. She reports maintaining sobriety, but she was recently fired from her job when a random urine drug screen detected methadone, which registered positive for opioid use.

The client began using drugs and alcohol at age 14. She has a history of polysubstance use, including alcohol, stimulants, and heroin. This progressed to frequent heroin use beginning 2 years ago, after a sexual assault. The client was walking home from a bar late one evening when she was approached by a group of acquaintances. The client has little recollection of the encounter due to severe alcohol intoxication; she recalls that, when she woke up early that morning, she did not know where she was, but she recalls bits and pieces of the assault. She did not report the abuse to the police, has stated that she continues to feel shame, and blames herself for the incident.

The client reports that she continues to remain sober for the most part but has not complied with her inpatient aftercare plans. She states that she didn't like 12-step programs and just "gave up" after losing her dream job as a veterinary technician. This has contributed to sadness and anhedonia. She currently admits to heavy alcohol use and occasional misuse of prescription opioids; however, she believes that her heroin use is under control. She agrees to counseling to help with depression, but she states that she does not want to re-engage with treatment for drug and alcohol use. The client also states that she has worked hard to put the sexual assault behind her and is not open to processing past trauma, stating that this has been a trigger for increased substance use and sleeplessness in the past.

9. The counselor is looking for an assessment tool that would assess the client's drug and alcohol use in the past 30 days in the following domains: medical, employment, legal, family, and interpersonal status. Which instrument would meet these qualifications?

a. The Prescription Opioid Misuse Index
b. The Opioid Risk Tool
c. The Addiction Severity Index
d. The Tobacco, Alcohol, Prescription Medication, and Other Substance Use (TAPS) tool

10. When used in isolation, a standardized risk assessment for opioid use is found to be superior to which one of the following?

a. Collateral reports
b. Urine drug screen
c. Mental status exam
d. Biopsychosocial assessment

11. Harm reduction strategies for opioid use disorder are least compatible with which one of the following?

a. 12-step group philosophies
b. Psychosocial programs
c. Community reinforcement
d. Methadone maintenance

12. The client likely has a co-occurring mental disorder. Of the following choices, which diagnosis is most likely?

a. Acute stress disorder
b. Major depressive disorder
c. Post-traumatic stress disorder
d. Bipolar I disorder

13. The NAADAC Code of Ethics (2021) states that addiction professionals (APs) must first disclose the legal and ethical limits of confidentiality during which of the following?

a. When informed consent is provided
b. When the treatment plan is formulated
c. When access to client records is requested
d. When an initial intake evaluation appointment is requested

14. When experiencing mental health concerns, from whom are racial and ethnic minorities LEAST likely to seek help?

a. A primary care physician
b. A counselor
c. Religious clergy
d. A traditional healer

15. The American Society of Addiction Medicine (ASAM) views addiction as:

a. An acute medical disease
b. A treatable medical disease
c. A psychosocial medical disease
d. A developmental medical disease

16. Careful assessment of suicidal and non-suicidal self-injury (NSSI) is conducted to help providers clearly articulate limitations to confidentiality. Which one of the following is least likely to qualify as NSSI?

a. Cutting
b. Scratching
c. Biting
d. Piercings

17. When a counselor asks, "Did you always feel this way?" it is an example of:

a. Probing
b. Reframing
c. Clarification
d. Open-ended questioning

18. Your client does not seem to be meeting treatment goals after a substantial period of time in therapy. What should you do?

a. Terminate therapy
b. Terminate therapy and refer the client to another therapist
c. Continue therapy
d. Document that the patient is not improving and continue treatment

19. A 32-year-old female client with OUD recently checked out of an intensive outpatient treatment center against medical advice. The client's counselor, who the treatment center employs, terminated services without providing the client with a referral. Which one of the following is likely true of the counselor's conduct?

a. The counselor acted unethically by abandoning the client.
b. The counselor acted ethically by respecting the client's autonomy.
c. The counselor acted unethically by not remaining objective.
d. The counselor acted ethically by honoring nonmaleficence.

20. There are multiple pathways of recovery. Which one of the following is an example of a nonclinical pathway?

a. Equine therapy
b. Relapse prevention
c. Contingency management
d. Education/collegiate recovery programs

21. Trauma-informed care requires a shift from a pathology-oriented perspective to a resilience-oriented perspective. This is reflected by asking the client:

a. "What is wrong with you?"
b. "What has happened to you?"
c. "How long have you had these feelings?"
d. "How can I help you today?"

22. Which one of the following effects occurs when a person undergoes significant clinical and functional impairment from neuronal adaptation after repeated substance use?

a. Intoxication
b. Withdrawal
c. Dependence
d. Tolerance

23. Which one of the following is an example of person-centered language?

a. The client suffers from alcoholism.
b. The client is a person who is unqualified to parent.
c. The client is a person in recovery.
d. The client is an addict who experienced trauma.

24. Which one of the following is based on the transtheoretical model of behavioral change?

a. Drug Abuse Screening Test
b. Drug Use Decisional Balance Scale
c. Substance Abuse Subtle Screening Inventory
d. Adult Substance Use Survey

25. Which one of the following can be detected on a urine drug screen after 7 days from the last use?

a. Amphetamines
b. Short-acting benzodiazepines
c. Cocaine
d. Phencyclidine

26. The purposes of counselor self-disclosures include all of the following EXCEPT:

a. Mitigating a therapeutic impasse
b. Validating the client's experience
c. Fostering the counselor's professional confidence
d. Conveying to clients that they are not alone

27. Which one of the following is NOT a form of counselor self-disclosure?

a. A counselor's social media postings
b. A counselor's framed diploma
c. A counselor's tattoos
d. A counselor's wedding ring

28. According to the NAADAC Code of Ethics (2021), APs have an ethical responsibility to address societal prejudice, stereotypes, misconceptions, and stigma toward individuals with substance use disorder through which of the following?

a. Providing research and evidence-based practices
b. Engaging in self-care and cultural humility
c. Legislative and educational advocacy
d. Active collaboration with other healthcare professionals

Refer to the following for questions 29-32:

Kennedy and Sara recently took a 7-day cruise to Greece and Italy to celebrate their 10th wedding anniversary. They have been together for 14 years and were married 10 years ago, after same-sex marriage became legal. The couple shares custody of their son from Sara's previous marriage. They requested to be seen for couples counseling after Kennedy, who had been sober for 12 years, relapsed on their vacation. Kennedy admits to a "slip" and states that she called her sponsor the next day and has not had a drink since. Sara is concerned that Kennedy is minimizing her relapse and has become increasingly upset after discovering that Kennedy had also been gambling on their trip.

Kennedy denies having a problem with gambling. She states that, before the cruise, she had gone to horse races and casinos, where she placed $2 bets or casually played the slot machines. Kennedy relays that she decided to play roulette on the cruise. After the ball landed on black 10 consecutive times, she placed all of her money on red. When the next roll came up black, she lost a substantial amount of money. Kennedy is frustrated with Sara for "making a big deal out of nothing," believing that Sara is "just looking for a reason to be upset."

During their first session, the counselor determines that Kennedy is being treated for bipolar I disorder and is working with a psychiatrist to regulate her medication. Kennedy has a history of AUD and is also a smoker. Sara has been diagnosed with depression but states that it is well managed with medication. She drinks sporadically and does not use other substances. Both are committed to their relationship; however, Sara is adamant about "not dragging my son through this again" because her ex-husband has been in and out of rehab for SUD. The counselor works to engage the couple, notably Kennedy, to further explore relevant issues.

29. The percentage of individuals diagnosed with gambling disorder who also have a mental disorder is nearly:

a. 25%
b. 50%
c. 75%
d. 100%

30. Kennedy would NOT be assigned the diagnosis of gambling disorder if her gambling behavior is found to be:

a. Influenced by her alcohol use
b. Better explained by the symptoms of her mental disorder
c. Financed only through legal versus illegal activities (e.g., theft, embezzlement)
d. Mentally distressing anytime within the past 12 months

31. The counselor seeks to engage Kennedy in the counseling process to help ensure that the couple will return and adhere to treatment. This can best be accomplished by the counselor:

a. Asking open-ended questions
b. Affirming her desire to change
c. Reassuring her that she will be okay
d. Providing information on smoking cessation

32. Kennedy engages in irrational thinking when playing roulette at the casino. This is an example of:

a. The halo effect
b. The gambler's fallacy
c. The bottom-dollar effect
d. The cashless effect

33. The primary purpose of person-centered language is to:

a. Reduce stigma
b. Increase self-esteem
c. Improve access to treatment
d. Underscore personal responsibility

34. Clients who know that they must stop using substances can vacillate between wanting and not wanting to change for extended periods, even years. These same clients may still be using substances but are considering a change soon. Using Prochaska and DiClemente's stages of change model, these clients would be in the:

a. Maintenance stage
b. Preparation stage
c. Precontemplation stage
d. Contemplation stage

35. The primary purpose of a harm reduction model of care is to:

a. Enhance client decision-making skills
b. Promote abstinence-based principles
c. Decrease rates of severe mental illness
d. Reduce client mortality and morbidity rates

36. Which stage of addiction is characterized by cravings and deficits in executive functioning?

a. Intoxication
b. Binge
c. Preoccupation/anticipation
d. Withdrawal/negative effect

Refer to the following for questions 37-40:

Jamie is a 24-year-old server at a local restaurant and bar who identifies as genderqueer and uses the pronouns they/them. Jamie seeks counseling for symptoms of depression and anxiety. The counselor uses various evidence-based screening instruments, including a screener for suicidality. Jamie's responses to the counselor's selected questionnaire indicate that, in the past few weeks, there were periods when they wished they were dead, periods when they felt like their family would be better off if they were dead, and periods when they wanted to kill themselves. The screening instrument also indicates that Jamie has no history of suicide attempts and is not presently considering killing themselves.

Jamie explains that their depression and anxiety worsened 2 months ago after an episode at work. They explained that they were closing the bar around 2:00 AM when a group of drunk and belligerent men approached them. Jamie states, "Earlier that night, the men kept asking me if I had a penis and which sexual positions I preferred. The more they drank, the cruder they became. I tried to ignore them but eventually had a coworker take over their tab." Jamie begins to cry as they recount taking out the trash and seeing the men approach from the back alley. A confrontation ensued at which time Jamie was struck repeatedly with a pistol, as each of the men took turns sexually assaulting them.

Since the incident, Jamie has had difficulty sleeping and has been unable to return to work. They have experienced nightmares and distressing memories and have begun to cope by using alcohol daily. Jamie is hypervigilant and has had difficulty concentrating. Jamie did not report the incident because "I know from experience that nothing would be done about it, or worse, they wouldn't believe me. I'm not ready to put myself through that." Since the assault, Jamie feels like no one can be trusted.

37. Jamie identifies as genderqueer, meaning:

a. They are fluid with their sexual orientation.
b. They do not subscribe to conventional gender binary distinctions.
c. They were born with both male and female genitalia and internal sex organs.
d. Their external appearance (e.g., clothing, behavior) does not conform to their assigned gender.

38. Which evidence-based screening instrument was administered by Jamie's counselor?

a. ASQ
b. PHQ
c. BDI
d. CAGE

39. Given the information presented, which DSM diagnosis would the counselor likely assign?

a. Acute stress disorder
b. Post-traumatic stress disorder
c. Generalized anxiety disorder
d. Major depressive disorder

40. Which one of the following counselor statements would best affirm Jamie's gender identity?

a. "My pronouns are she/her/hers."
b. "Your preferred pronouns are important to me."
c. "It doesn't matter which pronouns you use for me."
d. "It's really hard for me to get used to using the pronoun 'they.'"

Refer to the following for questions 41-44:

Clyde is a 32-year-old graphic designer who lives with his girlfriend of 2.5 years, Faith. Clyde met Faith on a dating website, and they bonded over their love of craft beer, nature, and hiking. Faith became concerned that Clyde had become increasingly hostile and moody 6 months ago. Around the same time, she began to notice unpaid bills and that Clyde would go for days without sleeping.

After an especially explosive argument, Faith confronted Clyde and learned that he had been smoking and snorting cocaine and amphetamines. Clyde vowed to change but continued to use. He eventually lost his job, and they received notice that their house was in danger of foreclosure. Clyde begged for forgiveness and consented to regular urine drug screens. The results of confirmatory drug screens indicated the presence of cocaine, amphetamines, and opioids. Clyde emphatically denied purchasing or using opioids.

Faith reached her point of desperation and arranged an intervention. A trained professional helped Faith hold a safe and conflict-free intervention with the goal of repairing family relationships through psychoeducation and contingency management. Faith was also led to Al-Anon, and she learned to lead a purposeful life independent of Clyde's recovery status. She continued enjoying hiking and other outdoor activities. This gave Clyde the space and time to work on his sobriety and engage with a recovery community of his own.

41. The effects produced by cocaine last longest with which method of administration?

a. Injecting
b. Smoking
c. Snorting
d. Swallowing

42. Cocaine is classified as a:

a. Schedule I drug
b. Schedule II drug
c. Schedule III drug
d. Schedule IV drug

43. Clyde's confirmatory drug screen indicates the presence of cocaine, MA, and opioids, but Clyde denied using opioids. Which one of the following is a likely explanation?

a. Clyde's urine sample was tampered with or adulterated.
b. Clyde used opioids but had no memory of doing so.
c. Clyde purchased stimulants contaminated with opioids.
d. Clyde's pattern of drug use resulted in a broad therapeutic index.

44. The trained professional assisting Faith with the intervention likely specializes in which one of the following?

a. The Johnson method of intervention
b. Unilateral family therapy
c. Relapse prevention
d. Crisis counseling

45. In screening clients, what does a cutoff score refer to?

a. A criteria-based score beyond which a client must be turned away
b. The threshold above which a more thorough assessment is indicated
c. A score that is incomplete, having been cut off prematurely
d. The final score that supersedes any other screening score obtained

Refer to the following for questions 46-49:

An employee assistance program counselor assesses a 28-year-old male for alcohol use disorder (AUD). The client is employed by an insurance agency, and he works from home reviewing claims. After receiving his second DUI charge, the client was referred to an employee assistance program. He believes that he should not have received a DUI charge because he was not driving but instead was found asleep in the driver's seat of his vehicle. His blood alcohol concentration (BAC) was 0.23. He reports that his first DUI occurred after an altercation with his then-girlfriend 3 years ago. He has never been married and states that he goes on a few dates a month but is not interested in settling down. The client refused to sign a release form authorizing the counselor to communicate with his employer because of the "ridiculousness of these bogus charges."

The client is the youngest of four children and reports that his oldest brother has been in recovery for nearly 8 years. The client is familiar with Alcoholics Anonymous and 12-step programs through his brother but has no interest in "sitting in a dark church whining about my problems." He admits that he cannot picture himself without alcohol but believes he can control his drinking.

The client states that he has struggled with depression "off and on" and was hospitalized as an adolescent for a suicide attempt but did not provide any further details. He displays an irritable affect and states that he should not have to attend counseling. After the assessment, the counselor contacted the client's employer, limiting the discussion to the client's confirmed diagnosis of AUD and his resistance toward attending future sessions. The counselor recommended that the client attend 90 AA meetings in 90 days instead of participating in counseling. The counselor provided this recommendation to the client's employer in writing, along with statements of his diagnosis and the client's refusal to participate.

46. The counselor chose to administer the Alcohol Use Disorders Identification Test-Concise (AUDIT-C) to screen for alcohol use disorder (AUD). All of the following questions are included in the AUDIT-C EXCEPT:

a. How often did you have a drink containing alcohol in the past year?
b. Have you ever had a drink first thing in the morning to steady your nerves or get rid of a hangover?
c. How many drinks did you have on a typical day when you were drinking in the past year?
d. How often did you have six or more drinks on one occasion in the past year?

47. Which one of the following symptoms is associated with a BAC of 0.23?

a. An overall feeling of well-being, lowered inhibitions, and relaxation
b. Needing assistance with walking, dysphoria, and vomiting
c. Gross disorientation and loss of consciousness
d. Coma and potential for respiratory arrest and death

48. How does the Alcoholics Anonymous (AA) program differ from the Rational Recovery (RR) approach?

a. AA emphasizes an admission of powerlessness, whereas RR emphasized personal control over addiction.
b. AA advocates for controlled drinking, whereas RR was abstinence-based.
c. AA believes addiction is not a progressive disease, whereas RR did not.
d. AA leaders are trained volunteers, whereas RR was led by its members.

49. Which choice best describes the counselor's adherence to the NAADAC (the Association for Addiction Professionals) Code of Ethics (2021) regarding mandated clients?

a. The counselor acted ethically by limiting recommendations and interventions to the problems outlined by the client's employer.
b. The counselor acted ethically by recommending AA as an alternative to counseling.
c. The counselor acted unethically by not including family members and collateral sources.
d. The counselor acted unethically when disclosing the client's diagnosis and his resistance to treatment to his employer without a signed release of information form.

50. Which one of the following is true of adverse childhood experiences (ACEs)?

a. The likelihood of negative behavioral health outcomes decreases as the number of ACEs increases.
b. Although adverse effects are not preventable, interventions can reduce the adverse effects of ACEs.
c. Sexual and physical abuse are associated with greater instances of SUDs than other ACEs.
d. ACEs are traumatic events that happen before the age of 21.

51. Group cohesion is to group therapy as:

a. Self-disclosure is to individual therapy
b. Collaboration is to individual therapy
c. The therapeutic alliance is to individual therapy
d. Autonomy is to individual therapy

52. A client experiencing opiate withdrawal becomes agitated, exhibits pressured speech, and threatens an intake counselor. Which one of the following is the strongest predictor of violence for this client?

a. A history of violence toward others
b. Current symptoms and clinical presentation
c. The type of substance producing withdrawal symptoms
d. Any co-occurring diagnosis or medical condition

53. Use of benzodiazepines as a treatment for anxiety is likely NOT effective after which of the following?

a. Six weeks
b. Four months
c. One year
d. Eighteen months

54. Experts suggest that naloxone should be offered during stimulant withdrawal due to the commonly concurrent presence of which one of the following?

a. HIV infection
b. Opioid use
c. Alcohol use
d. Suicidality

55. How might a counselor help motivate a client to move into the preparation stage of Prochaska and DiClemente's stages of change model?

a. Use a decisional balance strategy
b. Ask open-ended questions
c. Offer a menu of options
d. Use an importance ruler

56. Which one of the following concepts refers to the ongoing process of self-examination and self-critique coupled with a willingness to adopt an other-oriented perspective?

a. Cultural competence
b. Cultural humility
c. Cultural encapsulation
d. Cultural awareness

57. Which of the following may occur when cocaine is used regularly at increasing doses?

a. Psychosis
b. Depression
c. Mental acuity
d. Lethargy

58. APs aspire to develop values useful for ethical decision-making, including giving back the good received from others. This refers to which one of the following?

a. Beneficence
b. Gratitude
c. Justice
d. Stewardship

59. Because of the tendency to self-medicate with CNS depressants, polysubstance detoxification is advised for individuals withdrawing from which of the following?

a. Inhalants
b. Alcohol
c. Cocaine
d. Hallucinogens

60. The phrase "Let me see if I understand so far..." is an example of:

a. Reframing
b. Interpretation
c. Summarization
d. Active listening

61. In adherence to Principle III-13 of the NAADAC (the Association for Addiction Professionals) Code of Ethics (2021), APs provide services within their scope of practice and should only offer services characterized by all of the following EXCEPT those that are:

a. Evidence-based
b. Outcome-driven
c. Trauma-informed
d. Science-based

62. Which part of the brain is responsible for a substance's rewarding and pleasurable effects?

a. Amygdala
b. Prefrontal cortex
c. Basal ganglia
d. Cerebellum

63. In the GATE model for suicidality, GATE is an acronym that stands for gather information, access supervision:

a. Take responsible action, and extend the action
b. Treatment plan construction, and evaluate the plan
c. Target suicidality, and enlist family members
d. Trauma identification, and express concerns

64. How would a counselor best address ambivalence with clients in the contemplation stage of change?

a. Normalize ambivalence
b. Explore denial as a defense mechanism
c. Uncover feelings contributing to resistance
d. Help the client develop a change plan

65. Which one of the following is a religious-based mutual help support group?

a. Celebrate Recovery
b. Women for Sobriety
c. Alcoholics Anonymous
d. LifeRing Secular Recovery

66. Stimulant use increases the production of catecholamines, which include all of the following EXCEPT:

a. Norepinephrine
b. Serotonin
c. Epinephrine
d. Dopamine

Refer to the following for questions 67-70:

Carl is a 31-year-old client referred to a behavioral health center by his case manager. The case manager explains that Carl often experiences homelessness and has been in and out of jails and psychiatric hospitals for the past 3 years. Carl recently received temporary medical care after connecting with a "street medicine" outreach program. Carl is diagnosed with bipolar disorder and does not receive his medication consistently. He is also diagnosed with epilepsy and has had difficulty accessing specialized care.

Carl explains that he was employed as a chef at a local restaurant until he began experiencing tonic-clonic seizures. He was diagnosed with epilepsy and was not permitted to drive, forcing him to quit his job. He reports that he felt depressed after losing his job and that he started binge drinking, which quickly escalated to daily drug use. Most recently, he began using crack cocaine and amphetamines. Carl states that his drug use is problematic, and he is ready to stop; however, he is not prepared to stop drinking due to a fear of withdrawal.

Carl relays that he couch surfed for a bit, lived in about a dozen homeless shelters, and was periodically on the streets. He explains that he turned to panhandling but was threatened, called derogatory names, and spit at by passersby. His arrests include refusing to leave an encampment area, verbal aggression toward police officers, and stealing from grocery stores and local businesses. He is motivated to end the cycle of homelessness and was provided with a complete biopsychosocial assessment to determine how to meet his complex behavioral health needs. He is hesitant to commit to counseling services and admits that he does not want to risk being judged for situations that previous counselors have been "simply unable to understand." Carl's concrete needs are evaluated, and various housing services are considered.

67. Carl's pattern of homelessness is categorized as:

a. Transitional
b. Chronic
c. Acute
d. Episodic

68. Carl's counselor uses the Stages of Change Readiness and Treatment Eagerness Scale (SOCRATES) to obtain more information on his desire to change, with results yielding scores in all of the following domains EXCEPT:

a. Ambivalence
b. Problem recognition
c. Personal responsibility
d. Taking steps

69. Which housing services would be most appropriate for Carl?

a. Damp housing
b. Dry housing
c. Sober housing
d. Wet housing

70. Which component of trauma-informed care would best help engage Carl in the counseling process?

a. Behavioral skills training
b. Pharmacotherapy
c. Job skills training
d. Peer support services

71. APs adopting NAADAC's ethical decision-making model engage in which one of the following during the model's final step?

a. Implementation and reflection
b. Reflection and supervision
c. Supervision and deliberation
d. Deliberation and implementation

72. Clients with an extensive substance abuse history often struggle with impulse control and anger. If a client becomes verbally agitated, angry, and elevated with a counselor, what is the BEST response?

a. Threaten to call law enforcement unless he or she calms down.
b. Cite the right to expel him or her from treatment if he or she misbehaves.
c. Validate his or her affect but not expression (if threatening).
d. Ignore the behavior so as not to further escalate his or her emotions.

Refer to the following for questions 73-76:

Estelle is a 76-year-old patient in a short-term medical rehabilitation facility. She was admitted after a hospital discharge, where she was treated for vertigo and a hip fracture. She has been a patient at the rehab for the past 3 months. Estelle was previously active with her bridge club and enjoyed gardening and out-of-town visits with her grandchildren. She relays that in her younger years, she was described as the "life of the party." Estelle had a slower-than-anticipated recovery, which left her discouraged and in chronic pain. Estelle's primary care provider has prescribed a benzodiazepine for sleep and anxiety. She is also prescribed hydrocodone for pain and fluoxetine for depression.

During his frequent visits to the rehab facility, Estelle's son, Frank, reports that he is concerned that his mother has declined cognitively. He states that he is unsure if the changes are typical age-related changes or something more serious. Frank explains that he first noticed issues with her memory soon after she broke her hip. Estelle explains that since her fall, she's been unable to do the things she once enjoyed, leaving her apathetic and depressed.

The counselor meets with Estelle and Frank, conducts a biopsychosocial assessment, and uses standardized measures to evaluate Estelle's memory. When asked about any substance use, Estelle states that she drinks two glasses of wine in the evenings. She denies illicit substance use. She dismisses her son's concern over her memory and says he is "overreacting." During the interview, the counselor notices that Estelle sometimes repeats the same question and has difficulty concentrating. Estelle will follow up with her primary care provider to rule out any underlying health conditions.

73. Which one of the following is a symptom of Alzheimer's disease rather than a reflection of the normal aging process?

a. Occasionally missing a bill payment
b. Sometimes getting lost in a familiar part of town
c. Misplacing items from time to time
d. Difficulty multitasking

74. Which one of the following is the most commonly misused substance among older adults?

a. Cannabis
b. Tobacco
c. Alcohol
d. Prescription opioids

75. Engaging in drug and alcohol use can be risky for older adults for all of the following reasons EXCEPT:

a. Older adults metabolize and eliminate substances at different rates.
b. Older adults have a higher tolerance to substances, requiring higher doses to produce the same effect.
c. Older adults tend to have chronic health conditions that exacerbate the adverse effects of substance use.
d. Older adults tend to take more prescribed medications that exacerbate the adverse effects of substance use.

76. All of the following instruments assess for orientation (e.g., time, date, place) EXCEPT the:

a. Mini-Cog
b. Saint Louis University Mental Status Examination
c. Montreal Cognitive Assessment
d. Mini-Mental State Examination

77. In certain circumstances, APs may engage in the ethical practice of conscientious refusal. This is best exemplified by an AP's refusal to follow an employer's directive to:

a. Treat an openly racist client
b. Treat an LGBT client
c. Deny youth gender-affirming client care
d. Diversify the client caseload

78. The DSM-5-TR outlines 11 criteria for substance use disorder (SUD) that are grouped in all of the following categories EXCEPT:

a. Risky use
b. Legal problems
c. Social problems
d. Impaired control

79. Motivating an addict to enter treatment is often difficult. Which treatment entry method uses the intervention network as part of its motivational process?

a. The Johnson method
b. Community reinforcement training (CRT)
c. The ARISE method
d. The community reinforcement approach (CRA)

80. What is the key feature that differentiates a substance abuse counselor who merely practices in the field from one who succeeds in changing clients' lives?

a. The knowledge of addiction issues
b. The ability to be empathetic
c. The skill to set clear boundaries
d. The capacity to firmly confront

81. What is the main purpose of Title 42 of the Code of Federal Regulations (CFR) Part 2?

a. To allow clients with OUD to receive medication-assisted treatment without employment penalties
b. To protect clients in treatment for substance use against adverse consequences in domestic or criminal proceedings
c. To permit disclosures of protected health information with written consent for continuity of care purposes
d. To provide privacy and confidentiality protection for a client's educational records

82. If a person is dependent on amphetamines, there is an increased likelihood of cross-tolerance with which one of the following?

a. MDMA
b. Opioids
c. Sedative-hypnotic drugs
d. Peyote (mescaline)

83. A client states, "I'm really hurting today. It's hard to face everything I destroyed when I was using." Which counselor response best reflects appropriate empathy?

a. "You are really hurting today, and it's hard to face everything you destroyed when you were using drugs."
b. "If I understand correctly, you are in tremendous pain over all that was lost when you were using drugs."
c. "I understand; when I was active in my addiction, the guilt and shame seemed insurmountable."
d. "You are heartbroken over relationships and opportunities that were lost as the result of your drug use."

84. Which one of the following only detects recent drug use (i.e., within a few hours or days)?

a. Urine test
b. Hair test
c. Saliva test
d. Blood test

Refer to the following for questions 85-88:

AJ is a 62-year-old male living with HIV/acquired immunodeficiency syndrome (AIDS). He receives ongoing counseling to address his stress and anxiety related to chronic experiences of stigma and discrimination. AJ relays his feelings of isolation and despair while he has had to learn how to navigate life as a gay person of color. He explains, "I've been spit on, beaten up, and called derogatory names my whole life." He reports that he began drinking at age 11 to cope with unwanted negative feelings. He recalls, "Alcohol was the only thing I found that would numb the pain." AJ reports that alcoholism exists on both sides of his family. He never knew his father, and his mother was "an alcoholic who never found recovery." He continues, "I was kicked out of my house at age 17 and was estranged from my family for most of my life."

AJ had tried multiple times to stop drinking throughout his adulthood. In his mid-30s, he began to show symptoms of HIV; however, he delayed treatment because of internalized stigma and medical mistrust. When his symptoms worsened, he contacted his healthcare provider and was prescribed dronabinol, an FDA-approved Schedule II medication for HIV-related weight loss. Around the same time, he checked himself into rehab for AUD. Once discharged, he planned to reside in a government-funded recovery house. However, he was denied residence when dronabinol was detected in his urine drug screen. He recalls, "I remember when they called and said, 'Your drug test came back dirty.' I was devastated. It tapped into all of my shame, rejection, and self-hatred. I relapsed and quickly reached rock bottom. I knew alcoholism was going to kill me if I didn't get help."

Today, AJ is a grateful recovering alcoholic with 24 years of sobriety. He states, "One of the gifts of the program is that I was able to make amends to my mother and be with her during her dying days." AJ complies with a daily antiretroviral therapy regimen, and his viral load is "durably undetectable." He and his partner live together and have plans to travel "as much as possible" when they retire in a few years. Although he struggles at times, counseling has provided a supportive environment that allows him to avert internalized stigma and successfully cope with day-to-day interactions within his community.

85. Drugs controlled by the federal government are placed into five distinct schedules or classifications, taking into account all of the following EXCEPT:

a. The substance's potential for abuse
b. The substance's potential for dependency
c. Whether the FDA regulates the substance
d. Whether the substance has acceptable medical uses

86. Dronabinol contains which one of the following?

a. Opioids
b. Stimulants
c. Cannabinoids
d. Antiviral agents

87. AJ reports being called derogatory names based on his race and sexual orientation. This is an example of a:

a. Microinequity
b. Microinsult
c. Microinvalidation
d. Microassault

88. AJ's placement in the recovery house was denied based on his urine drug screen results. Would AJ be protected by the Americans with Disabilities Act (ADA)?

a. No, dronabinol qualifies as an illegal substance.
b. Yes, but only if the facility has 15 or more employees.
c. No, the facility has the right to deny residency based on a positive urine drug screen.
d. Yes, he has a previous history of AUD that limits his functioning.

89. Defining patient goals takes place during which point in counseling?

a. After rapport is established
b. During the treatment process
c. Within the assessment stage
d. At the end of each session

90. A client with alcohol use disorder (AUD) would like to abstain from alcohol rather than reduce consumption. Which one of the following US Food and Drug Administration (FDA)-approved medications would best assist this client?

a. Naltrexone
b. Disulfiram
c. Buprenorphine
d. Acamprosate

Refer to the following for questions 91-94:

Amari is a 24-year-old computer technician who meets with an online counselor to address symptoms of panic disorder. Amari reports that she began having panic attacks a year and a half ago while riding a city bus. She describes symptoms that include heart palpitations, trembling, and feeling as if she were having a heart attack. During this time, she becomes lightheaded and has difficulty breathing. Amari reports that she avoids the city bus, which is difficult because she does not own a car. Amari recalls that she eventually went to her doctor after having several panic attacks, and he prescribed a benzodiazepine.

Amari reports that the benzodiazepine became ineffective over time, and she began using alcohol to increase its effectiveness. She acknowledges that this is only a short-term solution and has started feeling hopeless. She recalls, "It was to the point where I wasn't leaving my house. Whenever I had a panic attack, it was like I would leave my body. I thought I was going crazy. I started feeling depressed, and my parents started to worry." Amari reports moving home for a few months but found it difficult to stay with her parents and has now returned to her apartment.

When asked about medical conditions, Amari reports that she was diagnosed with subclinical (mild) hyperthyroidism, which she has managed with dietary changes. Amari states that she drinks most nights and began using ecstasy and experimenting with hallucinogens at age 21. She reports that she enjoys dancing at local clubs and is friends with one bartender, who supplies Amari with MDMA. She states, "It's the only time I feel free. I've had a couple of bad trips, but it's worth it."

91. The DSM-5-TR diagnostic criteria for panic disorder include:

a. Intense fear or discomfort that reaches its peak within seconds
b. Intense fear or discomfort that reaches its peak within minutes
c. Intense fear or discomfort that reaches its peak within hours
d. Intense fear or discomfort with intermittent peaks and valleys

92. MDMA (aka ecstasy [pill form] or Molly [crystal form]) intoxication and panic attacks share which one of the following symptoms?

a. Dystonia
b. Dyssynergy
c. Disinterestedness
d. Depersonalization

93. The best way to differentiate between a substance-induced mood disorder and an independent anxiety disorder in an individual with overlapping symptoms is by:

a. Determining the onset of overlapping symptoms
b. Providing standardized diagnostic assessments
c. Ascertaining the pharmacological properties of the substance
d. Examining the results of a confirmatory drug screen

94. According to the DSM-5-TR, which one of the following symptoms differentiates panic disorder from other anxiety disorders (e.g., social anxiety, generalized anxiety disorder)?

a. The panic attacks are unexpected.
b. The panic attacks are situational.
c. The panic attacks co-occur with substance-induced anxiety disorders.
d. The panic attacks occur in the presence of medical conditions.

95. Prior to modifications, the MAST was used to screen a client's potential dependency on which of the following?

a. Cocaine
b. Opioid
c. Methamphetamine
d. Alcohol

96. What does a treatment frame assist both the counselor and clients to establish and maintain?

a. An effective theoretical orientation
b. Healthy boundaries in treatment
c. Shared meanings and definitions
d. An effective treatment focus

97. Which circumstance is most likely to result in a client waiving their right to confidentiality or privileged information?

a. When the client's attorney requests information
b. When the client brings public charges against a counselor
c. When the client's spouse contacts the counselor to report a client's relapse
d. When the client refuses the counselor's recommendations for treatment to address a co-occurring anxiety disorder

98. You are a trained substance abuse counselor working with a client diagnosed with alcohol use disorder. As treatment progresses, you begin to see indications of bipolar disorder in your client. What should you do?

a. Refer to, or consult with, a clinician trained in bipolar disorder
b. Treat the bipolar disorder as well as the alcohol use disorder
c. Discontinue treatment
d. Continue to treat for the alcohol use disorder only

99. Perinatal transmission (i.e., mother to child) of the human immunodeficiency virus (HIV) can be reduced if the mother takes medication during pregnancy and childbirth and provides medication to her baby for 4–6 weeks after birth. When mothers take HIV medications as prescribed, the risk of transmission is:

a. Slightly reduced
b. Moderately reduced
c. Significantly reduced
d. Nearly eliminated

100. Pyramiding is a form of anabolic steroid misuse described as:

a. Taking steroids off and on, providing rest periods at specific intervals
b. Using various methods of administration with several steroids at once
c. Slowly increasing the steroid dosage and then titrating down after reaching a maximum peak
d. Overlapping the use of different steroids and different methods to prevent tolerance

101. Which of the following subcategories of alcohol use disorder onset is NOT found in late adulthood?

a. Late-onset alcoholism
b. Delayed-onset alcoholism
c. Late-onset exacerbation drinking
d. Early-onset alcoholism

102. Which one of the following is associated with sudden sniffing death syndrome (SSDS)?

a. Cocaine
b. Heroin
c. Butane
d. Spice

103. Research indicates that behavioral therapies for SUD are effective for all of the following substances EXCEPT:

a. Marijuana
b. Cocaine
c. Benzodiazepines
d. Inhalants

Refer to the following for questions 104-107:

Candace is a 28-year-old pregnant person who is a long-term opioid user. Her obstetrician referred her after a urine drug screen detected the presence of opioids. She also disclosed to her doctor that she smokes cigarettes but she cut down when she discovered she was pregnant. Candace occasionally uses marijuana but says that she has avoided it during pregnancy.

Candace's referral reads, "Patient with dirty drug screen. She is a known opioid addict and is pregnant with her fourth child—all with different fathers. The child's father is an imprisoned crack addict. Her last child was born addicted and suffered from neonatal abstinence syndrome. She continues to abuse substances despite causing harm to her unborn child."

After Candace missed her initial appointment, an in-home counselor and peer support specialist (PSS) were assigned to her case. Candace expressed distrust in the medical community and was skeptical about receiving treatment for opioid use. She relayed that she felt judged by her obstetrician, which left her feeling belittled, ashamed, and alone. The counselor and peer specialist used respectful, person-first language and discussed harm reduction treatment models. Candace was surprised to hear about treatment options for neonatal opioid withdrawal syndrome (NOWS). A case manager was assigned and helped Candace find a medical provider sensitive to her treatment needs.

Candace remained connected to her treatment team throughout her pregnancy and responded well to trauma-informed care and a strengths-based approach. She has joined with her treatment team in an effort to help address stigma among pregnant persons with opioid use disorder. Candace publicly shares her personal experiences with healthcare providers to dispel myths, misconceptions, and stereotypes surrounding treatment for pregnant persons and their newborn infants.

104. Clinical recommendations for the treatment of long-term opioid use or opioid use disorder among pregnant persons include:

a. Abruptly stopping opioid use during pregnancy
b. Providing supervised withdrawal during pregnancy
c. Using medications for opioid use disorder (e.g., methadone) during pregnancy
d. Using behavioral alternatives for pain management during childbirth

105. Harm reduction is an approach used to help pregnant persons access treatment with the primary goal of:

a. Preventing abuse and neglect
b. Reducing mortality and morbidity rates
c. Decreasing stigma and discrimination
d. Providing a safe treatment environment

106. Although often used interchangeably, the terminology *neonatal opioid withdrawal syndrome* (NOWS) is preferred over the term *neonatal abstinence syndrome* (NAS) to help:

a. Provide treatment to those who earnestly seek it.
b. Emphasize that abstinence is a medical condition.
c. Eliminate connotations derived from the term *abstinence*.
d. Emphasize that addiction is a freely chosen moral condition.

107. Which ethical principle states that APs shall address societal stigma and prejudice impeding access to care by working with the public to dispel myths, stereotypes, and misconceptions about SUDs and the people who have them?

a. Research
b. Education
c. Advocacy
d. Professional development

108. What does the SOAP progress note acronym stand for?

a. Subjective, Overview, Actions, and Plan
b. Subjective, Objective, Assessment, and Plan
c. Subjective, Observation, Assessment, and Plan
d. Subjective, Overview, Attention, and Plan

109. There are no documented withdrawal symptoms noted in the DSM-5-TR for all of the following substances EXCEPT:

a. Inhalants
b. Caffeine
c. Hallucinogens
d. PCP

110. When must an AP working with mandated clients disclose legal and ethical limitations to confidentiality?

a. During the initial intake evaluation
b. Before the start of the service relationship
c. Upon constructing a client's treatment plan
d. In the event of treatment refusal

111. When behaviorally assessing for a co-occurring disorder, what is the MOST important variable to consider?

a. Alcohol or drug toxicity or withdrawal symptoms
b. The client's denial of any psychiatric problems
c. The client's family history of psychiatric disorders
d. The client's immediate behavior

112. Case managers help clients determine treatment options by balancing client safety with which of the following?

a. Timely follow-up
b. Multiple referral sources
c. Client autonomy
d. The least restrictive level of care

Refer to the following for questions 113-116:

Juan is a 23-year-old male in his third year of medical school. He grew up in foster care and received merit-based college and medical school scholarships. He reports feeling like he never fit in, stating, "I was often the only Latino in my college classes, as well as my medical school cohort." Juan says he previously used stimulants to keep up with his hectic schedule and that he occasionally smokes marijuana.

In the fall, Juan began his clinical rotation in psychiatry, working with children and adolescents at an inpatient psychiatric unit. He explains that he was doing rounds one day for his patient, an 8-year-old Hispanic male with a history of sexual abuse, when "out of the blue," he had an intrusive memory resurface involving his own childhood sexual abuse. He said he excused himself from rounds and proceeded to have a panic attack. Since then, Juan has used alcohol daily. At the request of his fiancé, Juan has made an appointment with an AP.

The AP discovers that Juan is in the precontemplation stage regarding his drinking. Juan reports that he would first like help with intrusive thoughts and anxiety to see if that helps with his alcohol use. The AP agrees with Juan's request but suggests that he attend AA meetings. Juan agrees to go to AA but never follows through. He states that, as a medical school student, it is "too risky" to attend meetings open to the public. On another occasion he states, "A buddy of mine said there were no Latinos at those meetings."

The AP arranges for peer support services with a Latino provider to engage Juan in treatment and support his recovery. Juan needs clarification about the provider's benefits and role but is open to it. The AP also provides Juan with information on caduceus group meetings, which are closed 12-step groups for recovering medical professionals. Juan eventually connects with others, enlarges his recovery capital, and gives back to his community through sponsorships and participation in outreach programs.

113. Juan's addiction professional (AP) agrees to begin meeting to address anxiety rather than placing the sole emphasis on his alcohol use, thus honoring the principle of:

a. Justice
b. Autonomy
c. Stewardship
d. Honesty and candor

114. An individual who has successfully navigated recovery and is now certified or trained to help others with similar experiences is known as a:

a. Peer worker
b. Peer navigator
c. Peer mentor
d. Peer specialist

115. Which one of the following interrelated concepts describes occurrences involving a peer support specialist (PSS) performing tasks outside the scope of their job?

a. Role drift
b. Role strain
c. Role confusion
d. Role conflict

116. Recovery capital refers to an individual's:

a. Risk factors
b. Socioeconomic assets
c. Strengths and weaknesses
d. Available internal and external resources

117. When used as a part of a relapse prevention strategy, the term "bookend" refers to which of the following?

a. Discussing a trigger event with a support person before and after it occurs
b. Keeping a difficult issue on the shelf until it can be better dealt with
c. Remaining steadfast in recovery, even in the face of temptation
d. Attending ninety 12-step meetings in ninety days

118. Which one of the following terms describes what occurs in the healthy body in the absence of substance abuse?

a. Homeostasis
b. Therapeutic index
c. Pharmacokinetics
d. Psychoactive mechanisms

119. Which of the following is NOT a typical stage in the development of cocaine addiction?

a. Compulsive use
b. Experimental use
c. Isolated use
d. Social use

120. Which one of the following is true of risk and protective factors?

a. They are relational, are fixed, and have multiple outcomes.
b. They are independent, isolated, and weakened over time.
c. They are correlated, cumulative, and influential over time.
d. They are interactional, developmental, and predictable over time.

121. What is the ADS scale used to measure?

a. Alcohol dependence
b. Anomalous drug use
c. Readiness for treatment
d. Substance use minimization

122. Which of the following is NOT a group in the Matrix Model of treatment?

a. Early recovery skills groups
b. Relapse prevention groups
c. Family education groups
d. Stress management groups

123. Which of the following medications is NOT commonly used in the treatment of alcohol abuse?

a. Disulfiram
b. Buprenorphine
c. Acamprosate
d. Naltrexone

124. Which one of the following substances is frequently linked to risky sexual behaviors and HIV among men who have sex with men?

a. Lysergic acid diethylamide (LSD)
b. MDMA
c. Amyl nitrite
d. Synthetic cathinones (i.e., bath salts)

Refer to the following for questions 125-128:

Heather, a 22-year-old female, seeks counseling to address symptoms of panic and anxiety. During her initial intake assessment, Heather reported that she has taken LSD multiple times, with a recent increase in use as she joined friends to follow their favorite band from coast to coast. She explained that, "This is their final tour, so we were all going to make the best of it." She reports that she smokes marijuana and has tried MDMA but states that LSD is the most accessible drug during concerts, and she has enjoyed having transcendent experiences. A detailed drug history reveals that she has averaged one tab of LSD up to four times weekly over the past 3 months.

Heather states that LSD provides her with a long-lasting high and the ability to see zigzags, spirals, and colors. She enjoys a heightened connection to the music and with the other concertgoers. However, she recently experienced a bad trip, leaving her paranoid and panicky. She states, "The last time I tripped on acid, I thought aliens had possessed my boyfriend. I remember hyperventilating and having a panic attack." She states that, despite abstaining from the substance, she continues to have flashbacks.

Heather explains that, when experiencing a flashback, she realizes the hallucinations are not real but continues to experience the same terror and fear that originally characterized her bad trip. She says that she has not used LSD in 2 weeks. When asked about her mental health history, she stated that she has felt suicidal occasionally but has no history of anxiety. She was diagnosed with ADHD when she was younger but has managed it without medication. Her treatment plan goals are to improve on her coping skills when experiencing panic attacks. Her initial homework assignment is to keep a journal to document her flashbacks and rate the severity of the associated symptoms.

125. The diagnostic criteria for hallucinogen persisting perception disorder include all of the following EXCEPT:

a. Symptoms must occur during acute intoxication.
b. Symptoms must involve functional impairment.
c. Symptoms must not be attributable to a medical condition.
d. Symptoms must not be explained by a mental disorder.

126. Clinicians who encounter clients actively experiencing a bad trip during LSD intoxication must first ensure that the client and others are safe, followed by:

a. Requesting medication-assisted treatment
b. Providing close supervision to monitor for withdrawal
c. Arranging for physical restraints to prevent unintended harm
d. Placing the client in a calm, isolated environment to provide reassurance and support

127. LSD has the potential for all of the following EXCEPT:

a. Toxicity
b. Physical cravings
c. Tolerance
d. Psychological dependence

128. To substantiate a diagnosis of hallucinogen-induced anxiety disorder, the symptoms must:

a. Predate hallucinogen use
b. Occur during intoxication and abstinence
c. Predominate in the clinical presentation
d. Not be severe enough to warrant individual attention

129. Of the following choices, which one is the most effective strategy for improving treatment engagement and retention among individuals experiencing homelessness?

a. Sequencing services and interventions according to client readiness
b. Addressing structural racism and residential segregation
c. Ensuring communication and collaboration with multiple providers
d. Offering medication-assisted treatment for OUD

130. Ethical dilemmas often involve conflicts between the principle of autonomy and which one of the following?

a. Honesty
b. Beneficence
c. Confidentiality
d. Informed consent

131. Individuals with the highest prevalence of tobacco use include those diagnosed with which one of the following disorders?

a. Schizophrenia
b. Anorexia nervosa
c. Post-traumatic stress disorder (PTSD)
d. Attention-deficit/hyperactivity disorder

132. Client outcome measures should be conducted with which of the following frequencies?

a. Initial and ongoing
b. Only initially
c. Initially and finally
d. Only as indicated

133. Addiction professionals (APs) can best guarantee that confidentiality will be maintained in which one of the following circumstances?

a. A counselor provides couples counseling at the client's request to address infidelity.
b. A counselor provides group therapy for clients with co-occurring disorders.
c. A counselor provides professional consultation to another counselor to understand a client's cultural experiences.
d. A counselor provides family therapy before termination to assist with a client's relapse prevention.

Refer to the following for questions 134-137:

The client is a 74-year-old Vietnam War veteran who is currently being admitted to an inpatient psychiatric hospital to assess his mental status and provide crisis support. The client was initially admitted to the ED after his wife found him unresponsive, prompting her to call 911. First responders were called to his residence and administered naloxone, which quickly restored his breathing. The ED clinician used a screening, brief intervention, and referral to treatment approach, which led to his hospital admission.

The inpatient psychiatric hospital counselor conducts a comprehensive assessment. The clinical interview reveals that the client is a heavy smoker and engages in episodic binge drinking. He states that he drinks a 12-pack of beer 4–5 nights per week. The client's alcohol use escalated 5 years ago after he received a call informing him that his brother had been reported missing. The client drove to his brother's apartment and found him dead. His brother's decomposed body triggered memories of the Vietnam War. The client reports experiencing distressing dreams and flashbacks every night and day. He states that he feels guilt and shame related to events that he witnessed in combat, and he often wonders why he survived and others did not. He takes cannabidiol to help with sleep and memory. He denies suicidal ideation.

The client reports that he once saw a therapist who asked him to write an impact statement about his exposure to traumatic events and how the events have affected his life. He did not complete the assignment, nor did he return to therapy. The client's wife explains to the counselor that "he bottles everything up and avoids talking about any of it." The client is assigned a diagnosis of post-traumatic stress disorder (PTSD) and a preliminary diagnosis of alcohol use disorder (AUD), moderate.

134. You are the supervisor of the psychiatric counselor. Upon reviewing the client's DSM diagnoses, you note that the counselor may have missed symptoms of which one of the following?

a. Opioid use disorder
b. Neurocognitive disorder
c. Cannabinoid use disorder
d. Avoidant personality disorder

135. The ED counselor uses the screening, brief intervention, and referral to treatment approach, which leads to a psychiatric referral. Which one of the following is a full screening instrument used to assess alcohol use or misuse in older adults?

a. DAST-1
b. TAPS-1
c. C-SSRS
d. SMAST-G

136. The client explains that his previous therapist asked him to write an impact statement about his experiences of trauma and how the events have affected his life. This intervention is associated with which one of the following?

a. Narrative therapy
b. Solution-focused therapy
c. Prolonged exposure therapy
d. Cognitive processing therapy

137. Best practices for developing treatment plan goals are reflected in which one of the following statements?

a. The client will experience fewer depressive symptoms, decreasing from four times a week to two times a week within 3 months.
b. The client will experience fewer distressing thoughts and flashbacks, decreasing from daily to four times a week within 3 months.
c. The client will experience less suicidal ideation, decreasing to zero times per day each day.
d. The client will talk to his wife about distressing feelings and report on his progress.

138. When assessing for prescription drug misuse, the biopsychosocial model can BEST be used to:

a. Determine the intergenerational etiology of substance misuse.
b. Identify environmental and sociocultural contributors to substance misuse.
c. Establish both psychological and physical components of substance misuse.
d. Provide a holistic view of interconnected causal factors of substance misuse.

139. Which one of the following substances activates dopamine, serotonin, and norepinephrine monoamines?

a. Cocaine
b. Marijuana
c. Alcohol
d. Prescription narcotics (e.g., oxycodone)

140. Which one of the following refers to counselors encountering situations in which attending to one obligation results in abandoning another one?

a. An ethical dilemma
b. A boundary violation
c. A dual relationship
d. A conflict of interest

141. Clients who may be inappropriate candidates for group therapy include all of the following EXCEPT:

a. Those exhibiting psychosis
b. Those unmotivated to participate
c. Those unable to follow group rules
d. Those currently using substances

142. Which one of the following is true of privacy protections for minors who receive treatment for SUD in school-based 42 CFR Part 2 federal programs?

a. Written consent must be obtained to authorize the disclosure of treatment information to parents and guardians.
b. Written consent is not required to authorize the disclosure of treatment information to insurance providers.
c. Written consent must be obtained before reporting suspected cases of child abuse and neglect.
d. Written consent is not required to notify parents of assessment and evaluation results.

143. Counselors using an integrated care model for SUD promote prevention, treatment, and referral to address each client's:

a. Basic needs
b. Medical needs
c. Holistic needs
d. Psychosocial needs

Refer to the following for questions 144-147:

John conducts group therapy for adolescent boys who are at risk for developing SUD. Participants have been selected based on several factors, including early substance use, underlying mental disorders, and lack of social connectedness. John uses an abstinence-based contingency management approach to reinforce prosocial behaviors and enhance the group's drug resistance skills.

Each participant must refrain from substance use and attend the group in exchange for monetary awards. Negative immunoassay urine drug screens are used to determine if the participants have remained abstinent. Per agency policy, group membership is terminated after missing more than one session and/or having a positive urine drug screen.

The group has been meeting weekly for 10 weeks, and the boys have begun to form bonds with one another. The boys' parents are also provided incentives for attending a concurrent psychoeducational group. The boys' group has eight cohesive members. One group member, Ricardo, initially presented as defiant and argumentative. Ricardo has since bonded with the boys, and today, he eagerly joins in the ice-breaker activity and is actively engaged with the group.

Ricardo's parents have supported the group from the beginning, telling him that his participation was nonnegotiable. Circumstances for Ricardo's parents have changed since the group began 10 weeks ago. His mother now must work second shift, and there is only one family car. This has caused Ricardo and his parents to miss one group session.

Today, Ricardo's urine drug screen is positive for amphetamines. Ricardo is adamant that he is abstinent, and his anger quickly becomes contagious. John has been told by his supervisor that he must adhere to the agency's policy and initiate an administrative discharge. The boys have all threatened to disband the group, placing full faith in Ricardo's abstinence. John is uncertain how to proceed.

144. John's group for at-risk youth uses which one of the following interventions?

a. Primary prevention
b. Secondary prevention
c. Tertiary prevention
d. Universal prevention

145. Contingency management is based on which one of the following principles?

a. Skills training
b. Operant conditioning
c. Motivational interviewing
d. Cognitive behavioral therapy

146. What is the advantage of John using urine drug screens (rather than other detection methods) to determine his clients' substance use?

a. The results are immediate.
b. There is a lower likelihood of receiving an adulterated sample.
c. They provide the same level of accuracy as more costly methods.
d. There is a longer window of detection than with other methods.

147. John is uncertain of how to proceed after Ricardo's positive drug screen. He begins by assessing the psychological impact for Ricardo and whether he is progressing with his treatment. Which ethical principles would best guide this process?

a. Honesty and candor
b. Discretion and nonmaleficence
c. Conscientious refusal and beneficence
d. Justice and gratitude

148. Many therapeutic approaches might be helpful in working with families of addicts. Of those commonly used, which brief therapeutic approach uses the miracle question technique?

a. Cognitive-behavioral therapy
b. Bowen family systems therapy
c. Multidimensional family therapy
d. Solution-focused family therapy

149. There are multiple theories that explain the co-occurrence of substance use disorder (SUD) and post-traumatic stress disorder (PTSD). Which one of the following posits that SUD is caused by a response to PTSD symptoms?

a. High-risk hypothesis
b. Self-medication hypothesis
c. Susceptibility hypothesis
d. Pandora's box hypothesis

150. Which one of the following best illustrates questioning consistent with the core motivational interviewing skills known by the acronym OARS?

a. "On a typical week, how much alcohol do you consume?"
b. "What has your alcohol use been like in the past week?"
c. "Did your husband encourage you to come today?"
d. "When would you like to quit drinking?"

Answer Key and Explanations

1. B: Compared to cocaine, methamphetamines (MAs) are metabolized at a much slower rate. MAs have plasma concentration levels that peak rapidly but decline less rapidly than cocaine. MAs have a longer half-life than cocaine, lasting 8–12 hours when smoked, compared to cocaine, which lasts 20 minutes when smoked.

2. D: For individuals with chronic or heavy methamphetamine (MA) use, symptoms of psychosis may persist for years after discontinuing use. This is known as post-acute withdrawal syndrome, which is most common in individuals with chronic or heavy use; symptoms of this syndrome can be continuous or intermittent and can last months to years.

3. B: Tweaking is a physical and psychological condition characterized by unpredictable and explosive behaviors when the individual requires more MA to attain the desired high and to avoid withdrawal. Delirium is associated with an overall lack of awareness and confusion associated with drug withdrawal, primarily alcohol and benzodiazepines, and various mental or physical conditions. Pharming is the use of several prescription drugs at once in order to achieve a high. A bender is a term used to describe a period of heavy drug and/or alcohol use.

4. D: Recreational methamphetamine (MA) use is associated with increased rates of sexually transmitted infections, such as HIV, through any route of administration. MA is known to heighten libido and increase risky sexual behavior, including having casual sex without a condom. Although sharing needles is associated with an increased risk of HIV and other sexually transmitted infections, recreational use of MA, whether injected, smoked, or snorted, increases sexual libido, and it is often followed by unsafe sexual practices.

5. C: Compared to females, males aged 12–17 are less likely to have alcohol use disorder. Men are more likely to report excessive alcohol use, are more likely to die as a consequence of alcohol use, and have higher instances of alcohol-related hospitalizations. Despite these statistics, alcohol consumption among males is declining, narrowing the gap between male and female alcohol use and alcohol use disorder. According to the National Center for Drug Abuse Statistics (2023), females aged 12–17 are 61.5% more likely to have alcohol use disorder than their same-aged male peers. This is a concerning trend because it places women at higher risk for experiencing the long-term effects of alcohol use, including breast cancer, heart disease, liver damage, brain damage, and pregnancy complications.

6. B: At this point in treatment, the counselor should support the client in his own pathway of recovery. According to Principle VII-17 of the NAADAC Code of Ethics (2021), APs must obtain supervision or consultation before disclosing personal recovery, and the disclosure must benefit the client rather than the AP. If the client and counselor belong to similar ethnic and racialized groups, self-disclosure may be beneficial later in the client's therapy. Providing information on NA is not the best response because the reasons for the client's hesitancy are unknown. Arranging to meet a new client at a local NA meeting may constitute a dual relationship and should be avoided.

7. C: Heroin is snorted to achieve a longer-lasting high among individuals with opioid use disorder (OUD). The most common form of heroin administration is injection, which is achieved by heating heroin powder to turn it into a liquid. Injection is also the quickest route. The second most common means of ingesting heroin is by smoking/inhaling it. Snorting heroin is most commonly coupled with cocaine and is less common because the high is longer but not as intense. When taken orally, heroin is converted to morphine, causing deacetylation and leading to significantly lower highs, making this form of administration unlikely among individuals with OUD.

8. C: Motivational interviewing (MI) was developed by Miller and Rollnick. It utilizes techniques derived from numerous theoretical approaches that clarify the progressive stages of recovery. MI is designed to explore and lessen the uncertainty about accepting treatment by using an empathic, client-centered, yet directive counseling approach. This frequently involves building on clients' prior successes and the problem-solving strategies and solutions that supported those achievements. To be successful, MI requires a nonjudgmental, collaborative style that reveals the often-disguised negative hazards and effects of substance abuse. Thus, the counselor serves as a coach or consultant, not as an expert or authority figure. Four basic MI principles are: (1) empathy—acknowledging and respecting the client's decisions yet noting the client's accountability for change; (2) discrepancy identification—contrasting current behavior with expressed ideals and goals; (3) resistance reduction—remaining neutral to client resistance, rather than confronting or correcting, to allow resistance to recede in the face of available information; (4) supporting self-efficacy—reflecting client strengths and encouraging a conviction that change can be achieved.

9. C: The Addiction Severity Index assesses drug and alcohol use in the past 30 days in the following domains: medical, employment, legal, family, and interpersonal status. The Prescription Opioid Misuse Index is a six-item assessment used to determine the likelihood of an opioid use disorder diagnosis. The Opioid Risk Tool is used to detect opioid misuse in patients who are prescribed opioids for chronic pain. TAPS is a four-item screening tool for tobacco, alcohol, prescription drug misuse, and substance use.

10. A: Using one instrument to assess the client's risk for opioid use is insufficient; however, when compared to subjective collateral reports, the standardized instrument is found to be superior. Best practices for assessing the risk of opioid use disorder include standardized instruments, a clinical interview/assessment, a biopsychosocial assessment, and a urine drug screen when indicated.

11. A: Harm reduction strategies for opioid use disorder are least compatible with 12-step group philosophies. Harm reduction programs, such as medication-assisted treatment, for opioid use disorder are designed to reduce overdose deaths and lessen illness. Harm reduction strategies, such as those allowing continued use of alcohol and prescription pills, are incompatible with the 12-step abstinence-based philosophy. Harm reduction strategies include psychosocial programs, community reinforcement, and methadone maintenance.

12. C: The client likely meets the DSM-5-TR criteria for PTSD. The counselor must first ensure that the client's symptoms are not caused by the physiological effects of a substance, which is likely because the client continues to use drugs and alcohol. The client's symptoms that coincide with PTSD include direct exposure to sexual violence, emotional distress after exposure to trauma, avoidance of trauma-related reminders, overly negative thoughts and assumptions about oneself or the world, exaggerated self-blame for the trauma, risky or destructive behavior after the trauma, and difficulty sleeping. Acute stress disorder includes similar symptoms; however, the symptoms must last less than 1 month. Major depressive disorder is less likely as the information provided did not mention when the symptoms began. Major depressive disorder requires the appearance of five symptoms in 2 weeks. The client exhibits the following four symptoms: depressed mood, anhedonia, and excessive/inappropriate guilt. There is a history of sleeplessness, but this is reported as a response to trauma triggers. Bipolar I disorder requires an episode of mania, which has not been reported.

13. A: Principle II-7 of the NAADAC Code of Ethics (2021) states that addiction professionals (APs) must first disclose the legal and ethical limits to confidentiality during informed consent. Informed consent is a process designed to supply clients with enough information to make a decision about the services being offered. Informed consent is first reviewed at the onset of treatment and continues throughout treatment as needed. Legal and ethical limitations to confidentiality differ for clients who receive mandated treatment. APs take appropriate steps to limit disclosures in scope by providing limited information (e.g., compliance with treatment, treatment progress) for mandated clients. Informed consent can be revoked at any time; however, for mandated clients, the consequences of withdrawing consent must be made clear at the onset of treatment. Limitations also include situations in which clients express the desire to harm themselves or others, and in suspected instances of child or elder abuse. Additionally, APs must adhere to HIPAA and CFR 42 Part 2 regulations regarding confidentiality.

14. B: Racial and ethnic minorities are less inclined to seek treatment from mental health specialists. They turn more often to primary care medical providers. Other more frequently selected sources of support include clergy, traditional healers, family, and friends. African Americans often rely on ministers, who may carry out a variety of mental health roles (e.g., counselor, diagnostician, and referral provider). When they do utilize mental health services, many African Americans prefer counselors of the same race or ethnicity. African Americans often prefer counseling over drug therapy, citing concerns of addiction, side effects, and effectiveness. In avoiding mental health professionals, 50 percent of African Americans cited a fear of treatment and hospitalization, as compared to 20 percent of whites with similar concerns. Mistrust arises from both historical and present-day struggles with racism and discrimination, including perceptions of mistreatment by medical and mental health professionals. A recent survey revealed that 15 percent of Latinos and 12 percent of African Americans felt a doctor or health provider had judged them unfairly or treated them with disrespect because of their race or ethnic background, as compared with 1 percent of whites expressing such feelings.

15. B: The American Society of Addiction Medicine (ASAM) defines addiction as "a treatable, chronic medical disease involving complex interactions among brain circuits, genetics, the environment, and an individual's life experiences." Additionally, ASAM adheres to the belief that individuals with substance use disorder (SUD) engage in compulsive behaviors despite adverse consequences. As with all chronic diseases, ASAM asserts that prevention and treatment for addiction can be successful and that ongoing treatment is necessary for more severe conditions.

16. D: Piercings are least likely to qualify as non-suicidal self-injury (NSSI) because they are socially sanctioned. NSSI refers to deliberately destroying one's body for reasons not socially sanctioned and without suicidal intent. Examples of NSSI include but are not limited to scratching, biting, punching, burning, head banging, and hitting. Careful assessment is critical for determining suicidal intent and for monitoring NSSI because individuals who engage in self-harm are at an increased risk for suicide and have higher levels of emotional distress than individuals who do not engage in self-harm. Counselors assess a client's risk for self-harm by evaluating the client's ideation, plan, and means. Informed consent must be obtained during the initial session to outline limits to confidentiality and examples of circumstances necessitating a confidentiality breach.

17. C: Asking "Did you always feel this way?" is an example of clarification. Clarification is a form of active listening used to elicit facts. Clarification is similar to probing, but they differ in that probing is used to encourage clients to think more deeply about specific subjects. If the client were to respond to the counselor by stating, "Yes, I have felt this way since childhood," the counselor could follow up with a probing question such as "Can you give me an example of how this played out in your childhood?" Reframing is used to reconceptualize a problem or difficulty by placing it in a more positive light. Lastly, the question posed is a yes-or-no question, making it closed-ended rather than open-ended.

18. B: The therapist has an ethical responsibility to terminate therapy when treatment is ineffective. When terminating, the therapist should also refer the client to another clinician. It is common practice to provide at least three referrals and document the need for alternative services. Documenting that the client is not improving and continuing therapy falls short of an AP's ethical obligation to provide culturally and linguistically appropriate services when unable to fully meet the client's biopsychosocial and spiritual needs.

19. B: The counselor acted ethically by respecting the client's autonomy. Upon admission to the treatment center, the client would have received informed consent information indicating that treatment is voluntary and that consent can be revoked at any time. The client is in an intensive outpatient program, which aligns with ASAM level 2 care, providing services that include family therapy, group therapy, and psychiatric medication management. The client's condition at the time of termination did not warrant medical management for opioid withdrawal, indicating that the client is not at imminent risk for harm. Despite being employed by the treatment center, there is no indication that the counselor's objectivity was impaired. Lastly, the principle of nonmaleficence, or do no harm, is not applicable.

20. D: An education/collegiate program is an example of a nonclinical pathway to recovery. Nonclinical pathways are recovery-oriented programs led by individuals without specialized clinical training. Education-based (i.e., collegiate-based) recovery programs assist high school and college students in the beginning stages of SUD. Services include emotional and social support, access to sober living arrangements, psychoeducation, and mutual self-help groups to help students live a substance-free life. Clinical pathways to recovery include holistic-based recovery services, such as equine therapy, which are led by experiential therapists with specialized training. Relapse prevention, a clinical pathway to recovery, uses a cognitive-behavioral therapy approach to assist individuals in maintaining sobriety. Lastly, contingency management, a clinical pathway, uses operant conditioning to help motivate and reinforce recovery-oriented changes.

21. B: Trauma-informed care requires a shift from a pathology-oriented perspective (e.g., asking "What is wrong with you?") to a resilience-oriented perspective (e.g., asking "What has happened to you?"). Rather than viewing the counselor as the "expert" and the client as a diagnostic label, trauma-informed counselors view the client's thoughts, feelings, and actions as adaptive responses to trauma. Using a strengths-based approach helps to provide the counselor and the client with an emotionally safe and therapeutic experience.

22. C: Substance dependence involves repeated substance use, leading to significant clinical and functional impairment. With substance dependence, there is an uncontrollable desire to use a substance despite harmful consequences. Intoxication refers to the emotional, physical, mental, behavioral, and psychological effects of drugs and alcohol. Withdrawal refers to the psychological and physiological symptoms that occur in the absence of an addictive substance, with symptoms ranging in severity and varying based on the substance and the length of time it was used. Individuals build tolerance when higher doses of a substance are required to experience its originally encountered effects.

23. C: An example of person-centered language is the statement, "The client is a person in recovery." Person-centered language is strengths-based and respectful. Instead of using the words "The client suffers from alcoholism," use "The client is a person recovering from (or experiencing) alcohol use disorder." Instead of labeling someone "unqualified to parent," use "a person experiencing obstacles to effective parenting." Instead of saying "addict," say "a person with substance use disorder."

24. B: The Drug Use Decisional Balance Scale is associated with motivational interviewing (MI) and the transtheoretical model of behavioral change (aka the stages of change model). This instrument guides clients from the contemplation to the preparation stage of change. The instrument uses a 1 to 5 Likert scale to evaluate where individuals fall in deciding on using drugs and alcohol. The Drug Use Decisional Balance Scale provides clinicians a tool to evoke change talk by building discrepancy between the client's values and substance use. The Drug Abuse Screening Test-10 is a 10-question inventory assessing consequences related to drug abuse. The Substance Abuse Subtle Screening Inventory is used to help screen individuals who may have SUD, and the Adult Substance Use Survey offers a more in-depth assessment of a person's perceived alcohol or substance use, as well as indicators for mental health functioning.

25. D: Phencyclidine (PCP) is most likely to be detected after 7 days from the last use. Also known as angel dust and rocket fuel, PCP is a hallucinogen known for its mind-altering, dissociative, and anesthetic effects. It can be detected by a urine drug screen up to 8 days from the last use. Amphetamines can be detected for 3 days, cocaine and opioids for 3–5 days, and short-acting benzodiazepines for 2 days. Short-acting benzodiazepines are used to treat insomnia and include estazolam, flurazepam, temazepam, and triazolam. Midazolam is a short-acting benzodiazepine generally administered in surgical patients for anxiety and sedation before anesthesia is given.

26. C: Ethically sound counselor self-disclosures benefit the client rather than the counselor. Effective self-disclosures are brief, intentional, and appropriately timed. Self-disclosures benefit the client and their clinical needs, reflect authenticity and professionalism, and convey to clients that they are not alone. Skillful use of self-disclosures can mitigate a therapeutic impasse. Experts caution against using self-disclosure during the intake, screening, and assessment phases of treatment for SUD to avoid influencing the client's responses.

27. B: A framed diploma is not a form of counselor self-disclosure. Self-disclosure is defined as a counselor revealing personal information to clients inside or outside of a professional setting. A counselor's framed diploma qualifies as professional rather than personal information. Self-disclosure would include a counselor's social media postings, tattoos, and wedding rings. Not all self-disclosures are verbal or avoidable. Effective self-disclosures focus on strengthening the therapeutic alliance, establishing trust, creating a collaborative dynamic, and normalizing client challenges. Infective self-disclosures compromise the client–counselor relationship and can lead to blurred boundaries, boundary crossings, or boundary violations.

28. C: Section III-29 and III-30 of the NAADAC Code of Ethics (2021) address the AP's ethical obligation to address societal prejudice, stereotypes, misconceptions, and stigma by willful engagement in the "legislative process, educational institutions, and public forums" to educate the public and "advocate for opportunities and choices for clients." Further, APs must actively participate in advocacy efforts with civic and community organizations to inform others of the impact of substance use disorders (SUDs). Advocacy efforts are designed to help individuals with equal access to treatment opportunities, resources, and services. APs are ethically responsible for providing research-based practices, engaging in self-care and cultural humility, and collaborating with other healthcare professionals; however, advocacy is most closely tied to addressing societal stigma and prejudice towards individuals with SUD.

29. D: The percentage of individuals diagnosed with gambling disorder who also have a mental disorder is estimated at 98%. This underscores the importance of universal screening for co-occurring disorders when individuals are treated for gambling disorder.

30. B: The DSM-5-TR provides diagnostic criteria for gambling disorder, which includes Criterion B: "the gambling behavior is not better explained by a manic episode." Kennedy's mental disorder is bipolar I, which includes manic episodes and is not currently managed with medication. Alcohol use may exacerbate gambling; however, that is not required for a formal diagnosis. The DSM-IV included the criterion of illegal acts used to finance gambling, but this criterion was eliminated in the DSM-5. The gambling behavior must have occurred at any time within the last 12 months.

31. A: The best way for the counselor to engage Kennedy in the counseling process is to ask open-ended questions. Motivational interviewing is an approach used to help engage clients through the core skills of open questions, affirmations, selections, and summaries. Open-ended or open questions can be offered through the structure of elicit-provide-elicit, which involves the counselor determining what information the client knows, asking permission to offer what they know, and evoking the client's response to the information provided. It would be premature to affirm Kennedy's desire to change because she does not acknowledge having a problem. Reassuring her that she will be okay also misses the mark since she is not distressed. Providing warnings or information without asking permission can lead to disengagement rather than engagement.

32. B: This form of irrational thinking is known as the gambler's fallacy, an interpretive bias that involves an inaccurate predictive outcome. The gambler's fallacy is the belief that a certain outcome will occur more or less frequently based on the frequency of similar preceding occurrences. The belief that the roulette wheel will land on red after landing on black 10 consecutive times is an example of gambler's fallacy. This is also known as negative recency or the Monte Carlo fallacy. The halo effect is a cognitive bias that occurs when positive impressions of people in one area (e.g., attractiveness) are generalized to other characteristics of that person (e.g., intelligence). The bottom-dollar effect is the belief that products that strain a person's budget are disliked more than affordable options. The cashless effect is the tendency to buy more and pay more for a transaction if physical dollars are not exchanged, explaining the tendency to place an item on a credit card rather than paying for it in cash.

33. A: Person-centered language, which focuses on the person rather than their disorder, has the primary purpose of reducing stigma. It is holistic, strengths-based, empowering, and respectful. For example, use the words "a person with substance use disorder" rather than "addict." Person-centered language avoids stereotypes associated with mental illness. For example, use the words "Jasmine has been diagnosed with bipolar disorder" rather than "Jasmine is bipolar." Although person-centered language may improve self-esteem, it primarily aims to change societal attitudes and stereotypes that drive stigma. It is one component of equitable access and treatment. Person-centered language seeks to counter societal attitudes toward people with SUD by changing the viewpoint that the SUD is a moral failing or that addiction is a personal choice or weakness of character; instead, it emphasizes that SUD is a chronic disease, just like diabetes or heart disease.

34. D: Clients who vacillate between wanting and not wanting to stop using substances are in the contemplation stage of change. Clients who are in the contemplation stage may even continue to use substances but are considering a change in the near future. Prochaska and DiClemente's stages of change model consists of the following stages: precontemplation, contemplation, preparation, action, and maintenance. In the precontemplation stage, clients may lack total or partial awareness of a problem and are usually unwilling to consider changing in the near future. In the contemplation stage, counselors help clients weigh the pros and cons and explore ambivalence. The preparation stage is characterized by the development of concrete and realistic plans to change. In the action stage, a specific strategy is adopted and clients are actively changing patterns of substance use and are committed to following strategies for improvement. Lastly, the maintenance stage is marked by efforts to sustain gains and remain committed to relapse prevention strategies.

35. D: The primary purpose of a harm reduction model of care is to reduce mortality and morbidity rates. The harm reduction model of care is a recovery-oriented approach focusing on meeting people where they are in their recovery to reduce death and illness among those with SUD and/or co-occurring physical or mental health conditions. Harm reduction is a compassionate, supportive, and person-centered approach used with individuals who may have the desire to stay sober or reduce risky behaviors, but who have not been successful with traditional abstinence-based approaches. The harm reduction model approaches recovery on a continuum, with incremental changes leading to improved outcomes. Medication-assisted treatment for OUD is an example of a harm reduction strategy.

36. C: The preoccupation/anticipation stage of addiction is characterized by cravings and deficits in executive functioning. The three stages of addiction are (1) the binge/intoxication stage, which is characterized by a person using substances to experience pleasurable or satisfying effects; (2) the withdrawal/negative effect stage, which involves experiencing negative emotional states when the substance is not in use due to decreases in dopamine; and (3) the preoccupation/anticipation stage, which is identified by an individual's pursuit of the substance (i.e., cravings) and the desire to obtain the drug (i.e., relapse) after a period of abstinence. The three stages all involve changes in different parts of the brain, and a person can cycle through these stages several times a day, month, or year, with each cycle intensifying over time.

37. B: Jamie identifies as genderqueer, meaning they do not subscribe to conventional gender binary distinctions. Individuals who are genderqueer do not see themselves as exclusively male or female. Genderqueer applies solely to gender rather than sexual orientation. Individuals who are intersex are born with both male and female genitalia and internal sex organs, as well as additional male and female hormones, chromosomes, and other sex traits. Gender expression is how a person's gender identity is expressed, including clothing, behavior, voice, or other gender-related characteristics.

38. A: Jamie's counselor used the Ask Suicide-Screening Questions (ASQ). The ASQ is a 5-item screening instrument inquiring about suicidality in the past few weeks. The ASQ asks individuals if they have had periods when they wished they were dead, if they have felt like their family would be better off if they were dead, and whether they have had thoughts of wanting to kill themselves. The screening also asks about a history of suicide attempts and current suicidal thoughts with a final acuity question. The Patient Health Questionnaire (PHQ) is a broad diagnostic instrument with high sensitivity to major depressive disorder. The Beck Depression Inventory (BDI) is a 21-item assessment for depression, with one question about suicidal thoughts and plans. The CAGE questionnaire assesses alcohol use with four questions relating to cutting down, annoyed feelings, guilty feelings, and eye-openers.

39. B: Jamie would likely be assigned the diagnosis of post-traumatic stress disorder (PTSD). Jamie's PTSD symptoms include exposure to sexual violence, intrusive memories and flashbacks, avoidance behaviors (i.e., not returning to work), hypervigilance, difficulty concentrating, and negative beliefs about the world (e.g., "no one can be trusted"). Symptoms of acute stress disorder must not exceed 1 month. Generalized anxiety disorder would not be assigned because its symptoms exist across a broad continuum and are not tied to a specific event. Major depressive disorder does not include the presence of trauma. A co-occurring diagnosis of major depressive disorder is also unsubstantiated because only four symptoms (out of the required five or more) are reported: depressed mood, insomnia, decreased concentration, and suicidal ideation.

40. A: The counselor statement that best affirms Jamie's gender identity is: "My pronouns are she/her/hers." Counselors are responsible for validating a client's use of gender pronouns by also introducing themselves with their pronouns to normalize the process and create an environment of inclusion. The statement: "Your preferred pronouns are important to me," conveys that pronouns are a preference. Instead, say, "their personal pronouns" or the "pronouns someone uses." The statement: "It doesn't matter which pronouns you use for me," may convey privilege in that the statement suggests that the person conforms to societal expectations of gender and does not need to worry about misgendering, thus invalidating experiences of those who struggle with getting others to use their correct pronouns. Stating, "It's really hard for me to get used to using the pronoun 'they'" minimizes the struggle of gender nonconforming or transgender persons.

41. C: The effects produced by cocaine vary based on the method of administration. Depending on the quality of cocaine and the individual's tolerance, the effects of cocaine can last up to 30–40 minutes when snorted, 15–20 minutes when injected, and 10–15 minutes when smoked. Swallowing cocaine is not a typical method of administration, with the exception of individuals ingesting large quantities to avoid an arrest or to smuggle cocaine through customs.

42. B: Cocaine is classified as a Schedule II drug. Schedule II drugs have a high potential for abuse and are known to cause severe physical and psychological dependence.

43. C: It is most plausible that Clyde purchased and used cocaine and methamphetamines contaminated with opioids. It is common for drug dealers to add opioids and opiates to stimulants to increase the drugs' potency or profitability, which is one form of adulteration. Adulterating a urine sample involves tampering with a urine specimen to create a false-negative result. A therapeutic index or threshold is the ratio between the drug's toxic dose and its therapeutic dose, which would not explain the presence of opioids.

44. B: The trained professional assisting with the intervention likely specialized in unilateral family therapy (UFT), which provides family members with support and guidance to motivate a family member with SUD to seek treatment. Clinicians using UFT provide motivational incentives to help individuals with SUD agree to treatment. UFT is a nonconfrontational approach designed to help family members learn about the disease of addiction and develop and maintain appropriate boundaries. The Johnson model of intervention is a family intervention approach using strategic confrontation to persuade a family member to enter treatment. The intervention encourages family members to express love and concern rather than anger and blame. UFT emphasizes treatment engagement rather than relapse prevention. Crisis counseling is typically not a part of UFT.

45. B: Intake screening tools are designed to identify those clients requiring a more thorough assessment in targeted matters of concern. Clinicians screen for substance use disorder to determine a pattern of use worthy of concern, a substance use disorder requiring treatment, or the likely presence of co-occurring disorders. Screening tools are not typically designed to define any particular mental disorder but rather the likelihood that a co-occurring mental disorder may exist. Screeners should be familiar with specific protocols for properly scoring screening instruments as well as protocols for specific steps to take when an individual breaches the cutoff threshold for substance abuse or a co-occurring mental disorder.

46. B: Questions on the Alcohol Use Disorders Identification Test-Concise (AUDIT-C) include (1) How often did you have a drink containing alcohol in the past year? (2) How many drinks did you have on a typical day when you were drinking in the past year? and (3) How often did you have six or more drinks on one occasion in the past year? The CAGE (which stands for cut down, annoyed, guilty, eye-opener) screening tool contains the question: Have you ever had a drink first thing in the morning to steady your nerves or get rid of a hangover?

47. C: Symptoms associated with a blood alcohol concentration (BAC) of 0.23 are gross disorientation and loss of consciousness. Lower BAC levels are associated with overall feelings of well-being, lowered inhibitions, and relaxation. As BAC levels reach 0.16–0.20, individuals require assistance with walking and experience dysphoria and vomiting. Once the BAC rises to its highest levels (0.25–0.30), individuals may experience coma, respiratory arrest, and death.

48. A: The Alcoholics Anonymous (AA) program differs from the Rational Recovery (RR) approach in that AA emphasizes an admission of powerlessness, whereas RR emphasized personal control over addiction. Because RR rejected the concept of powerlessness, there was no emphasis on a Higher Power's assistance. Additionally, AA is abstinence-based, whereas RR advocated for controlled drinking. AA asserts that addiction is a progressive disease, but RR did not. Lastly, RR leaders were trained in rational-emotive behavioral therapy, and AA is led by its members.

49. D: The counselor acted unethically by disclosing the client's diagnosis and his resistance to treatment to his employer without a signed release of information form. Unless otherwise specified, employee assistance program clients are afforded the same rights to confidentiality as any other client. Principle I-8 of the NAADAC Code of Ethics (2021) states that counseling services are voluntary for mandated clients. If the client refuses, then consequences should be instated. The counselor must clearly articulate the consequences for noncompliance during the informed consent process before establishing a treatment relationship. Without a signed release of information form, the provider would have acted unethically by providing a diagnosis and further recommendations. Employee assistance program counselors generally limit shared information to the client's attendance only. The counselor does not have an ethical responsibility to limit services to the problems related to alcohol use. In doing so, the counselor may have acted unethically by not conducting a suicide assessment. Lastly, while helpful for many clients, counselors are not ethically responsible for including family members and collateral sources.

50. C: It is true that sexual abuse and physical abuse are associated with greater instances of SUD than any other adverse childhood experiences (ACEs), which are traumatic events occurring before a person reaches age 18. ACEs include but are not limited to early exposure to parental substance use, child abuse and neglect, parental mental disorders, and intimate partner violence. As the number of ACEs increases, the likelihood of negative behavioral health outcomes, such as substance use, suicidality, diabetes, depression, obesity, cancer, and asthma, increases. The effects of ACEs are preventable, in part, by increasing protective factors and improving social determinants of health (SDOH).

51. C: Group cohesion is to group therapy as the therapeutic alliance is to individual therapy. Group cohesion refers to the "we-ness" of groups, indicated by the strength of emotional bonds and belonging and the coordinated efforts to achieve group tasks and goals. Similarly, the therapeutic alliance consists of three essential components: the emotional bond between the therapist and client, mutually agreed-upon treatment goals, and agreement on tasks. Self-disclosure, collaboration, and honoring client autonomy are all independent variables of the therapeutic alliance.

52. B: For clients who present as agitated and threatening, current symptoms and clinical presentation are the strongest predictors of violence. Agitation refers to excessive and repetitive motor activity paired with underlying psychological tension. It is an emergency situation that demands immediate attention. It is necessary for counselors to identify and assess the severity of the client's agitation and immediately implement appropriate deescalation techniques. In this moment, identifying whether the client has a history of violence, the substance causing withdrawal, or any co-occurring diagnosis or medical condition is secondary. Not all clients in withdrawal or intoxication have a history of violence. Additionally, the withdrawal symptoms of most drugs have the capacity to cause agitation, as does any underlying or co-occurring condition.

53. B: Benzodiazepine tolerance develops fairly rapidly. Consequently, anxiety cannot be treated effectively beyond four months, regardless of the dosage. Polydrug use is particularly problematic as using benzodiazepines in conjunction with pain medications, alcohol, and antihistamines can produce severe respiratory depression and even death. Due to the development of tolerance, even after use for as little as two to three weeks, individuals must be weaned away from benzodiazepines under medical supervision, most commonly over a period of months.

54. B: Experts suggest that naloxone should be administered or offered during stimulant withdrawal due to the common concurrent use of opioids. Naloxone is used to reverse opioid overdose. Individuals who inject stimulants are at a significant risk for contracting HIV. Although individuals who use stimulants often combine their use with central nervous system depressants, such as alcohol, naloxone only works to reverse opioid overdose. Individuals with stimulant use disorder have higher instances of impulsivity and subsequent suicidality.

55. A: Using Prochaska and DiClemente's stages of change model, counselors can help motivate clients to move from contemplation to preparation by using a decisional balance strategy. The decision to change characterizes the contemplation stage. Counselors work to tip the decisional balance toward change by maximizing change talk and minimizing sustain talk. The decisional balance sheet challenges the status quo by focusing on the client's reasons for changing. Asking open-ended questions is a general motivational interviewing strategy that is used in all stages of change. Offering a menu of options is a motivational interviewing strategy used to provide treatment information and help clients select from appropriate treatment options. Importance rulers, another motivational interviewing strategy, use a 1–10 Likert scale to measure the importance of changing patterns of substance use. This strategy can be used throughout all stages of change, but it is most commonly used to move a client from the precontemplation stage to the contemplation stage.

56. B: Cultural humility is an ethical principle that calls addiction professionals to redress power imbalances, understand and honor diverse worldviews and beliefs, and remain self-aware and willing to form partnerships to advocate for others effectively. Cultural competence, or knowledge of other cultures, differs from cultural humility in that it assumes that there is one majority culture and that competence of knowledge of minority cultures is something that can be mastered with a set end point. Cultural encapsulation is the failure to recognize cultural differences. Lastly, cultural awareness is the understanding of differences but does not include a willingness to adopt an other-oriented perspective.

57. A: Psychosis can occur when cocaine is used regularly at increasing doses. Long-term cocaine use can lead to restlessness, paranoia, panic, and eventually psychosis. Cocaine and other stimulant withdrawal symptoms begin with a "crash," followed by depression and lethargy.

58. B: The NAADAC Code of Ethics (2021) describes gratitude as giving back the good received from others. Beneficence refers to promoting the well-being of those served or acting in the best interest of others. Justice involves promoting equitable access to resources and behaving impartially toward others. Stewardship is expressed by judiciously allocating available resources to those in need.

59. C: Individuals withdrawing from cocaine are more likely to self-medicate with central nervous system (CNS) depressants, including alcohol, opiates, barbiturates, and benzodiazepines. Withdrawal from cocaine can occur after a period of dependency followed by an abrupt discontinuation of the substance. Compared to CNS depressants, fewer physiological withdrawal symptoms occur. Withdrawal symptoms from cocaine include irritability, cravings, nightmares, and psychomotor agitation. Individuals tend to use alcohol or other sedatives to handle symptoms of withdrawal and assist in "coming down" from a period of binge use.

60. C: "Let me see if I understand so far" is an example of summarization. Counselors use summarizations to bring together certain concepts and themes. They can also be used during transitions, such as at the end of the counseling session. Reframing is a counseling skill used to encourage clients to view situations or difficulties in a more positive light. Counselors use interpretation when sharing personal insight and introspection regarding a client's clinical presentation. Active listening involves verbal and nonverbal communication used to help the client feel validated and understood.

61. C: Principle III-13 of the NAADAC Code of Ethics (2021) requires that APs "only provide services within their scope of practice and competency and shall only offer services that are science-based, evidence-based, and outcome-driven." Only counselors working with clients experiencing trauma-related issues are obligated to practice trauma-informed care. Instead, APs provide services grounded in research and delivered to meet each client's cultural and linguistic needs.

62. C: The basal ganglia are responsible for controlling the rewarding and pleasurable effects of a psychoactive substance. There are two subregions in the basal ganglia—the nucleus accumbens and the dorsal striatum—which control motivation and habit formation. The amygdala is responsible for memory, emotions, and stress responses. The prefrontal cortex controls executive functioning, including thinking, planning, impulse control, problem-solving, and time management. Lastly, the cerebellum is responsible for coordination, movement, motor skills, and posture.

63. A: GATE (which stands for gather information, access supervision, take responsible action, and extend the action) is a four-step process model used to address suicidality among individuals with SUD. Gathering information comprises two steps: screening and asking follow-up questions. Next, the counselor must access supervision by assembling all gathered information, including past suicide attempts, risk and protective factors, and ongoing treatment issues. Taking action involves responsible, ethical, and legal interventions that align with the client's current level of risk, with particular attention paid to the client's intent, plan, means (i.e., methods), and lethality. The last step, extend the action, emphasizes that treatment for suicidality should be ongoing rather than a singular event. Counselors extend action by following up with referral sources, reassessing suicidality, and modifying interventions when necessary.

64. A: Viewing ambivalence as a normal response to change rather than resistance or denial creates an open channel for productive dialogue. One goal for clients in the contemplation stage is to tip the decisional balance toward change. Helping the client develop a change plan occurs in the preparation and action stages of change.

65. A: Celebrate Recovery is a biblically balanced religious mutual help group offering a progressive road to recovery through Jesus's Beatitudes, found in Matthew 5 in the Bible. Women for Sobriety is a secular support group offering abstinence-based help to women working to recover from SUD. The Women for Sobriety, New Life Program provides 13 acceptance statements to avoid destructive thinking and promote new ways of coping and thinking. Alcoholics Anonymous is a nonclinical, peer-based 12-step support group that provides opportunities for members to share their experiences, strength, and hope to help others recover. Alcoholics Anonymous is spiritual rather than religious; it suggests, but not require, that members seek a God of their understanding. Lastly, LifeRing Secular Recovery is an abstinence- and peer-based support group emphasizing a 3-S philosophy of sobriety, secularity, and self-help.

66. B: Stimulant use increases the production of catecholamines, which include norepinephrine, epinephrine, and dopamine. These are the main stress response hormones implicated in an individual's "fight or flight" responses. Examples of stimulants include cocaine, nicotine, amphetamines, methamphetamines, and caffeine. The mechanism of action for these psychoactive substances is an increase in central nervous system (CNS) activity. When the CNS is aroused, catecholamines are secreted from the adrenal glades. Substances that affect serotonin include MDMA, hallucinogens, and cocaine.

67. B: Homelessness is categorized as transitional, chronic, or episodic. Carl experiences chronic homelessness, which involves periods of homelessness lasting longer than 1 year or frequent instances of homelessness within the past couple of years. Transitional homelessness refers to episodes of homelessness that are less than 1 year, with periods ranging from a few weeks to months. Transitional homelessness is most common among individuals with recent displacement (e.g., individuals recently released from jail). Episodic homelessness is intermittent and repeated, occurring primarily among individuals with unstable housing.

68. C: The Stages of Change Readiness and Treatment Eagerness Scale (SOCRATES) yields scores in the following domains: ambivalence, problem recognition, and taking steps. SOCRATES 8A is for alcohol use, and SOCRATES 8B is for substance use. Participants are asked to use a 1–5 Likert scale, with 1 = "No! Strongly disagree" and 5 = "Yes! Strongly agree." Sample questions include, "Sometimes I wonder if I am an alcoholic," "I have already started making some changes in my drinking," and "My drinking is causing a lot of harm."

69. A: Damp housing would be most appropriate for Carl. There are three types of housing services, categorized by a person's readiness to change their substance use. Damp housing is appropriate for individuals in the contemplation or preparation stage. Carl is ready to change his drug use and is not prepared to change his alcohol use due to his hesitancy regarding withdrawal, placing him in the contemplation or preparation stage. Dry housing and sober living facilities are for individuals in the action or maintenance stage who are committed to abstinence-based living. Wet housing permits the use of legal substances and is for individuals in the precontemplation or contemplation stage.

70. D: Carl is hesitant to begin counseling and expresses a concern that he will be judged as he was with past therapists who were "simply unable to understand." Peer support services are a good option for engaging Carl in treatment and building trust. Peer support specialists are trained personnel with shared behavioral health care experiences. Carl would benefit from trauma-informed care due to his experience of homelessness, exposure to dehumanization while panhandling, and potential retraumatization by a previous therapist. Engagement may also help Carl with withdrawal symptoms, specialized care, and treatment for bipolar disorder. Pharmacotherapy, job skills training, and behavioral skills training are evidence-based practices for individuals experiencing homelessness and behavioral health disorders, but Carl must first engage with behavioral health services.

71. A: Principle VIII-3 of the NAADAC Code of Ethics (2021) outlines an ethical decision-making model to include the following steps: (1) upon identification of the dilemma, the AP should seek supervision and/or consultation; (2) consideration is then given to applicable laws, ethical guidelines, standards, and principles; (3) the AP engages in the deliberation of risks and benefits from each potential choice; (4) upon weighing the implications for all involved, the AP makes a decision; and (5) the decision is implemented, after which there is reflection and redirection when necessary.

72. C: Substance abuse clients, especially those with a history of being abused themselves, can struggle with impulse control and emotions, especially anger. Acting out anger cannot be tolerated. Usually, however, there are signs of agitation, elevation, and anger well before physical acting out occurs. At this earlier juncture, it can be helpful for the counselor to validate their affect without validating any given verbal expression ("I can see this is something difficult for you . . ." or "This brings up a lot of emotion for you, doesn't it?"). In this way, the counselor moves to constructive address of the client's emotions, defusing the need to act out physically. Prevention is particularly valuable—ground rules for conduct in group, with staff and on site, should be provided at the point of intake. Language, breach of confidentiality, threats, and physical aggression cannot be tolerated. Law enforcement may need to be called if safety becomes an issue. Clients should know in advance that serious threats are taken seriously and will be reported.

73. B: Getting lost in a familiar part of town, no matter the frequency, is more likely a sign of Alzheimer's disease rather than a reflection of the normal aging process. Individuals with Alzheimer's have difficulty paying monthly bills, including trouble handling money (e.g., depositing checks, making change). Misplacing items from time to time (e.g., phone, reading glasses) is common with normal aging. For people with dementia, misplacing items occurs with increased frequency, with an inability to retrace their steps. Difficulty multitasking is common among most older adults. For individuals with dementia, it is hard to focus on a single task.

74. C: Alcohol is the most commonly misused substance among older adults. The National Survey on Drug Use and Health (NSDUH) tracks data on substance use and mental disorders among subgroups. For individuals ages 65 and older, alcohol is the most commonly used substance, followed by tobacco, cannabis, and opioids.

75. B: Risky drug and alcohol use among older adults occurs for multiple reasons, including but not limited to differences in metabolism and elimination, with slower metabolism causing substances to remain in the body for longer periods; chronic health conditions exacerbating the adverse effects of substance use; and the tendency for negative interactions with prescribed medications. Tolerance to drugs and alcohol tends to decrease with age, with smaller doses producing the same effects as previous doses.

76. A: The Mini-Cog is a quick screener that assesses cognitive functioning by asking participants to recall three words and to draw a clock. A total of 5 points is possible, with 1 point for each of the three words recalled. Participants receive 1 point for correctly drawing a clock and 1 point for correctly positioning the numbers on the time requested (e.g., "Set the hands at 10 past 11"). The Saint Louis University Mental Status exam is a 20-item assessment used to determine the severity of dementia (e.g., mild, moderate, severe). The Montreal Cognitive Assessment produces scores in the following domains: visuospatial/executive, naming, memory, attention, language, abstraction, delayed recall, and orientation. Lastly, the Mini-Mental State Exam provides an assessment of the following domains: orientation (10 points), registration (3 points), attention and calculation (5 points), recall (3 points), and language and praxis (9 points).

77. C: The best example of conscientious refusal is an AP who refuses to follow an employer's directive to deny gender-affirming client care for youth. Conscientious refusal occurs when counselors refuse to carry out illegal or unethical directives. Research indicates that withholding gender-affirming care is harmful to youth. Gender-affirming care encompasses various interventions used to support an individual's gender identity. Examples include using pronouns to match an individual's gender identity, offering gender-neutral bathrooms, providing developmentally appropriate psychoeducation, and enlisting family support. Refusing to work with any client based on personally held convictions, regardless of whether one has deeply held convictions for or against an individual who is racist or individuals identifying as LGBT, is unethical (see Principle IV-4 of the NAADAC Code of Ethics [2021]). The request to "diversify" client caseloads is vague and is therefore not the best answer.

78. B: There are four primary categories used to group the 11 criteria for SUD: impaired control, social impairment, risky use, and pharmacologic symptoms. Legal issues were included in the DSM-IV criteria for SUD but were removed in the DSM-5. Examples of impaired control include the persistent desire to regulate substance use, cravings, and using the substance longer than intended. Social impairment refers to functional impairments at work, school, or home, including impaired interpersonal relationships, discontinuation of pleasurable activities (e.g., hobbies), and continued use despite social consequences. Risky use involves continued substance use in physically unsafe environments, despite knowledge of the potential for adverse physical and psychological consequences. Lastly, pharmacologic symptoms refer to symptoms of tolerance and withdrawal.

79. C: The ARISE method uses a three-level approach to motivate an addict to enter treatment. Level 1 (The First Call) begins with a telephone consultation, followed by a first meeting of an intervention network (IN). The IN consists of immediately involved significant others (spouse, family, and close friends) who then meet with the addict to encourage treatment. Faced with the collective encouragement of the IN, approximately 56 percent of addicts will then enter treatment. Level 2 (Strength in Numbers) expands the IN to include more family, friends, potentially even employers, and a therapist, citing specific examples of concerns and the need for treatment. The IN acts in concert to avoid no-win one-on-one contacts. Within two to five meetings, 80 percent will enter treatment. Level 3 (Formal Intervention) is more confrontational, as significant consequences of avoiding treatment are spelled out (all enabling behaviors to stop with more serious consequences to follow). Another 3 percent (i.e., 83 percent in total) will then accept treatment, and 61 percent of all will still be sober by the end of the first year.

80. B: The ability to work with genuine compassion for clients is the first essential feature of successful counseling, provided appropriate boundaries are also maintained. Skills, knowledge, and information specific to the client's situation and needs are essential but are substantially ineffective if not managed with compassion and care. The renowned psychologist Carl Rogers taught that every individual has a positive, trustworthy center if this psychological core can be accessed. Connecting with this center taps into an individual's resourcefulness and capability for self-understanding and positive self-direction. To this end, he promoted three keys: (1) congruence (genuineness); (2) unconditional positive regard (caring concern and compassion); and (3) accurate, empathetic understanding (the ability to meaningfully assume the client's subjective perspective). Using these tools, clients can be reached and motivated toward positive change.

81. B: The main purpose of Title 42 of the Code of Federal Regulations (CFR) Part 2 is to protect clients in treatment for substance use against adverse consequences in domestic or criminal proceedings. 42 CFR Part 2 offers privacy protections for treatment information for clients with SUD in federally funded programs. Although 42 CFR Part 2 protects treatment records for individuals receiving medication-assisted treatment for OUD, its main purpose is to provide privacy protection for all individuals with SUD to prevent ramifications such as loss of employment, criminal charges, housing loss, and loss of child custody. The Health Insurance Portability and Accountability Act of 1996 protects personal health information. Whereas 42 CFR Part 2 applies to substance use information for students in educational settings, the Family Educational Rights and Privacy Act protects educational records.

82. A: Amphetamine cross-tolerance is likely to occur with MDMA. Cross-tolerance happens when tolerance to one substance causes tolerance to a pharmacologically similar substance. MDMA acts as both a stimulant and a hallucinogen, making cross-tolerance probable with central nervous system (CNS) stimulants (e.g., amphetamines) because they share similar chemical structures. Cross-tolerance can occur with prescribed medications (e.g., antidepressants) and illicit drugs and is common with amphetamines, hallucinogens, and opioids.

83. D: The counselor response that best reflects empathy being used appropriately is, "You are heartbroken over relationships and opportunities that were lost as the result of your drug use." Counselors express appropriate empathy by reflecting an understanding of the client's thoughts and underlying feelings. The statement "You are really hurting today, and it's hard to face everything you destroyed when you were using drugs" is an example of parroting or mimicking, which should be avoided. The phrase "If I understand correctly" is an example of clarification. Lastly, stating, "I understand; when I was active in my addiction, the guilt and shame seemed insurmountable" is a poor example of empathy because the focus is on the counselor rather than on the client.

84. C: Saliva tests are limited because they can only detect recent drug use (i.e., within a few minutes or up to 48 hours). In general, the detection windows for each type of drug test vary based on factors including the substance used, when it was last used, and how long it was used. An individual's characteristics can also affect detection, including but not limited to ethnicity, hydration, body fat, and metabolic rate. Urine tests detect the presence of a drug's metabolites and are the most common method used in preemployment checks and random drug screens. A hair test can detect the presence of drugs in hair follicles months after use, giving them the widest detection window, with repeat drug use detected for up to 90 days. Hair tests can detect opioids, marijuana, cocaine, PCP, and amphetamines. Blood tests are the most effective for detecting alcohol concentration levels, showing levels of intoxication 24 hours after use.

85. C: The Drug Enforcement Administration (DEA), rather than the Food and Drug Administration (FDA), uses schedules to classify substances based on their potential for abuse, potential for psychological or physical dependency, and acceptable medical use. The Controlled Substances Act enables the DEA to categorize and oversee drug classifications (i.e., scheduling).

86. C: Dronabinol, an FDA-approved Schedule II medication for HIV-related weight loss, contains cannabinoids. Individuals taking dronabinol would have a positive urine drug screen suggesting the presence of cannabinoids. The FDA has not allowed other cannabis, cannabis-derived, or cannabidiol products to be made available to the general public.

87. D: Microassaults are verbal or nonverbal attacks that are purposeful, explicit, and overtly racist. Microinequity occurs when a person is dehumanized, disrespected, or overlooked because of race or gender. A microinsult refers to rude or insensitive remarks about a person based on the person's marginalized identity. Microinvalidation occurs when a person of marginalized status conveys experiences, thoughts, and feelings that are nullified or disbelieved. Microinequity, microinsults, and microinvalidations are often unconscious expressions, whereas microassaults are conscious.

88. D: AJ would be protected by the Americans with Disabilities Act (ADA) because he had a previous history of alcohol use disorder (AUD) that limited his functioning. Addiction is considered a disability when there is a current or past diagnosis of AUD or SUD. Because the facility is federally funded, they violated the ADA. Although dronabinol contains cannabinoids, it is a Schedule II medication that AJ's medical provider legally prescribed. The same protections apply to individuals receiving medication for opioid use disorder. Per Title I of the ADA, facilities with 15 or more employees are legally required to offer employment protection for individuals with disabling conditions. This requirement does not apply to federal housing protection.

89. C: Defining client goals should take place during the assessment phase. In this initial stage of counseling, a treatment plan is developed. In general, counselors do not need to establish rapport before constructing a treatment plan. The collaborative nature of treatment planning offers an initial opportunity for counselors to form a therapeutic alliance. Client goals must be established before treatment has begun, as they provide the focus for each session.

90. B: The US Food and Drug Administration (FDA) has approved disulfiram (Antabuse) as a second-line treatment for alcohol use disorder (AUD). Individuals who take disulfiram with alcohol become violently ill—experiencing severe headaches, vomiting, and shortness of breath. The FDA has also approved naltrexone and acamprosate for AUD. Naltrexone blocks alcohol-induced euphoria and intoxication, allowing a person to reduce alcohol consumption rather than abstain entirely. Naltrexone is an opioid antagonist and first-line treatment for individuals with moderate to severe symptoms of AUD who seek to reduce alcohol use and/or eventually abstain. The third FDA-approved medication for AUD is acamprosate, which is not impacted by alcohol use and can be given to individuals with hepatitis or additional comorbid liver conditions. For this reason, acamprosate is a first-line treatment recommended as an alternative for those with contraindications to naltrexone use (e.g., liver failure, concurrent opioid use). Lastly, buprenorphine is an FDA-approved medication for opioid use disorder (OUD).

91. B: The diagnostic criteria for panic disorder include intense fear or discomfort reaching its peak within minutes. In addition, panic attacks are recurrent, unexpected, and paired with perceptions that things are not real (i.e., derealization) and feeling disconnected from one's body (i.e., depersonalization). Panic attacks are accompanied by symptoms that include but are not limited to sweating, dizziness, trembling, and hyperventilation.

92. D: Depersonalization, or feeling as if one is separated from oneself or untethered from reality (e.g., having a distorted sense of time, emotional numbness), is a symptom shared with MDMA (aka ecstasy [pill form] or Molly [crystal form]) intoxication and panic attacks. Dystonia, which can be substance-induced, is a movement disorder that occurs with dopamine-blocking medications (e.g., neuroleptics, antiemetics). Dystonia may co-occur with depression and anxiety but is not associated with panic attacks. Dyssynergy refers to the tendency of one addiction to predispose a person to another form of addiction. Disinterestedness, or a state of impartiality, is not a symptom of panic attacks.

93. A: The best way to differentiate between a substance-induced mental disorder and an anxiety disorder is by determining the onset of overlapping symptoms. Similar or overlapping symptoms occur with severe intoxication or acute withdrawal. Transient substance-induced symptoms often improve with time. Symptoms caused by substances with a short half-life (e.g., cocaine) will improve faster than substances with a long half-life (e.g., methadone). Psychometric testing instruments are less likely to help confirm a diagnosis. Confirmatory drug tests help determine substance use but are not the best way to determine whether the effects of the substance have induced a mood disorder or if there is an independent mood disorder (e.g., generalized anxiety disorder, panic disorder). The pharmacological properties of substances are essential to determine because some substances are more closely related to anxiety symptoms than others; however, this is not the best way to differentiate between two diagnoses.

94. A: According to the DSM-5-TR, panic attacks differ from other anxiety disorders in that panic attacks are unexpected and cause considerable worry. Panic disorder is not diagnosed when panic attacks are situational or expected, such as those that occur with social anxiety or separation anxiety. Panic disorder is not diagnosed if the attacks are substance-induced or if they happen in the presence of a medical condition (e.g., hyperthyroidism).

95. D: The Michigan Alcoholism Screening Test (MAST) is used to detect the presence of alcohol dependency. The MAST was originally designed to screen for alcohol use disorder. The Michigan Assessment-Screening Test for Alcohol and Drugs (MAST/AD) was adapted from the original MAST to include dependency on other substances. Longer versions of the original MAST help clinicians understand the severity of alcohol use, consequences associated with alcohol use (e.g., legal, familial, occupational, health), and the potential for co-occurring disorders. Scores in the mid to high range indicate the need for a more comprehensive substance use disorder evaluation. Several variations of the MAST have been developed, including the brief MAST, the short MAST, and the self-administered MAST.

96. B: Clients with dense abuse histories often have difficulty establishing boundaries and have intense needs for approval, affection, and nurturing. Counselors can easily fall into trying to meet these needs, even while finding the relationship expanding to the point of role overload. To avoid this, counselors need to establish a treatment frame that helps set up and maintain reasonable boundaries. Key features of the treatment frame include: (1) an awareness that overinvestment fosters client dependency; (2) an understanding that clients must take responsibility for their own lives to grow; (3) establishing appointment times and durations in advance to limit encroachment; (4) enforcing start and closing session times; (5) refraining from giving out one's home phone number; (6) canceling sessions if the client is intoxicated; (7) limiting all contacts to the therapy session; (8) preventing intimate (sexual) boundary misinterpretations; (9) terminating if threats or acts of violence are experienced; and (10) insisting on proper and timely payment of session fees.

97. B: Confidentiality and privilege are waived when a client brings public charges against a counselor. This can occur, for example, in cases in which the client sues a counselor for malpractice or a counselor seeks a restraining order against a previous client. The counselor is the keeper of confidentiality in that the counselor is prohibited from disclosing client information. In contrast, the client is the keeper of privilege, prohibiting the counselor from disclosing client information in a court or other legal setting. Unless the client has signed an authorization enabling the counselor to speak to outside sources (e.g., a client's attorney or spouse), the counselor must honor client confidentiality. Lastly, unless considered to be a danger to themselves or others, clients refusing their counselors' treatment recommendations still have the right to have their confidentiality protected.

98. A: The AP should refer to, or consult with, a clinician trained in bipolar disorder. It is unethical for an AP to provide therapy to a client whose issues fall outside of the clinician's scope of practice. In this case, it would be best either to refer the patient to another therapist, or enter into co-therapy with a therapist trained in bipolar disorder. If the therapeutic alliance is strong, the therapist may want to refer the client for adjunctive services and remain the primary service provider, given that the client's bipolar disorder is apparently not severe.

99. D: Mothers who take human immunodeficiency virus (HIV) medications during pregnancy and childbirth and give the medication to their baby for 4–6 weeks after the birth can reduce the risk of transmission to 1% or less. HIV can be passed to an unborn baby through the placenta, blood, and other bodily fluids. Women can also reduce the chances of infecting their babies with HIV by electing to have a Cesarean birth and refraining from breastfeeding. In addition, testing pregnant women for HIV and immediately beginning treatment with an anti-HIV drug regimen has proven to decrease the number of babies born with HIV.

100. C: Pyramiding involves slowly increasing the steroid dosage, then titrating down after reaching a maximum peak. Cycling refers to taking steroids off and on and providing rest periods at specific intervals (generally between 6 and 16 weeks). Stacking involves using various administration methods with several steroids at once, whereas plateauing describes overlapping the use of different steroids and different methods to prevent tolerance.

101. D: Early-onset alcoholism refers to an onset of alcohol abuse in adolescence or young adult life. This represents about two-thirds of all individuals with an alcohol use disorder. Late-onset exacerbation drinking refers to individuals with an intermittent history of alcohol abuse that only became chronic in late adulthood. Late-onset alcoholism refers to individuals with no prior life history of alcohol abuse who developed an alcohol problem solely in later life. This category of alcoholism may be more amenable to treatment than the earlier-onset forms. Detoxification can be protracted in older adults, requiring a longer treatment stay, due to the metabolic changes of aging.

102. C: Butane is associated with sudden sniffing death syndrome (SSDS), which can occur almost immediately after inhaling butane, propane, or aerosols. When volatile substances are inhaled, an individual's body can go into shock, with a lack of oxygen causing heart failure. Individuals can experience SSDS from inhalants causing asphyxiation, suffocation, or altering adrenaline, which results in heart failure. SSDS can happen after prolonged use or after only one use.

103. D: More research is needed to determine if behavioral therapies can effectively treat inhalant use disorder. The National Institute on Drug Abuse supports using behavioral therapy with alcohol and other drugs, including but not limited to marijuana, cocaine, and benzodiazepines. The recommended behavioral therapies include digital therapeutics (i.e., mobile apps) to aid in outpatient retention, cognitive-behavioral therapy, motivational enhancement therapy, and contingency management.

104. C: Clinical recommendations for treating long-term opioid use or opioid use disorder among pregnant persons is to use medications, which include methadone and buprenorphine (without naloxone), that are recommended and safe for pregnant people. Abruptly stopping opioid use is contraindicated due to the risk of preterm labor, miscarriage, and fetal distress. Medications for opioid use disorder provide improved outcomes and are recommended over supervised withdrawal for long-term opioid use due to the reduced risk of a relapse. Behavioral alternatives for pain management are not indicated as a replacement for nonaddictive pain medications that can be used during childbirth.

105. B: Harm reduction is an approach used to help pregnant persons access treatment to reduce mortality and morbidity rates. Harm reduction is based on the premise that minimizing risks is beneficial—and indeed, life-saving—in situations in which it is challenging to alleviate all potential dangers. This approach involves meeting people where they are, recognizing multiple paths to recovery, and engaging with people to prevent overdose and improve behavioral health outcomes. Decreasing stigma and discrimination, preventing abuse and neglect, and providing a safe treatment environment are often by-products of harm reduction but do not reflect its primary purpose.

106. C: Although often used interchangeably, the terminology *neonatal opioid withdrawal syndrome* (NOWS) is preferred over *neonatal abstinence syndrome* (NAS) to help eliminate connotations derived from the term *abstinence* and to reduce stigma, reduce misconceptions, and increase access to treatment. NOWS emphasizes that withdrawal (rather than abstinence) is a medical condition, as opposed to implying that a newborn infant has a choice to abstain from substances. NOWS reinforces the disease recovery model with successful treatment strategies for infants born with the condition.

107. C: Principles III-29 and III-30 of the NAADAC Code of Ethics (2021) state that APs should be aware of and work to dispel societal stigma, prejudice, and misconceptions surrounding SUDs and the people who have them. It is suggested that APs actively advocate for equitable treatment, choices, and opportunities for all who seek assistance with SUD. This can be achieved through active participation in the legislative process, participating in public forums, or engaging with educational institutions.

108. B: The acronym SOAP stands for Subjective, Objective, Assessment, and Plan. The SOAP note was first generated in the 1970s to provide physicians with rigor, structure, and a way for practices to communicate with one another. *Subjective* provides a narrative summary of the client's current condition, usually including the presenting problem (why they came to be seen). Common elements include: (1) onset (if applicable); (2) chronology (improvements or worsening, variations in the problem, etc.); (3) symptom qualities (the nature of the symptoms, etc.); (4) severity (degrees of distress); (5) modifying factors (what helps or worsens the condition, etc.); (6) additional symptoms (whether related or unrelated to the presenting problem); and (7) treatments (prior treatments, if the client has previously been seen elsewhere). *Objective* captures key facts that are measurable, quantifiable, and repeatable aspects of the client's situation (physical symptoms, lab results, weight, etc.). *Assessment* refers to the clinician's early diagnostic impressions. *Plan* describes the clinician's next steps in response to the information obtained (further assessments, referrals, medications, interventions, etc.).

109. B: In the DSM-5-TR, there are no documented withdrawal symptoms for inhalants, hallucinogens, and PCP. Symptoms of caffeine withdrawal include headaches, irritable or depressed mood, sleep difficulties, sluggishness, and gastrointestinal issues. The DSM-5-TR does not acknowledge caffeine use disorder but has identified it as a condition warranting further study.

110. B: According to Principle I-8 of the NAADAC (the Association for Addiction Professionals) Code of Ethics (2021), APs working with clients who are mandated to treatment must inform the clients of the legal and ethical limitations to confidentiality before the start of the therapeutic or service relationship. The AP is also obligated to discuss confidentiality limitations for personal information shared during supervision or consultation. If a mandated client refuses services, the AP must discuss the potential consequences and honor client autonomy.

111. C: Clinicians assessing for co-occurring disorders attend to the client's clinical presentation after an initial period of abstinence. True psychiatric symptoms often become apparent during the early stages (during the first 30 days) of abstinence. Clinicians conduct ongoing, comprehensive biopsychosocial assessments, including but not limited to risk factors, protective factors, family history, mental status, history of substance or mental disorders, medical history, cultural and social influences, and occupational factors. The client's ongoing clinical presentation must prove or validate the diagnosis. Symptoms of withdrawal, as well as those of acute or chronic alcohol and drug toxicity, can readily present as a psychiatric disorder. They can also mask underlying psychiatric symptoms. Additional attention should be given to medications and medication compliance. As the assessment proceeds, caution must be taken to ensure the client is properly treated for any serious medical withdrawal problems and that all safety issues are carefully addressed.

112. C: Case managers help clients determine viable treatment options by balancing client safety with client autonomy or self-determination. Self-determination is most fully ensured when clients can take the lead in identifying their needs and choosing from resource options that most fully meet their personal goals and lifestyle. Flexibility is essential, as is adaptability, to ensure that referral providers and agencies are well-coordinated and adequately responsive. Clients should be assessed for their ability to apply for, access, and follow through with selected referrals, with the case manager providing assistance where needed. Informing, educating, and guiding clients through this process can ensure an overall least-restrictive level of care.

113. B: The AP honors the principle of autonomy by allowing Juan to address repressed memories and anxiety rather than placing the sole focus on his alcohol use. Autonomy refers to the capacity of a person to make their own decisions or choose their own destiny. Justice involves promoting equitable access to resources and behaving impartially toward others. Stewardship is the prudent allocation of available resources to those in need. Honesty and candor include telling the truth to clients, colleagues, and individuals in the community.

114. D: A peer specialist is a person who has been successful in recovery and is now certified or trained to help others with similar experiences. A peer specialist, or peer recovery support specialist, can be used to help engage individuals with recovery and assists with relapse prevention. Peer workers, peer navigators, and peer mentors provide nonclinical support services (i.e., without specialized training or certification). Peer support services assist individuals with SUDs, mental disorders, or a combination of both, with various roles (e.g., engagement, cultural support, recovery group facilitation) through volunteer or paid positions.

115. A: Role drift occurs when peer support specialists perform tasks outside their role (e.g., case management, therapy). Role strain involves the peer support specialist experiencing stress or pressure over poorly defined job responsibilities. Role strain often co-occurs with role drift or role confusion. Role confusion occurs when the peer support specialist is unclear about their role, whereas role conflict happens when two or more roles clash.

116. D: Recovery capital refers to an individual's available internal and external resources useful for initiating and sustaining recovery. This includes personal recovery capital (e.g., coping skills, self-efficacy, healthcare access), community recovery capital (e.g., peer support services, 12-step programs), cultural recovery capital (a form of community capital encompassing culturally prescribed external resources), and family and social recovery capital (e.g., interpersonal relationships, supportive family members). Recovery capital is a strengths-based model focusing on protective factors rather than risk factors or weaknesses. Socioeconomic benefits or assets are facets of recovery capital but do not encompass the full range of external and internal resources.

117. A: Trigger events are crises, stressors, or situations that have the potential to threaten a client's sobriety. Crisis situations can include divorce, job loss, an impending holiday, time with family, or visiting past friends who may encourage the client to use. Clients are encouraged to anticipate such events and then bookend them—talking about them with a trusted friend (e.g., a twelve-step sponsor, close confidant) both before and after they occur. In this way, the client can prepare to remain steadfast in their commitment to sobriety. This also offers the client a way to debrief and decompress. A counselor can be of further assistance, addressing the client's specific strengths and weaknesses in order to shore up the client's resolve. In this way, the client can be assisted in avoiding a return to past familiar dysfunctional responses.

118. A: Homeostasis is the balanced state that exists in the body in the absence of substance abuse. When substances are misused or overused, the body is unable to regulate or balance systems. Tolerance and dependence often occur after prolonged substance use. Once the substance is discontinued, the body must again acclimate to its removal, which occurs during withdrawal. The therapeutic index is used to measure the range between a substance's efficacy and its toxicity. Pharmacokinetics describes processes that occur from the time a substance enters the body to when it is eliminated. Psychoactive mechanisms describe how psychoactive substances affect the brain to change a person's mood, perception, behavior, thoughts, and feelings.

119. C: Individuals whose cocaine use is considered isolated do not go on to develop cocaine use disorder. Cocaine use disorder begins with experimental use, which is motivated by curiosity and characterized by non-punitive consequences. The second stage is frequent or social use. In this phase, individuals tend to use cocaine socially or turn to the substance when in emotional pain. In the third stage, individuals are less likely to have control over the amount used. Finally, dysfunctional use is characterized by preoccupation with drug use, chronic sleep and health problems, severe disruptions in social and family life, and work and financial issues. In the final phase, the person becomes dependent on cocaine and generally cannot stop without assistance.

120. C: Risk and protective factors are correlated, cumulative, and influential over time. Risk and protective factors have multiple outcomes and exist in multiple contexts (e.g., families, communities). In the context of substance use disorder (SUD), risk factors are those that increase the likelihood of developing SUD. In contrast, protective factors are associated with a lower chance of developing SUD. Risk and protective factors are correlational, with risk factors positively correlated with developing SUD, and protective factors producing a negative correlation. Risk factors are cumulative, with some leading to others; multiple risk factors exponentially increase the likelihood of developing SUD. Finally, risk and protective factors can be fixed (e.g., genetics) or variable (e.g., employment status), and each risk and protective factor can be experienced across an individual's lifetime.

121. A: The copyrighted Alcohol Dependence Scale (ADS) is composed of twenty-five items that provide a quantitative measure of alcohol dependence, with a score of nine being highly predictive of a DSM-supported diagnosis. The five-minute test can be self-administered and covers: (1) alcohol withdrawal symptoms, (2) reduced control over drinking, (3) compulsive drinking awareness, (4) increased alcohol tolerance, and (5) key drink-seeking behaviors. The ADS has been widely used in research and in clinical settings, and numerous studies have determined that the instrument is both valid and reliable. The ADS offers excellent predictive value in establishing a DSM diagnosis. It also produces a measure of dependence severity that is needed in treatment planning, particularly regarding the intensity of treatment needed. ADS instructions for administration request responses regarding alcohol used during the immediate past twelve months. However, other selected intervals (e.g., six months, twelve months, or twenty-four months) may be applied following treatment. Use of the ADS has primarily been among clinical adult samples. However, studies have also used the ADS with adolescents.

122. D: Stress and emotion management skills are integrated into the treatment process. Early recovery groups typically consist of new clients (first month of treatment) or those needing additional (or repeated) abstinence skills training. The primary goal is to educate clients about: (1) cognitive tools to reduce cravings; (2) classically conditioned biological cravings; (3) time management and scheduling skills; (4) essentials of secondary substance abstinence; and (5) needed community services linkages. Relapse prevention groups offer relapse education and supportive sharing. Topics focus on behavior change, altering cognitive and affective orientations, and establishing twelve-step program linkages. Social support groups consist of clients in the final month of treatment and focus on identifying drug-free activities and establishing and extending friendships with drug-free people. These groups are less structured, with content determined by group members' needs. Family education groups meet for twelve weeks to address topics such as: (1) addiction biology; (2) conditioned cues, extinction, and conditioned abstinence; (3) substance abuse health effects; and (4) addiction effects on the family.

123. B: Buprenorphine is used in the treatment of physical opioid dependence as a newer alternative to methadone. Disulfiram (Antabuse) and naltrexone (ReVia) are medications used in the treatment of alcohol dependence and most particularly in the avoidance of relapse. Disulfiram doses are effective for three days. Clients can receive the medication during group sessions, with additional doses sent home for use over the weekends. While early studies indicate that naltrexone does not reduce the frequency of relapses, it does appear to reduce the overall duration of relapse. It also helps to reduce the amount of alcohol consumed in a relapse episode. Of note, however, recent data suggest that naltrexone might not be effective for men with chronic and severe alcohol dependence. Another alcohol treatment medication, acamprosate (Campral), has been Food and Drug Administration (FDA)-approved for alcohol abstinence maintenance since 2004. Acamprosate decreases the amount, frequency, and duration of alcohol consumption during episodes of alcohol relapse. It also helps to reduce cravings, even if clients resume drinking.

124. C: Amyl nitrite is frequently linked to risky sexual behaviors and increased instances of HIV among men who have sex with men. For decades, the use of amyl nitrate (aka poppers) has been linked to sexually transmitted infections among gay and bisexual men. Amyl nitrite is known for increasing a person's sex drive and intensifying orgasm. Other substances linked to risky sexual behavior and HIV among men who have sex with men include alcohol, opioids, methamphetamine, and crack cocaine.

125. A: The diagnostic criteria for hallucinogen persisting perception disorder include reexperiencing perceptual alterations that were initially experienced during intoxication and now occur during cessation (i.e., when sober). Symptoms must cause clinically significant distress and functional impairment. The perceptual alterations must not be attributable to a medical condition or mental disorder.

126. D: To assist clients experiencing a bad trip, clinicians must first assess for safety, followed by placing the client in a calm, isolated environment to provide reassurance and support. This "talking down" approach involves providing clients with a stress-free environment and reassuring them that they are safe—that perceptions are not real. Although symptoms may be treated with benzodiazepines in extreme cases, medication-assisted treatment applies mainly to opioid and alcohol use. Haldol is not recommended due to an increased risk of adverse effects, including nightmares, hallucinations, and delirium. A flashback or bad trip is not considered a withdrawal symptom. Physical restraints are contraindicated for LSD intoxication due to the risk of hyperthermia and/or rhabdomyolysis (damage to muscle tissue).

127. B: LSD has the potential for toxicity, tolerance, and psychological dependence. Individuals who use LSD do not experience physical cravings, and it is atypical for individuals to use LSD daily. Therefore, psychological dependence, rather than physical cravings, occurs when individuals seek to reexperience the euphoria or good trips. LSD toxicity can lead to respiratory arrest, hyperthermia, and coma.

128. C: To substantiate a diagnosis of hallucinogen-induced anxiety, the symptoms must predominate in the clinical presentation or be severe enough to warrant separate clinical attention. Hallucinogen-induced anxiety is a function of hallucinogen use, so it would not predate substance use. Anxiety would occur only during intoxication, with abstinence differentiating it from hallucinogen persisting perception disorder.

129. A: The most effective strategy for improving treatment engagement and retention among individuals experiencing homelessness is to sequence services and interventions according to client readiness. Evidence-based practices for individuals experiencing homelessness include peer support, brief counseling, medication for OUD, case management, and use of a community reinforcement approach. Sequencing events would allow individuals to decide which services are most desirable. For example, some individuals may be open to peer support but opposed to case management. Addressing structural racism and racial segregation is not the most effective strategy for treatment engagement and retention. Communication and collaboration are effective for retention but not engagement. Offering medication-assisted treatment is an effective strategy for engagement and retention; however, not all individuals experiencing homelessness require this intervention.

130. B: Ethical dilemmas often involve a conflict between the principles of autonomy and beneficence. Autonomy is the right of every individual to make rational decisions and determine the direction of their lives through self-determination, without force or coercion. APs practice beneficence by promoting the well-being of the clients served. The obligation is to do good, or act in the client's best interest. The conflict occurs when the wants and desires of the client oppose what the AP believes is best for the client. When weighing this dilemma, client competence, preferences, and consequences must be considered and carefully weighed with the counselor's obligation to do no harm. Autonomy is the bedrock of honesty, confidentiality, and informed consent (Varkey, 2020).

131. A: Individuals with schizophrenia have the highest prevalence of tobacco use. The smoking rates of individuals with psychiatric disorders are higher than those in the general population, particularly among those with serious psychiatric disorders. The National Institute on Drug Abuse estimates that up to 70–85% of individuals with schizophrenia smoke. It also estimates that 50–70% of people with bipolar disorder smoke. The lifetime prevalence of individuals with anorexia nervosa who smoke is estimated to be approximately 30%. The prevalence of individuals with post-traumatic stress disorder (PTSD) and individuals with attention-deficit/hyperactivity disorder who also smoke is approximately 45%.

132. A: Client outcome measures should be conducted on an ongoing basis. Outcome measures and related assessments should be ongoing to review, evaluate, and adjust the client's treatment plan to reflect progress or determine if a change in approach is necessary. Outcome measures can be formal or informal. An example of a formal outcome measure is the OQ-45.2, which provides baseline screening measures, identifies areas of immediate concern, and assists in discharge planning. Informal outcome measures include things like scaling questions, interviews, and surveys.

133. C: Although confidentiality has limitations, an addiction professional (AP) can best guarantee confidentiality when providing or receiving consultation with other professionals. This is because both parties are ethically obliged to protect the client's privacy and confidentiality. Principle II-16 of the NAADAC Code of Ethics (2021) states that APs cannot guarantee the maintenance of confidentiality when providing group, family, or couples therapy. APs must convey this risk to clients and explain the roles and responsibilities of all involved parties.

134. A: The counselor may have missed symptoms of opioid use disorder. First responders administered naloxone, which quickly restored the client's breathing. Naloxone only works on opioid overdose. The information provided does not substantiate the diagnosis of neurocognitive disorder. Cannabinoid use disorder is not a DSM-5-TR diagnosis. Avoidant personality disorder is characterized by restraint within intimate partnerships, social inhibition, and viewing oneself as inferior. This criterion was not evident in the client's clinical presentation.

135. D: The Short Michigan Alcohol Screening Test—Geriatric (SMAST-G) is a 10-item full screening tool used to determine alcohol use or misuse in older adults. The questions assess an individual's difficulty controlling drinking, how others view their drinking, physical symptoms of excessive alcohol use, and alcohol use in response to loneliness and loss. The Drug Abuse Screening Test (DAST-1) is a one-question prescreening instrument that asks, "In the last 12 months, have you used drugs other than those required for medical reasons?" The Tobacco, Alcohol, Prescription Medication and Other Substance Use (TAPS-1) tool is another initial screener for commonly used substances. If the person admits to substance use, then TAPS-2 is administered, which assesses the risk for each substance used. Lastly, the Columbia Suicide Severity Rating Scale (C-SSRS) is a suicide risk assessment measuring the severity, intensity, and lethality of suicidal ideation or intent.

136. D: Recommended for the treatment of post-traumatic stress disorder (PTSD), cognitive processing therapy helps clients reconceptualize traumatic events to reduce their negative consequences in the present day. It is a structured intervention that begins with teaching clients about the effects of trauma. The next step is processing the event(s), which involves clients writing detailed narratives of their most traumatic event. Counselors then guide clients in processing the events to modify maladaptive thinking and improve overall functioning. Narrative therapy uses personal accounts to externalize events and to recreate healthy narratives. Narrative exposure therapy is designed specifically for PTSD sufferers. Solution-focused therapy is a strengths-based approach to problem solving. Prolonged exposure therapy is a behavioral approach used to instruct clients to gradually experience memories, emotions, and circumstances surrounding their trauma.

137. B: Best practices for developing treatment plan goals are reflected in the statement: The client will experience fewer distressing thoughts and flashbacks, decreasing from daily to four times a week within 3 months. Treatment plan goals must be measurable, observable, and quantitative. They must also be consistent with the client's diagnosis or problem statement. The goal for decreasing depressive symptoms is measurable, but it is not consistent with the client's diagnosis. The goal for decreasing suicidal ideation is not appropriate because the client denied suicidal ideation and the client's ED admission is more likely due to an accidental opioid overdose rather than a suicide attempt. Lastly, discussing distressing feelings with his wife is not a quantitative, measurable goal.

138. D: The biopsychosocial assessment provides a holistic view of interconnected causal factors of substance misuse, including but not limited to the client's age, genetics, medical history, any underlying mental disorder, environmental conditions, sexual orientation, spirituality, cultural norms, gender identity, family relationships, interpersonal relationships, and socioeconomic status. Clinical biopsychosocial assessments provide a collaborative, strengths-based, and holistic approach to diagnosing substance misuse (i.e., prescription drug misuse).

139. A: Cocaine activates the dopamine, serotonin, and norepinephrine monoamines. Dopamine is responsible for movement, memory, concentration, and pleasure; serotonin regulates emotional happiness, sexual desire, learning, sleep, and digestion; and norepinephrine controls movement, sleep, memory, and anxiety. Marijuana alters the endogenous cannabinoids, influencing movement, cognition, and memory functions. Alcohol affects the neurotransmitters glutamate and gamma-aminobutyric acid (GABA), with glutamate acting on excitatory functions and GABA acting on inhibitory functions. Lastly, prescription narcotics such as oxycodone modify the endogenous opioids (i.e., endorphins and enkephalins), causing sedation, altered moods, stress responses, diminished pain, and cardiovascular regulation.

140. D: A conflict of interest occurs when providers encounter situations in which attending to one obligation results in abandoning another one. Counselors who are unable to avoid conflicts of interest are at risk of impaired objectivity. Conflicts of interest may result in ethical dilemmas or involve boundary violations and dual relationships, but many do not, as in cases in which a counselor's actions result in personal gain. For example, a provider with financial difficulties continues therapy with a client longer than necessary or bills for services that were not delivered. Boundary violations are harmful and exploitative and occur when counselors cross the line between personal and professional roles. Dual relationships refer to a counselor's direct relationship with the client or someone close to the client and occur in one or more settings (e.g., personal, professional, or community).

141. B: Clients who may not be appropriate candidates for group therapy in substance use treatment include those who exhibit psychosis, those unable to follow group rules, and those currently using substances. Other clients who may be ineligible for group therapy include those who exhibit mania, those diagnosed with disorders affecting communication (e.g., intellectual disability, dementia), and those with irregular attendance. Clients who are deemed inappropriate candidates for groups should be reassessed if their circumstances change. Clients who are unmotivated to participate are appropriate for SUD groups because most use motivational interviewing, cognitive-behavioral therapy, and psychoeducation to improve outcomes among clients in all stages of change.

142. A: Minors receiving treatment for substance use disorder (SUD) must provide written consent to authorize the disclosure of information to parents and guardians. Students are entitled to protections under the Family Educational Rights and Privacy Act and 42 CFR Part 2. 42 CFR Part 2 requires written consent from students treated for SUD to authorize communication with third parties, including parents, guardians, insurance providers, and school personnel. Exceptions include cases of suspected child abuse or neglect and concerns for a school-based applicant's safety. An individual is considered an applicant when they are in the process of seeking services. For example, in cases in which a student in the process of seeking treatment for substance use is deemed a harm to themselves, the program director is permitted to inform the parents of the counselor's concerns.

143. C: Counselors using an integrated care model promote prevention, treatment, and referral to address each client's holistic needs. Integrated care involves collaboration and communication with primary care and behavioral health providers to ensure that recovery-oriented services are delivered across a continuum of care. Client services range from ambulatory and medical detoxification to inpatient psychiatric care, residential treatment, and step-down services (e.g., peer support, community-based services). Basic, medical, and psychosocial needs are all incorporated in integrated treatment.

144. C: John's group for at-risk youth uses interventions for tertiary prevention. Tertiary prevention reduces the negative consequences of substance use and prevents its recurrence. The participants have engaged in substance use, and the group's purpose is to reinforce prosocial behaviors and enhance drug use resistance skills. Primary prevention is used to prevent substance use by targeting all susceptible people or populations. Secondary prevention aims to reduce the likelihood of substance use among persons with risk factors (e.g., lack of connection, poor academic achievement, sexual abuse). Universal prevention is a primary prevention strategy used to deter the onset of substance use by providing information and skills to prevent the problem.

145. B: Contingency management uses principles of operant conditioning to increase or decrease behaviors through immediate rewards or consequences. Contingency management programs function by identifying a target behavior (e.g., substance use), monitoring the behavior (e.g., with drug screens), and reinforcing improved behavior (e.g., by using monetary rewards) or punishing the behavior (e.g., by administrative discharge). Skills training is a behavioral intervention that uses a didactic approach to teach drug-resistance skills. Motivational interviewing is used to engage clients and determine their readiness for change. Cognitive-behavioral therapy involves identifying and changing automatic thoughts. Contingency management can incorporate skills training, motivational interviewing, and cognitive-behavioral therapy components, but operant conditioning serves as its basis.

146. A: The advantage of using urine drug screens for contingency management is that the results are immediate. Immediacy is necessary for effectively reinforcing target behaviors. Drugs can be detected using urine, hair, blood, saliva, and sweat samples. Of the methods used, there is an increased likelihood of receiving adulterated urine samples that have been diluted or otherwise tampered with or manipulated. Drug screens using blood as a detection method are the most reliable. Hair, saliva, and sweat tend to have longer detection windows than urine.

147. C: Conscientious refusal and beneficence would best help John determine his next steps. John must decide if it is ethical to adhere to his supervisor's mandate and initiate an administrative discharge. It will be necessary to first examine the program's drug testing protocol. The drug screens that the program uses are immunoassay urine drug screens, which can produce false positives, particularly when detecting amphetamines. Ricardo benefits from the group, which has been meeting for 10 weeks, supporting the principle of beneficence. Conscientious refusal involves declining to carry out illegal or unethical actions. Although Ricardo's discharge is not illegal, it can be argued that it is unethical to terminate his participation rather than to perform a confirmatory drug test. Other principles that may apply include justice and nonmaleficence. Autonomy is a possibility when considering informed consent/assent and parental pressure to attend the group.

148. D: This form of brief therapy focuses on helping clients to identify solutions to vexing problems. Asking clients to recall a time when the problem was not present or so severe, and then asking what they or others had done differently, can help in identifying potential solutions. Further, asking about exceptions to the problem (when it could have occurred but did not) can also be helpful. Using the miracle question involves asking this: "If a miracle occurred and the problem went away, what would be the first sign (and then what signs would follow)?" Scaling questions allow clients to scale a problem from 0 (worst) to 10 (resolved) and then to discuss why they selected that number to find clarity (comparing couples or family answers can also help). Coping questions ask "How have you managed to carry on to this point?" to find strengths. Using consultation breaks at the half-session mark and pondering the answers, followed by compliments, encouragement, and ideas, can also help. Compliments and a future focus (instead of focusing on the past) keep the work positive and solution focused.

149. B: Although multiple theories explain the co-occurrence of substance use disorder (SUD) and post-traumatic stress disorder (PTSD), the self-medication hypothesis has the most robust empirical support. The self-medication hypothesis theorizes that individuals use substances to counteract or cope with symptoms of PTSD. The high-risk hypothesis states that people who use substances place themselves in high-risk situations, resulting in exposure to traumatic events. The susceptibility hypothesis states that individuals with SUD are more biologically predisposed to developing PTSD after exposure to a traumatic event than those who do not use substances. Lastly, the Pandora's box hypothesis purports that separate treatment of SUD and PTSD, particularly in the initial stages of SUD, is preferable to concurrent treatment. Proponents of this theory, which lacks empirical evidence, fear that asking about trauma is akin to opening Pandora's box and that treating PTSD during the early stages of SUD will perpetuate a relapse.

150. B: "What has your alcohol use been like in the past week?" is an open-ended question, which is consistent with the core motivational interviewing skills known by the acronym OARS (which stands for open-ended questions, affirmations, reflections, and summarization). Open-ended questions are used to encourage back-and-forth dialogue between the counselor and client and require more than a "yes," "no," or simple response. The question, "On a typical week, how much alcohol do you consume?" is closed-ended and requires a simple response. The respondent may be more inclined to expand on their answer, but the question itself is not open-ended. The question, "Did your husband encourage you to come today?" is a closed-ended question, yielding a "yes" or "no" response. The question "When would you like to quit drinking?" is closed-ended and requires a simple response.

How to Overcome Test Anxiety

Just the thought of taking a test is enough to make most people a little nervous. A test is an important event that can have a long-term impact on your future, so it's important to take it seriously and it's natural to feel anxious about performing well. But just because anxiety is normal, that doesn't mean that it's helpful in test taking, or that you should simply accept it as part of your life. Anxiety can have a variety of effects. These effects can be mild, like making you feel slightly nervous, or severe, like blocking your ability to focus or remember even a simple detail.

If you experience test anxiety—whether severe or mild—it's important to know how to beat it. To discover this, first you need to understand what causes test anxiety.

Causes of Test Anxiety

While we often think of anxiety as an uncontrollable emotional state, it can actually be caused by simple, practical things. One of the most common causes of test anxiety is that a person does not feel adequately prepared for their test. This feeling can be the result of many different issues such as poor study habits or lack of organization, but the most common culprit is time management. Starting to study too late, failing to organize your study time to cover all of the material, or being distracted while you study will mean that you're not well prepared for the test. This may lead to cramming the night before, which will cause you to be physically and mentally exhausted for the test. Poor time management also contributes to feelings of stress, fear, and hopelessness as you realize you are not well prepared but don't know what to do about it.

Other times, test anxiety is not related to your preparation for the test but comes from unresolved fear. This may be a past failure on a test, or poor performance on tests in general. It may come from comparing yourself to others who seem to be performing better or from the stress of living up to expectations. Anxiety may be driven by fears of the future—how failure on this test would affect your educational and career goals. These fears are often completely irrational, but they can still negatively impact your test performance.

Elements of Test Anxiety

As mentioned earlier, test anxiety is considered to be an emotional state, but it has physical and mental components as well. Sometimes you may not even realize that you are suffering from test anxiety until you notice the physical symptoms. These can include trembling hands, rapid heartbeat, sweating, nausea, and tense muscles. Extreme anxiety may lead to fainting or vomiting. Obviously, any of these symptoms can have a negative impact on testing. It is important to recognize them as soon as they begin to occur so that you can address the problem before it damages your performance.

The mental components of test anxiety include trouble focusing and inability to remember learned information. During a test, your mind is on high alert, which can help you recall information and stay focused for an extended period of time. However, anxiety interferes with your mind's natural processes, causing you to blank out, even on the questions you know well. The strain of testing during anxiety makes it difficult to stay focused, especially on a test that may take several hours. Extreme anxiety can take a huge mental toll, making it difficult not only to recall test information but even to understand the test questions or pull your thoughts together.

Effects of Test Anxiety

Test anxiety is like a disease—if left untreated, it will get progressively worse. Anxiety leads to poor performance, and this reinforces the feelings of fear and failure, which in turn lead to poor performances on subsequent tests. It can grow from a mild nervousness to a crippling condition. If allowed to progress, test anxiety can have a big impact on your schooling, and consequently on your future.

Test anxiety can spread to other parts of your life. Anxiety on tests can become anxiety in any stressful situation, and blanking on a test can turn into panicking in a job situation. But fortunately, you don't have to let anxiety rule your testing and determine your grades. There are a number of relatively simple steps you can take to move past anxiety and function normally on a test and in the rest of life.

Physical Steps for Beating Test Anxiety

While test anxiety is a serious problem, the good news is that it can be overcome. It doesn't have to control your ability to think and remember information. While it may take time, you can begin taking steps today to beat anxiety.

Just as your first hint that you may be struggling with anxiety comes from the physical symptoms, the first step to treating it is also physical. Rest is crucial for having a clear, strong mind. If you are tired, it is much easier to give in to anxiety. But if you establish good sleep habits, your body and mind will be ready to perform optimally, without the strain of exhaustion. Additionally, sleeping well helps you to retain information better, so you're more likely to recall the answers when you see the test questions.

Getting good sleep means more than going to bed on time. It's important to allow your brain time to relax. Take study breaks from time to time so it doesn't get overworked, and don't study right before bed. Take time to rest your mind before trying to rest your body, or you may find it difficult to fall asleep.

Along with sleep, other aspects of physical health are important in preparing for a test. Good nutrition is vital for good brain function. Sugary foods and drinks may give a burst of energy but this burst is followed by a crash, both physically and emotionally. Instead, fuel your body with protein and vitamin-rich foods.

Also, drink plenty of water. Dehydration can lead to headaches and exhaustion, especially if your brain is already under stress from the rigors of the test. Particularly if your test is a long one, drink water during the breaks. And if possible, take an energy-boosting snack to eat between sections.

Along with sleep and diet, a third important part of physical health is exercise. Maintaining a steady workout schedule is helpful, but even taking 5-minute study breaks to walk can help get your blood pumping faster and clear your head. Exercise also releases endorphins, which contribute to a positive feeling and can help combat test anxiety.

When you nurture your physical health, you are also contributing to your mental health. If your body is healthy, your mind is much more likely to be healthy as well. So take time to rest, nourish your body with healthy food and water, and get moving as much as possible. Taking these physical steps will make you stronger and more able to take the mental steps necessary to overcome test anxiety.

Mental Steps for Beating Test Anxiety

Working on the mental side of test anxiety can be more challenging, but as with the physical side, there are clear steps you can take to overcome it. As mentioned earlier, test anxiety often stems from lack of preparation, so the obvious solution is to prepare for the test. Effective studying may be the most important weapon you have for beating test anxiety, but you can and should employ several other mental tools to combat fear.

First, boost your confidence by reminding yourself of past success—tests or projects that you aced. If you're putting as much effort into preparing for this test as you did for those, there's no reason you should expect to fail here. Work hard to prepare; then trust your preparation.

Second, surround yourself with encouraging people. It can be helpful to find a study group, but be sure that the people you're around will encourage a positive attitude. If you spend time with others who are anxious or cynical, this will only contribute to your own anxiety. Look for others who are motivated to study hard from a desire to succeed, not from a fear of failure.

Third, reward yourself. A test is physically and mentally tiring, even without anxiety, and it can be helpful to have something to look forward to. Plan an activity following the test, regardless of the outcome, such as going to a movie or getting ice cream.

When you are taking the test, if you find yourself beginning to feel anxious, remind yourself that you know the material. Visualize successfully completing the test. Then take a few deep, relaxing breaths and return to it. Work through the questions carefully but with confidence, knowing that you are capable of succeeding.

Developing a healthy mental approach to test taking will also aid in other areas of life. Test anxiety affects more than just the actual test—it can be damaging to your mental health and even contribute to depression. It's important to beat test anxiety before it becomes a problem for more than testing.

Study Strategy

Being prepared for the test is necessary to combat anxiety, but what does being prepared look like? You may study for hours on end and still not feel prepared. What you need is a strategy for test prep. The next few pages outline our recommended steps to help you plan out and conquer the challenge of preparation.

Step 1: Scope Out the Test

Learn everything you can about the format (multiple choice, essay, etc.) and what will be on the test. Gather any study materials, course outlines, or sample exams that may be available. Not only will this help you to prepare, but knowing what to expect can help to alleviate test anxiety.

Step 2: Map Out the Material

Look through the textbook or study guide and make note of how many chapters or sections it has. Then divide these over the time you have. For example, if a book has 15 chapters and you have five days to study, you need to cover three chapters each day. Even better, if you have the time, leave an extra day at the end for overall review after you have gone through the material in depth.

If time is limited, you may need to prioritize the material. Look through it and make note of which sections you think you already have a good grasp on, and which need review. While you are studying, skim quickly through the familiar sections and take more time on the challenging parts.

Write out your plan so you don't get lost as you go. Having a written plan also helps you feel more in control of the study, so anxiety is less likely to arise from feeling overwhelmed at the amount to cover.

Step 3: Gather Your Tools

Decide what study method works best for you. Do you prefer to highlight in the book as you study and then go back over the highlighted portions? Or do you type out notes of the important information? Or is it helpful to make flashcards that you can carry with you? Assemble the pens, index cards, highlighters, post-it notes, and any other materials you may need so you won't be distracted by getting up to find things while you study.

If you're having a hard time retaining the information or organizing your notes, experiment with different methods. For example, try color-coding by subject with colored pens, highlighters, or post-it notes. If you learn better by hearing, try recording yourself reading your notes so you can listen while in the car, working out, or simply sitting at your desk. Ask a friend to quiz you from your flashcards, or try teaching someone the material to solidify it in your mind.

Step 4: Create Your Environment

It's important to avoid distractions while you study. This includes both the obvious distractions like visitors and the subtle distractions like an uncomfortable chair (or a too-comfortable couch that makes you want to fall asleep). Set up the best study environment possible: good lighting and a comfortable work area. If background music helps you focus, you may want to turn it on, but otherwise keep the room quiet. If you are using a computer to take notes, be sure you don't have any other windows open, especially applications like social media, games, or anything else that could distract you. Silence your phone and turn off notifications. Be sure to keep water close by so you stay hydrated while you study (but avoid unhealthy drinks and snacks).

Also, take into account the best time of day to study. Are you freshest first thing in the morning? Try to set aside some time then to work through the material. Is your mind clearer in the afternoon or evening? Schedule your study session then. Another method is to study at the same time of day that you will take the test, so that your brain gets used to working on the material at that time and will be ready to focus at test time.

Step 5: Study!

Once you have done all the study preparation, it's time to settle into the actual studying. Sit down, take a few moments to settle your mind so you can focus, and begin to follow your study plan. Don't give in to distractions or let yourself procrastinate. This is your time to prepare so you'll be ready to fearlessly approach the test. Make the most of the time and stay focused.

Of course, you don't want to burn out. If you study too long you may find that you're not retaining the information very well. Take regular study breaks. For example, taking five minutes out of every hour to walk briskly, breathing deeply and swinging your arms, can help your mind stay fresh.

As you get to the end of each chapter or section, it's a good idea to do a quick review. Remind yourself of what you learned and work on any difficult parts. When you feel that you've mastered the material, move on to the next part. At the end of your study session, briefly skim through your notes again.

But while review is helpful, cramming last minute is NOT. If at all possible, work ahead so that you won't need to fit all your study into the last day. Cramming overloads your brain with more information than it can process and retain, and your tired mind may struggle to recall even previously learned information when it is overwhelmed with last-minute study. Also, the urgent nature of cramming and the stress placed on your brain contribute to anxiety. You'll be more likely to go to the test feeling unprepared and having trouble thinking clearly.

So don't cram, and don't stay up late before the test, even just to review your notes at a leisurely pace. Your brain needs rest more than it needs to go over the information again. In fact, plan to finish your studies by noon or early afternoon the day before the test. Give your brain the rest of the day to relax or focus on other things, and get a good night's sleep. Then you will be fresh for the test and better able to recall what you've studied.

Step 6: Take a Practice Test

Many courses offer sample tests, either online or in the study materials. This is an excellent resource to check whether you have mastered the material, as well as to prepare for the test format and environment.

Check the test format ahead of time: the number of questions, the type (multiple choice, free response, etc.), and the time limit. Then create a plan for working through them. For example, if you have 30 minutes to take a 60-question test, your limit is 30 seconds per question. Spend less time on the questions you know well so that you can take more time on the difficult ones.

If you have time to take several practice tests, take the first one open book, with no time limit. Work through the questions at your own pace and make sure you fully understand them. Gradually work up to taking a test under test conditions: sit at a desk with all study materials put away and set a timer. Pace yourself to make sure you finish the test with time to spare and go back to check your answers if you have time.

After each test, check your answers. On the questions you missed, be sure you understand why you missed them. Did you misread the question (tests can use tricky wording)? Did you forget the information? Or was it something you hadn't learned? Go back and study any shaky areas that the practice tests reveal.

Taking these tests not only helps with your grade, but also aids in combating test anxiety. If you're already used to the test conditions, you're less likely to worry about it, and working through tests until you're scoring well gives you a confidence boost. Go through the practice tests until you feel comfortable, and then you can go into the test knowing that you're ready for it.

Test Tips

On test day, you should be confident, knowing that you've prepared well and are ready to answer the questions. But aside from preparation, there are several test day strategies you can employ to maximize your performance.

First, as stated before, get a good night's sleep the night before the test (and for several nights before that, if possible). Go into the test with a fresh, alert mind rather than staying up late to study.

Try not to change too much about your normal routine on the day of the test. It's important to eat a nutritious breakfast, but if you normally don't eat breakfast at all, consider eating just a protein bar. If you're a coffee drinker, go ahead and have your normal coffee. Just make sure you time it so that the caffeine doesn't wear off right in the middle of your test. Avoid sugary beverages, and drink enough water to stay hydrated but not so much that you need a restroom break 10 minutes into the test. If your test isn't first thing in the morning, consider going for a walk or doing a light workout before the test to get your blood flowing.

Allow yourself enough time to get ready, and leave for the test with plenty of time to spare so you won't have the anxiety of scrambling to arrive in time. Another reason to be early is to select a good seat. It's helpful to sit away from doors and windows, which can be distracting. Find a good seat, get out your supplies, and settle your mind before the test begins.

When the test begins, start by going over the instructions carefully, even if you already know what to expect. Make sure you avoid any careless mistakes by following the directions.

Then begin working through the questions, pacing yourself as you've practiced. If you're not sure on an answer, don't spend too much time on it, and don't let it shake your confidence. Either skip it and come back later, or eliminate as many wrong answers as possible and guess among the remaining ones. Don't dwell on these questions as you continue—put them out of your mind and focus on what lies ahead.

Be sure to read all of the answer choices, even if you're sure the first one is the right answer. Sometimes you'll find a better one if you keep reading. But don't second-guess yourself if you do immediately know the answer. Your gut instinct is usually right. Don't let test anxiety rob you of the information you know.

If you have time at the end of the test (and if the test format allows), go back and review your answers. Be cautious about changing any, since your first instinct tends to be correct, but make sure you didn't misread any of the questions or accidentally mark the wrong answer choice. Look over any you skipped and make an educated guess.

At the end, leave the test feeling confident. You've done your best, so don't waste time worrying about your performance or wishing you could change anything. Instead, celebrate the successful completion of this test. And finally, use this test to learn how to deal with anxiety even better next time.

Review Video: Test Anxiety
Visit mometrix.com/academy and enter code: 100340

Important Qualification

Not all anxiety is created equal. If your test anxiety is causing major issues in your life beyond the classroom or testing center, or if you are experiencing troubling physical symptoms related to your anxiety, it may be a sign of a serious physiological or psychological condition. If this sounds like your situation, we strongly encourage you to seek professional help.

Additional Bonus Material

Due to our efforts to try to keep this book to a manageable length, we've created a link that will give you access to all of your additional bonus material:

mometrix.com/bonus948/adc

Made in the USA
Coppell, TX
21 January 2025